THE CINEMA 4D R10® HANDBOOK

WITHDRAWN

THE CINEMA 4D R10®
HANDBOOK

ANSON CALL

CHARLES RIVER MEDIA

Boston, Massachusetts

Cover Design: Tyler Creative

CHARLES RIVER MEDIA
25 Thomson Place
Boston, Massachusetts 02210
617-757-7900
617-757-7951 (FAX)
crm.info@thomson.com
www.charlesriver.com

This book is printed on acid-free paper.

Anson Call. *The Cinema 4D R10® Handbook.*
ISBN-10: 1-58450-522-2
ISBN-13: 978-1-58450-522-8

Library of Congress Cataloging-in-Publication Data
Call, Anson.
  The Cinema 4D R10 handbook / Anson Call. -- 1st ed.
     p. cm.
  Includes index.
  ISBN-13: 978-1-58450-522-8 (pbk. with cd-rom : alk. paper)
  ISBN-10: 1-58450-522-2 (pbk. with cd-rom : alk. paper) 1. Computer graphics. 2. Computer anima-
tion. 3. Three-dimensional display systems. 4. Cinema 4D XL. I. Title.

  T385.C345 2007
  006.6'93--dc22
                                    2007006230

Printed in the United States of America
07 7 6 5 4 3 2

To my family:
Cris, Julia, Selina and the Bobs,
who make it worthwhile.

CONTENTS

ACKNOWLEDGMENTS

Thanks to Jenifer Niles, who was again patient and wonderful to work with.

Thanks to all the artists who contributed to this book and for being inspirational to all of us.

Thanks to Nigel Doyle for his great feedback and expertise.

Thanks to my students, who let me know what didn't work the last time.

PREFACE

WHY THIS BOOK?

With any software package, a number of benefits arise from taking a fresh perspective on the tool and its uses. MAXON's CINEMA 4D R10 is no exception. Despite its overall ease of use, C4D is also an incredibly powerful and diverse package. As such, its uses—and the methods of using it—are diverse. Not that any one method is the "right" way. In fact, the flexibility of being able to achieve powerful projects in a variety of ways is part of the strength of C4D.

Exploring these paths is the primary function of this book. Included with your copy of C4D software is documentation that provides a useful reference filled with definitions of all the tools. This documentation is great to have, and this book is not intended to replace the documentation. Instead, the book provides hands-on methods for analyzing the functions of C4D's many tools. The book takes a project-based approach that allows you to create impressive projects as you learn C4D's array of tools and functions.

WHAT'S NEW?

CINEMA 4D R10 is a major upgrade. This release focuses on character animation tools, but there are updates or improvements to most facets of the program. This multitude of new functions can be dizzying to get through. Some new functions are close to the old way of doing things but just different enough to be confusing. This volume works with, but is not limited to, most of the new tools within C4D R10 including the following:

- Interface changes and enhancements
- Enhanced Object Manager and new Layer Manager
- New animation tools
- 3D painting through BodyPaint 3D
- Enhanced OpenGL
- Interactive renderer
- Advanced rendering enhancements
- MOCCA 3, new and improved character animation tools
- Hair
- Dynamics
- Many other updates

Although there are far too many function and tools in C4D to cover all of them in this book, the core concepts are all here. All of the major tools for creating 3D are covered to allow you to produce great work.

What Is Covered?

In this book, all of the major areas of C4D and its uses are covered. Some light is also shed on many of the little-understood and underexplored corners of the program. Beginning with the general tools and tool layout, you learn how to maneuver through the 3D space and C4D's interface. However, this book doesn't attempt to cover every nook and cranny of this truly diverse package. There just isn't enough space to truly get to every part of the program; however, great care has been taken to explore nearly all of the most powerful and frequently used aspects.

Next, standard C4D workflow is covered, including where and how to start, and how to manage your projects. Then the real fun begins—the modeling tools within C4D. Modeling is covered, from primitive methods and NURBS, NURBS editing, polygon creation, and HyperNURBS. Thus, not only do we cover the modeling tools, but we also analyze a variety of ways to use them, giving you a wide scope of potential methods to try and perfect.

After creating the shapes of our dreams, we put C4D's powerful texture capabilities to work. You'll learn how they work, when they should be used, and what sorts of effects can be created with simple textures. New to this book are instructions on how to use the 3D painting and UV layout tools provided through BodyPaint 3D, which is now included in the core application, regardless of the bundle. You'll quickly learn the strengths and benefits of this powerful new addition.

After creating and texturing objects, we'll dive into lighting techniques, including three-point lighting, Area lighting, Global Illumination, and HDRI. We'll cover some basic lighting theory along with tool coverage to help you learn what you need to know about C4D's lighting. We'll even show you some tricks and techniques to help you speed things up, while keeping the quality of your renderings as high as possible.

Moving along, we'll get into the complex and powerful animation tools contained in C4D. These sections cover the new Timeline, Power Slider, and F-Curves. C4D R10 has new, improved tools to utilize within the Timeline, so we'll explore how to use these tools and also look at when, where, and why to use them. How to organize animation is also explained, as this can make the difference between a project nightmare and an enjoyable experience.

Also included is a brand new section on character animation. C4D is not often recognized as a character animation powerhouse, but with the new tools present in C4D R10, the possibilities have skyrocketed. In this section, we'll teach you how to use the new MOCCA 3 tools, including building a basic rig from scratch, creating facial animation, and using basic controller organization.

We'll cover the basics of dynamics so that you can add realism to your scenes. We'll explore C4D's Soft and Hard Dynamics and how to avoid the pitfalls that can often occur.

Toward the end of the book, we'll look at areas that truly lift C4D above the level of a mere 3D animation package. You'll put cloth on animated characters, hair on a character, and learn how Sketch and Toon can transform your models into stylized drawings. Finally, you'll learn the power of customization and how C4D can be bent to your will.

THE COMPANION CD-ROM

ON THE CD

Included with this book is a CD-ROM that contains all the project files you will need to complete the tutorials. Also present is the C4D demo application for Macintosh and PC, full color figures, and bonus tutorials from past iterations of the *C4D Handbook*.

WHAT IS IN IT FOR YOU?

This book is best for beginners. It reviews many of the tools within C4D and explains how best to use them. Through intensive tutorials, you will learn ideas and techniques not covered in the manuals. You'll also learn about the theory and why things work the way they do, so that by understanding the theory behind the tools, you can better utilize the ideas within them.

This book is also great for intermediate users. If you've been using C4D for a while now, you've probably already gone through the tutorials contained within the manuals and have a fairly good grasp on how the tools work. This book will put a new spin on the same tools and give you a chance to see how the tools are used in ways you may not have tried. The tutorials in the latter half of the book are intense enough that they provide an excellent learning challenge if you have not mastered complex 3D ideas such as animating the human form. Especially if you have been using earlier versions of C4D, this volume will get you quickly up to speed with the new tools and functions.

Additionally, this book is great for advanced users. Those of you who are C4D experts and have delved deeply into the depths of digital domains will still find useful information here. Have you ever thought it would be great if C4D just had a tool that would allow you to do x? Well, included here are tutorials by the programming wonder Donovan Keith and chapters on writing your own expressions with XPresso (on the companion CD-ROM) as well as some in-depth analysis of making your own plug-ins.

ON THE CD

Even if you are not interested in programming as an advanced user, you can find out about some of the tricks various artists throughout the world have tweaked and mastered (bonus chapters on the companion CD-ROM).

ON THE CD

And if you are comfortable and effective in C4D, this volume will provide some further enhancing techniques. If you are upgrading from older versions of C4D and just want to get up to speed with the new tools, this is your book.

So young or old, novice or experienced, amateur or professional, this book provides you with tools, techniques, and tricks that will increase your C4D productivity and workflow.

This book assumes you have the Studio bundle for some of the later chapters. It assumes you have the XL bundle for Chapter 5 "Materials and Textures."

INTERFACE

In This Chapter

- The Main Window
- Command Palettes
- Managers
- The Object Manager
- The Layer Browser
- The Attribute Manager
- The Viewport
- Configure the Viewport
- C4D's Built-in Layouts
- Object Manipulation
- The Coordinate Manager
- C4D Help

Upon opening CINEMA 4D® (from now on referred to as C4D), you are presented with an interface that incorporates all major areas of the 3D creation process: modeling, texturing, lighting, cinematography, animation, and rendering. In this chapter, rather than go through the entire list of tools (there's too many for this book!), we will look at groups of tools and the major interface elements. Later, using tutorials, you'll learn both the practical and theoretical applications of the tools in C4D.

R10 introduces new interface icons and schemes. Some early chapters of this book will use the "Classic" scheme because it provides better contrast between visual elements. Later chapters will use the default "Light." You can change the interface scheme in the main menu, by choosing Edit > Preferences. After the Preference dialog box opens, choose the Common tab, and then select your scheme. There is no functionality difference between schemes. The screenshots in this chapter will be listed as Classic or Light.

The new Help system is a wonderful addition, which will help you tremendously in learning C4D, and this book does not pretend to replace it. In addition, and where appropriate, this book may refer you to it. You can access the new Help system by choosing Help > Help.

In the Print Me directory on the CD-ROM, you'll find a file called Shortcuts that you can print and use as a reference throughout this book.

ON THE CD

Earlier versions of C4D will not open R10 files. You should, however, be able to open older files with R10.

THE MAIN WINDOW

C4D has a powerful collection of tools organized in a fairly intuitive format for general use. The interface, or *main window* (see Figure 1.1), is organized into command palettes on three sides (top, left, and bottom) containing clusters of tools. These command palettes live most happily on a screen that is running at least 1280×1024 (higher resolutions are recommended). However, if you have a smaller screen, you can still get to all the tools on a given palette. If you move your mouse up to the divider line separating palettes that contain tools out of the range of your screen, your mouse pointer will change to a small white pan hand when you click and drag (click-drag) to the left and right (for command palettes along the top) or up and down (for command palettes along the side) to scroll through the tools visible in the palettes (see Figure 1.2).

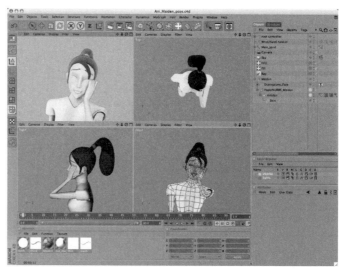

FIGURE 1.1   C4D main window. (Light scheme.)

FIGURE 1.2   Pan hand. (Light scheme.)

Although these visible tools are completely customizable, C4D pro-vides excellent presets for the major tasks, such as modeling, animating, and texturing. After you have learned more about C4D, check out Chapter 13, "Customizing the C4D Interface," on how to personalize the interface. For now, it is recommended that you learn the default layouts.

COMMAND PALETTES

In C4D, the pull-down menus contain *commands*. Each of these commands performs different functions that allow you to work in and manipulate the digital 3D space. Along the top and left side of the default C4D interface are *command palettes* (see Figure 1.3). These icon palettes are set up to allow you to reach often-used commands quickly.

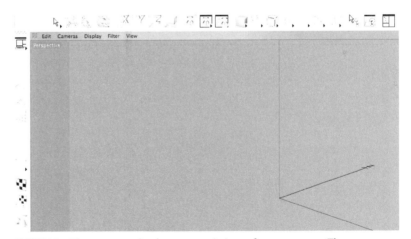

FIGURE 1.3   The command palettes contain icons for easy access. They are sometimes referred to as *icon palettes*. (Classic scheme.)

At the bottom-left corner of the interface is an area where little bits of text appear. This is a real aid when you are first starting to use C4D, as it helps you remember the names of tools within command palettes. As you move your mouse over any tool, the name of the tool or command will appear in this area. In the tutorials in this book, if you are having a hard time remembering which tool is being called for, be sure to take a look at this helpful area.

MANAGERS

In C4D, it's all about the *managers*. Managers are windows that represent program elements within C4D. Managers run at the same time and share information so the flow of data is smoothly automated. There are actually so many managers within C4D, that there is simply not enough room to display all of them at once. As a result, some of them are placed *beneath* other managers. You can access "buried" managers easily by clicking on the corresponding tab. When a tab is clicked, that manager is brought to the foreground (see Figure 1.4). Let's look at the most commonly used managers.

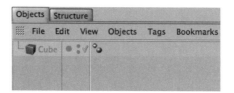

FIGURE 1.4 Tabs make getting to covered managers easy. Just click on the tab to reveal the manager. (Classic scheme.)

 *MAXON® refers to its Managers in the singular in their documentation but plural in the interface, for example, **Object** Manager (documentation) versus **Objects** Manager (interface). When referring to the interface, this book uses the plural in most cases.*

THE OBJECT MANAGER

The objects in the scene are named and organized in the Object Manager, which is normally located on the upper-right side of the main window. When you import objects into the scene, they will appear here as a name in a list. The objects can be linked to create *hierarchies*, which are a combination of parent/child objects. Hierarchy in the Objects Manager is critical for many functions. Objects also receive material and other property tags in the Objects Manager. New to R10 is the added search functionality, which allows you to quickly locate objects in a large list. You can also spawn multiple Objects Managers by clicking on the box with the plus sign in the upper-left corner of the manager (see Figure 1.5).

The new Filter options let you see your objects by objects, tags, and layers. This also means that, at some point, the manager may not show you everything that is in your scene. If that is the case, check to make sure your filters aren't hiding anything. You can access the filter by choosing View > Show Filter in the Objects Manager's menu. Or you can click on the closed eye (making it an open eye) as shown in Figure 1.6.

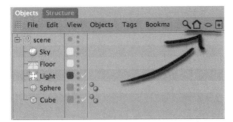

FIGURE 1.5   A typical hierarchy in the Objects Manager with an arrow pointing to the location of new R10 features. (Light scheme.)

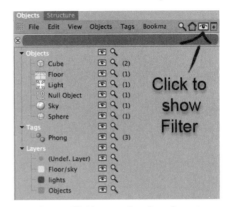

FIGURE 1.6   Clicking on the closed eye in the Objects Manager turns it into an open eye and reveals the Filter options. If you hide certain objects, tags, or layers, those types will no longer show up in the Objects Manager. (Light scheme.)

THE LAYER BROWSER

The *Layer Browser* is R10's answer to layer management. This wonderful tool helps you organize and keep track of both large and small scenes. The Layer Browser is not visible by default but can be accessed in several ways. You can access the Layer Browser by choosing Window > Layer Browser in the main menu or by single-clicking on the gray circle next to each object in the Objects Manager. When you click on it, a list will pop up (see Figure 1.7). From this list, you can add the object to existing layers, add it to a new layer, or open the Layer Browser.

FIGURE 1.7   Objects have a new gray circle next to them. When you single-click on it, you'll get access to the Add to Layer, and Add to New Layer, and Layer Browser. (Light scheme.)

The Layer Browser keeps track of your layers and lets you manage the layers into groups through linking, just like you do in the Objects Manager (see Figure 1.8). You can also turn on/off Animation, Expressions, Deformers, Generators, Lock (which protects unwanted edits to that layer), Visible in Render, Visible in Editor, or you can activate Solo Mode, which hides all the other layers and the objects in them, from both the editor and the Objects Manager. As such, it acts somewhat like the Filter.

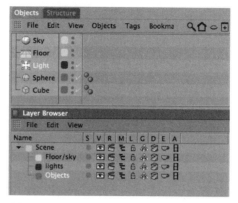

FIGURE 1.8   The Layer Browser. (Light scheme.)

THE ATTRIBUTE MANAGER

The Attributes Manager displays information about objects, tools, tags, and anything else. It normally sits right under the Objects Manager (lower-right side of the main window). If you click on a tool or an object, its properties are displayed in the Attributes Manger. Be mindful of this, as throughout the tutorials in this book you will be prompted to edit information in the Attributes Manager. In C4D R9, this manager was not labeled by default. In R10, it is labeled. Remember, it is always displaying information about a tool, object, or other attribute (see Figure 1.9). To experiment with the manager, follow these steps.

1. Make sure C4D is open, with a blank document.
2. From the main menu, select Objects > Primitives > Cube, or click on the Cube icon in the top command palette. A cube appears in the Objects Manager.
3. Notice the Object Properties in the Attributes Manager for the Cube (see Figure 1.9): Size, Segments, Separate Surfaces, Fillet, and a few more options. There are also Basic Properties about the Name of the object and its shading properties. Now notice the row of buttons labeled Basic, Coord., Object, and Phong along the top of the manager. A white button means that information is being displayed, and a gray button means it is not. You can click on a button to display its information or shift-click multiple buttons to display more than one. Ctrl-clicking deselects while maintaining your other button selections.
4. Observe the attributes of other objects or tools by clicking on them. Remember, the Attributes Manager almost always displays the last tool or object you click on.

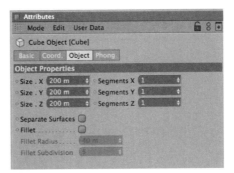

FIGURE 1.9   The Attributes Manager contains editable information about objects, tags, tools, and many other attributes. (Light scheme.)

If you want the Attributes Manager to keep its current object or tool, then you can click on the Lock icon. This will tell the Attributes Manager to keep displaying that particular information. This can be very useful, for example, when you need to edit attributes for a particular tool but still need to change tools often. You can also spawn multiple Attributes Managers by clicking on the box with a plus sign in the upper-right corner of the manager.

THE VIEWPORT

The space that takes up the most visual real estate is the large *Viewport* (see Figure 1.10). This window is your link to the digital world. Objects that you model will appear within this space. This window is like the viewfinder of a camera that allows you to view objects and their relationships to other objects. As with an ordinary camera, there are several ways to adjust how this camera works.

Remember those early math classes where you were given a series of *coordinates* to allow you to plot points in a graph where *x* represented the horizontal and *y* represented the vertical? Well, a computer thinks of digital space in much the same way. However, because we are dealing in 3D, there are more than just two directions.

Using the *Euclidean Geometry Model,* the computer keeps track of digital space along three axes: the *x*-axis (horizontal), the *y*-axis (vertical), and the *z*-axis (depth). Therefore, the computer thinks of an object's location as a defined point within these three axes. This is important to remember as we begin looking at maneuvering within the space and moving objects within the view panels. Whenever you start up C4D or open a new document, you'll see a guide in the middle of your view panel defining these three axes (see Figure 1.11).

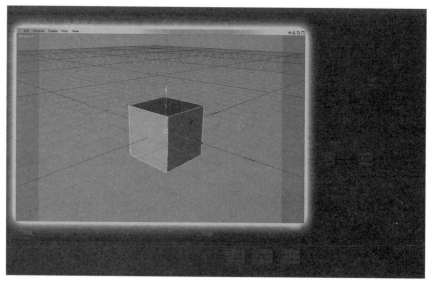

FIGURE 1.10 The Viewport. (Classic scheme.)

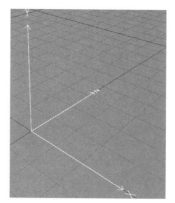

FIGURE 1.11 The *x-, y-, z*-coordinate symbols. (Classic scheme.)

Notice that the view panel has its own collection of pull-down menus as well as a set of four tools within the upper-right corner (see Figure 1.12). These four tools are important. They allow you (the camera person) to control where the virtual camera is, where it is pointing, and what "lens" you are using.

FIGURE 1.12 Viewport pull-down menus and camera tools. (Classic scheme.)

The Camera Tools

The following is a list of the name and function of the symbols for the four Camera tools. Experiment as you read what each tool does.

Camera Move: The four-arrow symbol *pans* the camera. Click-drag it to move the view up, down, left, or right (see Figure 1.13a).

Camera Zoom: The triangle *zooms* the camera. Click-drag it to zoom in or out (see Figure 1.13b).

Camera Rotate: The rounded arrows *rotate* the camera. Click-drag it to rotate around your scene. The center of rotation is whatever object (even groups, or elements of an object) you have selected. If nothing is selected, the origin (0,0,0) is the center of rotation (see Figure 1.13c).

Toggle Active View: The rectangle *toggles* between a single layout and a four-view layout. Single-click to activate it (see Figure 1.13d).

FIGURE 1.13   (a) Camera Move, (b) Camera Zoom, (c) Camera Rotate, and (d) Toggle Active view. (Classic scheme.)

Keyboard Shortcuts

Luckily, instead of having to move your mouse over to the Camera tools each time you want to change your view, there are some handy shortcuts. Experiment and memorize these, as they will literally save you hours of editing time. You might not think that moving your mouse over for 3 or 4 seconds means much. But, do that a thousand times in a row, and you'll quickly understand it's a big deal. In any given project, you might do it a lot more! Here are a few shortcuts for the Camera tools, separated by whether you are using a three-button mouse or a one-button mouse.

If You are Using a Three-button Mouse

- Simultaneously hold down the Alt key (Option for Mac) and left mouse button, and drag in the Viewport to rotate. This only works in the Perspective view.
- Simultaneously hold down the Alt key (Option for Mac) and middle mouse button, and drag in the Viewport to pan. Works in all views.
- Put your cursor over any Viewport, and single-click with the middle mouse button to toggle between that view and a four-view layout.
- Simultaneously hold down the Alt key (Option for Mac) and right mouse button, and drag in the Viewport to zoom. Mice with scroll wheels can scroll the zoom. Works in all views.

These shortcuts might look familiar. They are the same ones for Maya®, another popular 3D application. This shows a lot of brains on the part of MAXON, the makers of C4D, because it helps others who have used Maya (and a lot of people have!) learn C4D. It also means that C4D users will feel more at home with Maya (and that means C4D users will get more done!). MAXON generally tries very hard to make sure its users are spoiled by playing nice with other apps.

If You are Using a One-button Mouse

- Simultaneously hold down the 1 key and the mouse button, and drag in the Viewport to pan.
- Simultaneously hold down the 2 key and the mouse button, and drag in the Viewport to zoom.
- Simultaneously hold down the 3 key and the mouse button, and drag in the Viewport to rotate.

If you are serious about doing 3D, you should not use a one-button mouse! A three-button optical mouse is highly recommended. Right-click can, however, be invoked with the Command-click (Macintosh) for one-button mouse users.

Options for the Camera Tools

When you click on the Camera tool icons (see Figure 1.13), there are a couple of different ways to modify the action. Ctrl+Rotate will use the camera itself as the center of rotation. Right-clicking on the Camera Zoom changes the focal length for the camera. This doesn't actually move it, but it changes how much is visible in the Viewport. Right-clicking on the Camera Rotate tilts the view.

Function Keys

The function keys, F1 through F5, will toggle Perspective-, Top-, Right-, Front-, and four-view layouts. F6 through F8 control animation playback.

Configure the Viewport

In C4D R10, many of the view's preferences have moved to the Attributes Manager as compared to R8 and previous versions. To access the Viewport attributes, choose Edit > Configure (see Figure 1.14). The view's settings will now be displayed in the Attributes Manager (see Figure 1.15). As you do the tutorials in this book, you may be asked to edit these settings.

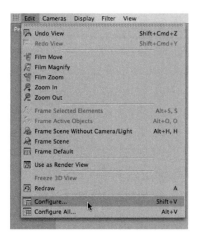

FIGURE 1.14   The shortcut for the Viewport attributes is Shift+V. (Classic scheme.)

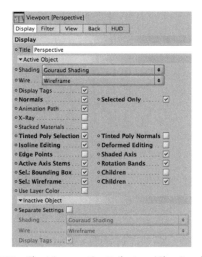

FIGURE 1.15   The Viewport's attributes. (Classic scheme.)

Notice that there are several buttons in the Attributes Manager. Although there are way too many settings to cover in this book, let's look at some important ones:

1. Press F1 to make sure you are in the Perspective view. From the Viewport's menu set, choose Edit > Configure.
2. In the Attributes Manager, click on the View button and locate the options for Title Safe and Action Safe listed underneath. These options put boxes into the Perspective view and indicate safe rendering zones when outputting to video or other media. Render Safe is on by default and is indicated by the darker bands on both sides of the Perspective Viewport.

3. Click on the Back button. Here you can load images into C4D to use as guides and reference images for modeling. Notice it is grayed out for the Perspective view because you can only load images in the orthographic (Top, Right, Front, and so on) views. You can fine-tune the grid here as well.

4. Click on the Filter button. Here is a list of things that you can edit depending on what you want displayed.

5. Click on the HUD button. Uncheck and recheck the Projection option several times. Notice that the word "Perspective" in the Perspective view disappears and reappears. You can completely customize what is shown in the Viewports. For more information on customization see Chapter 13.

C4D's Built-in Layouts

In recognition of the large number of tools available but not visible, C4D R10 includes several prebuilt layouts. At the top-left side of the command palette is a button that allows you to pick several different layouts depending on the task ahead (see Figure 1.16). Unless otherwise stated, use the Standard layout.

FIGURE 1.16   The default layouts, including the Standard layout. (Light scheme.)

Resetting the Layout

As you play around with the interface, you might find that things have become confusing. Windows may have been moved or have disappeared, and in general, you might feel lost. C4D is so changeable that after a while, you might not recognize it anymore. Resetting the layout will restore C4D to the Standard interface.

To reset the layout, select Window > Layout > Reset Layout from the main menu, or select the Standard layout using the Revert to Default Layout button just below the Undo button in the upper-left corner of the interface (see Figure 1.16).

OBJECT MANIPULATION

When you create objects, you need to be able to select them, change their position in 3D space, and scale and rotate them. This object manipulation is not to be confused with the changing of the camera views. The manipulation tools are found on the top command palette on the left side of the screen (see Figure 1.17).

The Live Selection tool (see Figure 1.17c) allows you to select objects and elements in the scene. Notice that clicking on the tool brings up its options in the Attributes Manager. Use the Shift key to select multiple objects. The Ctrl key deselects while maintaining your selections. The shortcut for the live selection is the spacebar, which will also toggle with whatever tool you are using.

The Move tool (see Figure 1.17d) allows you to change the position of objects. This tool lets you move an object by selecting any of its three directional, colored arrows (see Figure 1.18a). If you do not click on the directional handles, then the object will not be restricted to the x-axis, y-axis, and z-axis. If you are new to 3D, it is highly recommended that you use the arrows as you learn to navigate the 3D space. The shortcut for this tool is the E key.

The Scale tool (see Figure 1.17e) is represented by three boxes, one for each axis (see Figure 1.18a). Clicking on any of the boxes will constrain the scale to its corresponding axis. The shortcut for this tool is the T key.

The Rotate tool (Figure 1.17f) places three circles around the selected object (see Figure 1.18a). Click-dragging on these colored circles will constrain the rotation to the corresponding axis. The shortcut for this tool is the R key.

Holding down the Shift key while using the Move, Scale, or Rotate tools will quantize the results. Quantize amounts can be edited in the Attributes Manager > Snap Settings for these tools. Primitive 3D objects, like the cube, will only scale uniformly using the Scale tool (in conjunction with the Model tool). Use the primitive object's Object Properties in the Attributes Manager for a nonuniform scale.

THE COORDINATE MANAGER

Any given object or element has position, size, and rotation values, which are found in the Coordinates Manager (see Figure 1.18b). The Move, Scale,

FIGURE 1.17   (a) Undo (b) Redo (c) Live Selection, (d) Move, (e) Scale, and (f) Rotate tools. (Light scheme.)

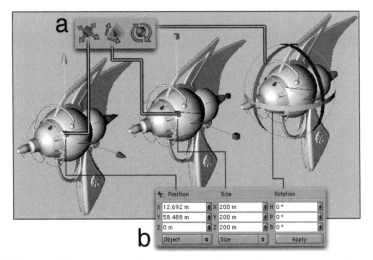

FIGURE 1.18   (a) The tools and their corresponding handles that surround the object. (b) The Coordinates Manager is affected by these tools. (*Note:* This figure represents the Classic scheme's Move, Scale, and Rotate icons for R9.)

and Rotate tools affect these numbers, which can also be entered in manually. Objects can be set to Object or World positions. Coordinates for selected objects can also be found in the Attributes Manager but are local only.

Axis Lock/Unlock and Use World/Object Coordinate System

Right next to the manipulation tools are icons for Axis Lock/Unlock and Use World/Object Coordinate System (see Figure 1.19). The X, Y, Z icons are on by default, which means you can move, scale, and rotate objects in any direction. Turning any of these off will disable manipulation for that axis (these are overridden by the Move, Scale, and Rotate tools' axis handles).

FIGURE 1.19   X, Y, Z Axis Lock/Unlock and Use World Coordinate System. (Light scheme.)

The Use World/Object Coordinate System button is set to Object by default. All objects have *two* independent coordinate systems: Object and World. When set to Object, the tools are constrained to the object's coordinate system. When set to World, the tools are constrained to the World coordinate system.

A word of caution: The X, Y, and Z keys will toggle the disable/enable for these axes. It's very easy to accidentally tap one of these keys and then later become frustrated because you can't move an object or element in a particular direction. Double-check the X, Y, and Z toggles if you're having trouble moving.

C4D Help

C4D has a new help system that makes accessing information about the features you don't understand quick and painless. To access Help, in the main menu, choose Help > Help to see the Help window (see Figure 1.20). This window essentially contains the manuals for C4D. You can also right-click on any of the main icons and choose Show Help from the pop-up menu (see Figure 1.21). The Help window will then appear with information on that particular icon. You can also press Ctrl+F1 for context-sensitive help on commands such as menu commands. Just hover your mouse over a command, and press the Ctrl+F1 simultaneously (Mac users use Command+F1).

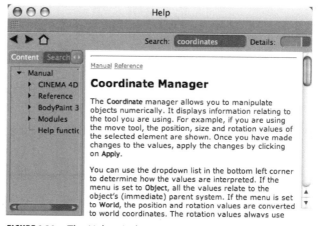

FIGURE 1.20   The Help window. Notice the search features along with the browsable content. (Light scheme.)

FIGURE 1.21 Right-click on any major icon, and then select Show Help to find out more information. (Light scheme.)

CONCLUSION

Cinema 4D has been recognized time and again for its ease of use for beginning and advanced users alike. Its intuitiveness doesn't stop here. As you'll see in the next chapter, C4D has a large library of 2D and 3D shapes that are easy to manipulate and that provide exciting capabilities.

BEGINNING MODELING

In This Chapter

- 3D Construction Theory
- Primitives
- Modeling Tools
- NURBS

We've looked at ways to manipulate the 3D world. We've looked at the basic layout, how to control the Viewports, and basic object movements. Now that you know how to look at the virtual world, it's time to look at how to create within it.

3D is technically heavy and challenging, but if any application makes it easier to understand, it's CINEMA 4D. This chapter is dedicated to covering some of the basic ideas behind 3D object construction. Try not to become discouraged as you read through the ethereal, abstract theory analysis. There are many fun, upcoming projects, but it's important to lay out the basics.

3D Construction Theory

The most basic building block of 3D objects is the *point* (see Figure 2.1). A point is analogous to the atom of our world. A point in 3D is visible in the Editor environment, yet it never renders. When two or more points are joined together, they are united by an *edge* (see Figure 2.2). When three or more edges are connected, they create a *polygon* (see Figure 2.3).

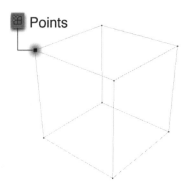

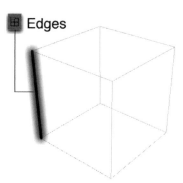

FIGURE 2.1   The point is the most basic element in 3D. It is also referred to as the vertex. Note the icon that allows you to edit points.

FIGURE 2.2   The edge is two connected points. It is sometimes called a polyline. Note the icon that allows you to edit edges.

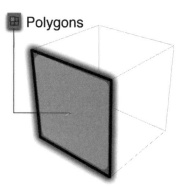

FIGURE 2.3   The polygon is the collection of points and edges. There are three kinds of polygons: triangles, quadrangles, and n-sided. Note the icon that allows you to edit polygons.

The polygon—this collection of points and edges—is the molecule of 3D objects. Polygons (polys) are either triangular, square (quadrangle), or n-sided (N-Gons) objects that are seen both in the *Editor* and in the *Renderer*. These polygons are paper-thin and rigid; this means that a polygon can be altered in shape by moving the elements that make it, but the polygon itself cannot be "bent." However, "quads," as they're often called, and N-Gons are either planar or nonplanar because these polygons are really just composed of triangles. When a large number of these rigid polygons are connected and placed at small angles to one another, a curved shape can be created (see Figure 2.4).

When points are used to create a polygon, they are also referred to as a *vertex*. The idea is that this point is at the vertex of two or more edges. These vertices—and the edges that meet at them—can be altered (pushed

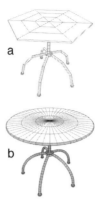

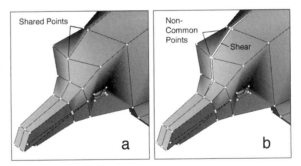

FIGURE 2.4   (a) A low number of rigid polygons placed together and (b) the same, smoother shape with a higher number of polygons.

and pulled in any direction) to change the shape of a polygon. Polygons also may "share" points and edges (see Figure 2.5a). When polygons share points, the result is a solid surface. If two adjacent polygons do not share two common points, there is technically no solid surface. The result can be shears, or holes, in a surface (see Figure 2.5b). Many polygons can come together to form a solid, 3D surface.

FIGURE 2.5   (a) A group of shared points that creates polygons. (b) Points that are noncommon may just be two, closely placed points. The result is a shear between edges.

The Concept of Poly-Count

The idea of polygons is central to 3D modeling. As illustrated in Figure 2.6, higher polygon counts (*poly-counts*) create smoother forms that are more pleasing and organic. However, the higher the poly-count, the more information your computer must keep track of. In a perfect world, your computer would not be limited or slowed by the number of polygons in your model or scene. However, as complex projects emerge and deal more and more with organic forms, the necessity of producing very rounded shapes becomes increasingly important. As these rounded shapes become ever more rounded, the poly-count may become so high that your computer simply cannot handle all the calculations fast enough to display them for you in the Editor (what you see through your view panel). Your *screen redraw time* (the time it takes your screen to "redraw" the information visible while you are in the Editor) can become painfully slow. In addition, C4D's usually speedy renderer can be slowed to a crawl when it must contend with huge amounts of polygons. It is important to note that even if you are working on broadcast-quality projects, keeping an eye on your poly-count will help maintain a snappy interface and smooth workflow. In Chapter 4, "Polygon Modeling," we'll show you how to keep track of your poly-count.

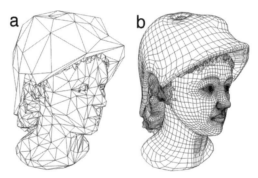

FIGURE 2.6   (a) Low poly-count and (b) higher poly-count. The high poly-count object renders smoother but much slower.

PRIMITIVES

Primitives are objects that C4D creates via mathematical formulas that create a shape based on determined values. Because of this dynamic mathematical nature, most primitives in C4D are said to be *parametric*, meaning the parameters of these primitive objects can be easily changed. This also means that although C4D uses polygons to display the objects in the Editor, you don't have direct access to the points, edges, and polygons of primitives. The benefit of this is that by altering the parameters, you can quickly get new shapes without having to alter the object at the polygonal level. The drawback is that you can only alter the shape according to C4D's parameter variables. There is a surprisingly large amount of possibilities in primitives. The best way to explore them is to create some and examine the possibilities. We'll do that soon.

Undo and Redo

Before we get too far into the intricacies of primitives, it's worthwhile to mention one of your soon-to-be (if it's not already) best friends—the Undo function. If your interface is still set up in the default setting, you have a command palette across the top of your screen. This palette is broken up into six sections that group the commands into clusters of similar tools. The first section with the two curved arrows contains the *Undo* and *Redo* commands (see Figure 2.7). C4D has what is called a *nondestructive* workflow, meaning (in part) that multiple undos are possible. With nondestructive workflows, C4D keeps information on parts of models and the method used to create shapes as you work. By default, you have 10 undo steps; you can change this by going to Edit > Preferences and then changing the Undo Depth setting listed in the Document area to your desired level of undos. Remember that all of these undos must be stored in your computer's memory—so if your computer doesn't have a large amount of available memory, keep this Undo Depth setting low or at its default.

FIGURE 2.7 Your new best friends, the Undo and Redo commands.

The Undo and Redo commands are two of the most-used 3D commands. Every artist, no matter how accomplished, works through a series of refining and retrying. Keep the Undo and Redo buttons handy, and know that there's no shame in undoing something just done. Indeed, many artists begin to develop cramps in their hands as they sit ready to hit the keyboard shortcuts for Undo (Ctrl+Z for PC, Command+Z for Mac) and Redo (Ctrl+Y for PC, Command+Y for Mac). As we work through the steps in the next section, we won't look at how to undo and redo, as these are fairly common concepts to computer work. However, keep in mind that this tool is available.

Creating Primitives

You can create primitives through menu selections (Objects > Primitive) or the icon palettes (see Figure 2.8). It doesn't matter which one you use, just be aware that all of the icons in the top command palette are mirrored in the menu options.

To create a cube, follow these steps:

1. Click on the Cube icon in the command palette, or choose Objects > Primitive > Cube from the main menu.
2. As you read along, observe the different aspects of the cube.

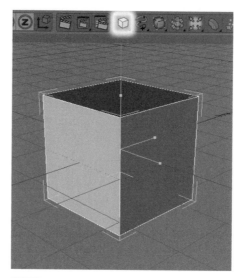

FIGURE 2.8   You can create a cube by single-clicking on its icon. It will appear in the Viewport Editor and the Objects Manager.

The Origin

There are several important things to notice right away about the C4D interface upon the creation of the cube. The first, of course, is the existence of a cube in the middle of the Editor window. However, the placement of this cube is also very important to note. Notice that the cube has been placed at exactly the center of known 3D space; that is, the center of the cube is at (0,0,0) in the *xyz* Cartesian coordinate grid. This is an important idea to remember in C4D. *When you are placing any new objects, the default location is at (0,0,0).* On the cube itself, notice the many visible tools available. The first visual tool is the red (orange with R10 default Light Scheme) corner pieces that C4D calls a *bounding box*. The bounding box defines the space that the 3D object takes up within digital space. These bounding boxes are not interactive, meaning that they are not functional tools to grab or alter. They are simply a visual communication tool between C4D and you.

Altering Parametric Primitives in the Editor

The next things to notice are the orange dots on the top and two sides of the cube (see Figure 2.9), which are interactive, functioning tools that allow you to adjust the parameters of this parametric primitive. These orange dots are only present on parametric primitives—you'll not see them on NURBS-based or polygonal-based objects. These parametric handles allow you to interactively change physical characteristics of the objects. This is actually a visual form of altering the mathematical variables described previously that create the shape. To use these interactive handles, simple click and drag them. For instance, if you want to make a cube wider, click on the orange dot on the side of the cube, and drag out to the desired size.

 Sometimes the orange dots for primitive objects disappear. This might be because you're using a particular kind of tool. Make sure you are using the Model tool and any of the main manipulation tools to see those orange dots.

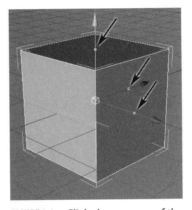

FIGURE 2.9   Click-drag on one of the orange dots to scale the primitive along an axis.

Object Properties

The cube's parameters, or *Object Properties,* are located in the Attributes Manager (see Figure 2.10). If you click on the Basic button, you'll see the Basic Properties (see Figure 2.10a), including the ability to enter a name other than the default name. It is important to keep track of your objects by naming them.

Clicking on the Object button reveals the Object Properties (see Figure 2.10b) for the cube primitive. The cube has X, Y, Z Size numbers that determine its volume. The Segments numbers tell the primitive how many polygons to generate on its surface. The default value of 1 means that each "face" will have one polygon. Higher numbers increases the polygon density of the primitive. Another option, Fillet, rounds the corners of the cube. When you activate this option, you'll see more orange dots on the cube in the Editor. Each primitive has unique Object Properties.

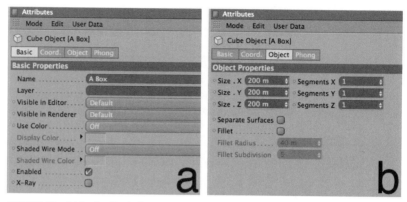

FIGURE 2.10   (a) In the Basic Properties section, you can name your objects, which will be reflected in the Objects Manager. (b) In the Object Properties section, you can change the parameters for the primitive.

Other Primitives

Some tools within command palettes contain other tools that are *folded* into the button. You can tell when other commands are folded by the small black triangle that appears at the bottom-right area of the command button.

The collection of primitive shapes that C4D creates is one example. These primitive shapes are actually nested (or folded) within the Primitive Cube command on the top command palette. If you click and hold on the Primitive Cube command button, a small subset of selections will appear showing you the other available primitives in C4D. To select a primitive, place it within your scene at (0,0,0), and list it in your Objects Manager, move your mouse over the desired form and click to select it (see Figure 2.11).

FIGURE 2.11   Click and hold on icons that have the little black triangle to get more options.

The primitive shapes available in C4D can also be accessed through the pull-down menu path of Objects > Primitive. The order in which they are listed is different from the order in which they are presented in the command palette. As this book isn't a manual, we won't be going over each primitive and each of its specific eccentricities. In general, primitives are great to get shapes started, but there is only so much you can do with them. In fact, you can often tell a beginning 3D user by the plethora of primitive shapes in their scene. That's all right. We all have to start somewhere. If you are new to 3D, now would be a good time to bring primitives into your scene and practice moving, scaling and rotating them.

MODELING TOOLS

C4D has many modeling tools from which to choose. Most of them are found on the left side of the interface. The following is a description of some of these.

Make Object Editable

Primitives are not polygons, but you can convert them. If you click the Make Object Editable button (see Figure 2.12) in the command palette on the left side of the screen, then the primitive is converted to a polygon object. Remember that this action is a destructive one, meaning that you will lose all of the parameters that the primitive had to offer. After you save and close the app or go beyond the reach of undos, that polygon object can never return to being a primitive. This is called *destructive* modeling not because the action can't be undone right away (it can); rather, it is destructive because there is no way to restore it much later in the process.

FIGURE 2.12   The vertical row of icons is found on the left side of the screen and provides access to the various modeling tools.

Point, Edge, and Polygon Tools

After you convert an object using the Make Object Editable tool (C for the shortcut), you can edit the object using Points, Edges or Polygons tools (see Figure 2.12). These tools access the same basic polygon elements talked about at the beginning of this chapter. There are a host of tools that will be explored further in Chapter 4 "Polygon Modeling."

Object Axis Tool

A primitive's center of rotation cannot be modified. You must covert it to a polygon object first. Afterwards, you can change the center of rotation using this tool (refer to Figure 2.12). Select it and then use the Move and Rotate tools to alter the center point.

Model Tool

The Model tool is the default tool that lets you move, rotate, and scale objects. After editing an object, remember to return to this tool because you will use it for most functions.

Tools Shortcut

C4D R10 utilizes pop-up menus for quick access to tools. The V key shortcut gives you a rapid way to access the different modeling tools. Press the V key and then go to the Tools section and choose whichever tool you need (see Figure 2.13). We'll get to the pop-up menus in later chapters.

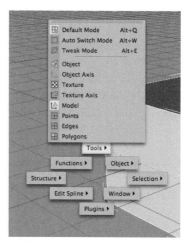

FIGURE 2.13   The V shortcut menu.

NURBS

In addition to polygonal modeling, C4D provides a form of modeling that allows for tremendous flexibility: NURBS. NURBS (an acronym, singular and plural) stands for Non-Uniform Rational B-Splines. NURBS are objects created by spline(s) and generators. A true team player, NURBS can make a pipe out of a circle, a vase out of a squiggle, and a vine from a line and a profile. In polygonal modeling, you actually work with the building blocks of 3D shapes—polygons. In contrast, with NURBS, you alter the source objects (splines) that create the final NURBS object, and C4D automatically calculates the final effect of the polygons that make up the NURBS object. This allows for a tremendous amount of flexibility. Very quickly—by merely altering a few parts of a constituent spline object—C4D can reorganize a large amount of polygons in the final NURBS object. This dynamic ability to change dramatically the shape of a 3D form without having to deal directly with polygons is one of the huge benefits to NURBS-based modeling.

However, there are some drawbacks. When you are using NURBS, you rely heavily on C4D's interpretation of how the NURBS algorithms are functioning. If you are in control of the parameters of the NURBS object, this can be to your advantage. However, while an object is part of a NURBS object, you do not have control over the object on a polygon-by-polygon basis. This can be frustrating if you need to make minute changes to the model. This is not a fatal flaw, however, as NURBS objects can be changed into polygonal objects if need be. We'll look much more at the power of NURBS in the next chapter.

Splines

The primary building tools of most NURBS objects are *splines*. Splines contain points that still have no geometry of their own. These points define the shape (linear, curvy) of the lines between the points. Furthermore, the lines that connect these points also have no inherent geometry; the manual describes them as "infinitely thin." The idea is that splines will never render. They are simply a collection of points connected by lines that exist within 3D space. The lines that connect these varying points in space create a shape referred to in C4D as interpolation. Although splines themselves have no geometry, they too can be used to create a wide variety of geometry. C4D has a diverse toolbox of spline-creation operations (see Figure 2.14).

FIGURE 2.14   The drawing tools.

CONCLUSION

So, let's move on. In Chapter 3, "NURBS," we will use splines to create NURBS objects (along with more modeling features), and we will bring all the theory you've read into concrete tutorials to put the theoretical discussion into practice.

NURBS

In This Chapter

- NURBS Generators
- TUTORIAL 3.1   Modeling a Castle
- Booleans
- TUTORIAL 3.2   Modeling a Desk Lamp

This technique is a powerful way of approximating common shapes. In C4D, linking a spline, or series of splines, to a NURBS generator makes NURBS geometries. This method is dubbed nondestructive modeling because you can still modify the spline or generator at any time. In any successful NURBS object, you'll find the generator and the spline(s).

In the first tutorial, you will create a basic shape using NURBS (see Figure 3.1), but first let's talk in more detail about this modeling method.

 This whole chapter uses the Classic interface. It provides better contrast for some of the screenshots. Don't worry, there's no loss of functionality. For this tutorial, you should switch to the Classic scheme by choosing Edit > Preferences. In the Common section, change the Scheme to Classic. For pre-R10 users, you'll feel right at home.

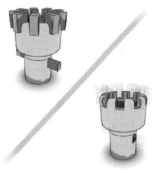

FIGURE 3.1   An illustration of the upcoming tutorial.

NURBS GENERATORS

The NURBS generators are Extrude, Lathe, Loft, and Sweep (see Figure 3.2). They are accessed either by choosing Objects > NURBS or by clicking and holding on the Add HyperNURBS icon in the top icon palette. HyperNURBS and Bezier NURBS are different from the NURBS generators. The Hyper-NURBS generator will not work with splines, only polygons. The Bezier NURBS already comes with geometry ready to be manipulated.

FIGURE 3.2 The NURBS generators with HyperNURBS and Bezier NURBS grayed out.

Splines

There are many splines to choose from (see Figure 3.3). The main differences are between the hand-drawn splines and spline primitives. For a more detailed look at each spline, refer to the C4D manuals or the Help feature.

FIGURE 3.3 The Spline icon menu.

For more information on splines, go to Help > Help. In the Help window, look for the Contents tab. Open up the triangles for each topic, and choose Manual > Reference > Objects > Create Spline, or type in Create Spline in the Search field.

How the Generators Work

Let's run through the steps for each generator and the splines that must accompany them in order for the NURBS geometry to be successfully created. There are certain steps, including the order of the hierarchy, which have to be followed.

Extrude NURBS

The Extrude NURBS gives depth to otherwise 2D splines and must have at least one spline linked to it (see Figure 3.4). You can use more splines if you wish, such as splines for a logo, but you must have Hierarchical checked under the Extrude NURBS Object Properties. Otherwise, just use one spline. For best default results, use the Front view to create or import your spline. If you create the spline in another view, for example, the Top view, then you have to change the Movement values in the Extrude NURBS Object Properties. We'll talk more about this later.

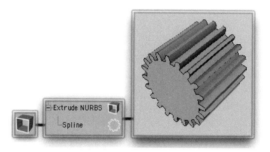

FIGURE 3.4   The Extrude NURBS icon, hierarchy, and example object.

Lathe NURBS

The Lathe NURBS (see Figure 3.5) revolves a profile spline around a center of rotation, like a potter's wheel, and can have only one spline linked to it. That spline should also, as good practice, be created in the Front or Right views and never in the Perspective or Top views. This generator uses the *y*-axis as its center of creation. It is usually wise to use the axis as a starting point, staying on one side and never crossing it. This is, of course, only a guideline, and there might be exceptions to this, depending on your modeling goals.

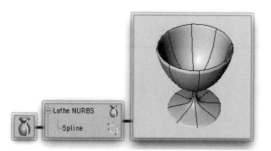

FIGURE 3.5   The Lathe NURBS icon, hierarchy, and example object.

Loft NURBS

The Loft NURBS (see Figure 3.6) acts like a skin that connects profile "ribs" together and needs two or more splines in the hierarchy. The number of splines allowable is dependent on the available RAM. In practicality, you can have as many as needed. The splines, or profiles, can ideally be created in any Viewport except Perspective. The order the splines are linked in the hierarchy is critical for the operation to give the desired results. You must link them in order.

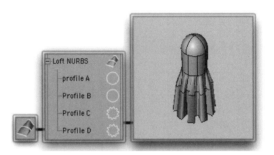

FIGURE 3.6 The Loft NURBS icon, hierarchy, and example object.

Sweep NURBS

The Sweep NURBS (see Figure 3.7) takes a profile and extends it along a path. Therefore, you must have only two splines linked to it. The profile is located above the path. If you get them reversed, you may get unwanted results. To get a default Sweep NURBS to work, create the path in the Top view, Right view, or Front view. Always create the profile in the Front view. Never link more splines, or any other geometry, to any NURBS generator than is necessary.

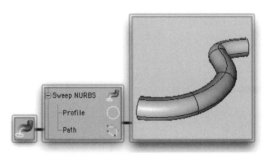

FIGURE 3.7 The Sweep NURBS icon, hierarchy, and example object.

Turning Off the Generators

Because each NURBS is a generator, it has a green checkmark by it, which indicates its On position. Click it to turn it off. You will see a red X denoting the Off position. Turning it off leaves the splines visible in the Editor (see Figure 3.8).

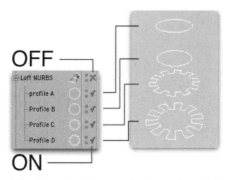

FIGURE 3.8   In this example, the Loft NURBS is turned off. The profiles are still visible in the Editor.

TUTORIAL 3.1	MODELING A CASTLE

In this tutorial, you take simple shapes—basic NURBS and cubes—and combine them to form a Boolean object, in this case a castle. Boolean modeling is a powerful way to take basic shapes and create much more sophisticated models. To begin, launch C4D or select File > New from the main menu. If you are not already doing so, make sure you are using the Classic scheme by choosing Edit > Preferences. In the Common section, change the Scheme to Classic.

The objectives of this tutorial are to show you:

- Boolean hierarchy and important functions
- Snap settings
- How to make simple 3D shapes from splines and NURBS
- The importance of hierarchy in the Objects Manager
- How to combine primitives and the Array tool
- How to access modeling features through keystrokes
- Spline creation and editing

These tutorials have been explicitly written so that you don't have to do any extra steps. If you do anything extra, things might turn out other than expected. For example, don't zoom in/out the Viewport windows, unless instructed. Otherwise, your object's size will be different than desired. But these things happen, so don't be afraid to try again or troubleshoot as best you can.

Create a Profile of the Castle Using the Bezier Spline Tool

To start, you create a spline using the Bezier Spline tool. You'll make a series of points to make the profile for the castle. You will also create rounded edges on parts of the spline.

Making the profile:

1. Press F4 to access a maximized Front view. (As a reminder, F1, F2, F3, and F4 invoke Perspective view, Top view, Right view, and Front view, respectively. F5 will return you to a four-view layout.)
2. To turn on Snapping, press the P key, and select 2.5D Snapping in the pop-up window (see Figure 3.9a). This turns on Snapping and ensures that the points will stay on the grid when you create the spline.
3. In the Front window's Viewport menu, select Filter > Axis to uncheck it (see Figure 3.9b). That way, the axis won't be in the way of the spline you are about to create. From the Front Viewport's menu, select Edit > Frame default to ensure that your spline will not be too large or too small. The keyboard shortcut to hide or reveal the axis is Alt+D.

FIGURE 3.9   (a) The Snap settings. (b) Turn off the Axis in the Viewports Display filter.

4. From the main menu, select Objects > Create Spline > Linear, or choose the Linear tool from the top Spline icon palette.
5. Create the profile (see Figure 3.10) by clicking in the Front window. Click and drag to make your first point. This will let you watch the point snap to the grid. You can click-drag like this for all the points. If

you make a mistake, just use the Undo function. Don't worry about being overly exact.

6. After you've made all your points, select the Move tool to edit them. Notice, you cannot click on the axis handles to make points. That's why it's important to turn it off for this operation. See the following Tip for extra help.

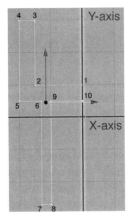

FIGURE 3.10   Click in the window starting at point 1, which lies exactly on the *y*-axis. Both the *y*-axis and *x*-axis have been emphasized.

If you prefer, zoom in slightly until you see finer grid divisions. Use the green y-*axis as your start and end. Don't cross it, as you will later see that the Lathe NURBS uses it as its center. Always use either the Front view or the Side view for creating splines to be used in conjunction with the Lathe NURBS. Using the Top view or the Perspective view can create undesirable shapes.*

To edit the spline, verify that you (1) have your object selected in the Objects Manager, (2) have selected the Move tool, and (3) are using the Points tool.

Ctrl-click on any part of the spline to create new points. Ctrl-clicking off the spline will create a new point connected to your last created point.

7. Make sure you have the Points tool selected. With the Live Selection tool, select points 4, 5, and 6 (see Figure 3.10 and Figure 3.11a). Hold the Shift key down if necessary.

8. From the main menu, select Structure > Edit Spline > Chamfer, or press V and then choose Edit Spline > Chamfer from the pop-up menu. Click and drag (from left to right, you may have to drag a lot) in the Front view to round these corners (see Figure 3.11b). Do not click on any axis handles. Chamfers are a great way to get perfectly rounded edges without hassle.

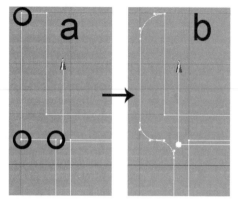

FIGURE 3.11 a) Selected points to be chamfered.
(b) The Chamfer rounds the selected points.

Feel free to further tweak the spline. Note that you can select and delete points with the Live Selection tool and the Delete key.

Don't worry if your spline doesn't look exactly like that shown in Figure 3.12. Only a general approximation is necessary.

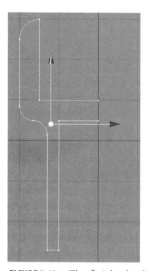

FIGURE 3.12 The finished spline.

Create the 3D Shape Using the Lathe NURBS

Now that you have created the spline, it is necessary to link it to a Lathe NURBS object in order for Cinema 4D to create the 3D geometry. The NURBS generators work with a linked spline or series of spline objects.

To create the 3D geometry:

1. From the main menu, select Objects > NURBS > Lathe NURBS, or select it from the icon palette.
2. In the Objects Manager, link the spline to the Lathe NURBS by dragging and dropping the word *Spline* onto the words *Lathe NURBS*. After you do this, the word *Spline* will become indented underneath *Lathe NURBS*. There will also be a connecting line indicating their parent/ child relationship (see Figure 3.13).

Hold down the Alt key while creating the Lathe NURBS object to make the spline a child of the Lathe NURBS object automatically.

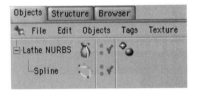

FIGURE 3.13   When you drag and drop the spline onto the Lathe NURBS, they become linked.

3. Change the name of the objects by double-clicking on their names (see Figure 3.14a). The name text becomes editable. Enter *Castle Base* for Lathe NURBS and *Castle Spline* for Spline (see Figure 3.14b).

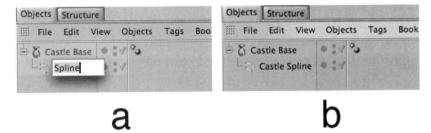

FIGURE 3.14   (a) Double-click on an object's name in the Objects Manager to rename it. (b) Rename the Lathe NURBS and the spline.

4. Change to the Perspective view (F1), and observe the new geometry. It should look similar to Figure 3.15. Feel free to zoom out a little and orbit around the object to see it better.

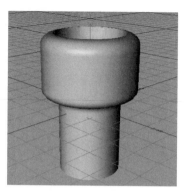

FIGURE 3.15   The result of the NURBS generator and spline.

Create the Top Gaps with the Array Tool

The castle base is the primary geometry, and everything else you make will become the negative spaces. For the top gaps, you will use ordinary cubes linked to an Array object. This will be placed where the negative spaces will be located.

Create and resize a cube:

1. From the main menu, select Objects > Primitive > Cube, or click on the Cube icon in the top icon palette. (You may not see the cube because it's inside the castle base.)
2. In the cube's Object Properties (in the Attributes Manager), change Size X to 60, Size Y to 130, and Size Z to 100 to shape the cube.

Create the array:

3. From the main menu, select Objects > Modeling > Array, or click on the Array icon in the icon palette.
4. Link the cube to the array by dragging and dropping in the Objects Manager. Your hierarchy and Viewport should look similar to Figure 3.16. You should also see not just one cube but eight of them. That's what the array does.
5. Select the array in the Objects Manager. In the Attributes Manager, change Radius to 170 and Copies to 8 copies, which means you will have 9 total.
6. Make sure Snapping is turned off. Press the P key, and select No Snapping from the pop-up menu. Select the array in the Objects Manager.
7. Bring back the axis by choosing Filter > Axis in the Viewport's menu.
8. Select the array in the Objects Manager.
9. Make sure you are using the Model tool (V > Tools > Model). Change the position of the array either manually using the Move tool or by entering in a value of 300 for the Y position (see Figure 3.17).

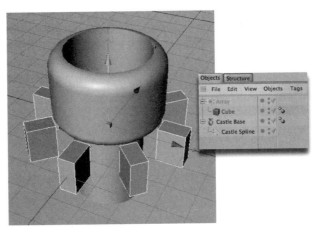

FIGURE 3.16   The array with the cube linked to it.

Don't select the cube and move it, just the array. If the castle base doesn't look like it's the right size, feel free to resize it with the Scale tool. It is common in 3D for objects to be resized. If it doesn't look like it's in the right place, move it. You want the cube array and the castle base to overlap.

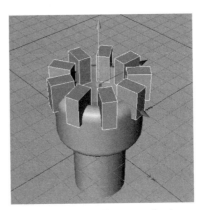

FIGURE 3.17   Move the array of cubes up so that they overlap slightly the top of the castle base.

Create the Negative Space for the Castle Window

Now that you've arranged the cubes, let's move onto the window. You will create an extrusion from a spline and place it so that it completely intersects the castle base. It is critical that the geometry used in the upcoming Boolean operation is overlapping.

To create the negative space for the window:

1. Press F4 to go to the Front view. From the main menu, select Objects > Spline Primitives > Rectangle, or choose it from the Spline Primitives icon palette.
2. In the Rectangle's Object Properties (found in the Attributes Manager), change Width and Height to 60.
3. Make sure the rectangle is selected, and then click on the Make Object Editable icon, or press the C key. This will transform the rectangle into a spline that can be edited.
4. Select the Points tool, and then select the top two points with the Live Selection tool. Press the V key.
5. Select Edit Spline > Chamfer from the pop-up menu. Click-drag, left to right, to round the top of the spline (see Figure 3.18).

 Right-clicking in the Viewport is another way to select tools and commands in C4D. The right-click menu is context sensitive depending on what you are doing.

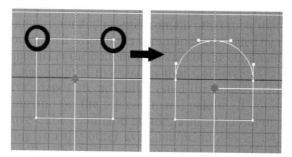

FIGURE 3.18   Select the top two points on the rectangle, and then round them.

6. From the main menu, select Objects > NURBS > Extrude NURBS, or choose it from the 3D icon palette.
7. Link the rectangle to the Extrude NURBS. Rename *Rectangle* to *Window Spline*, rename *Extrude NURBS* to *Window,* and then select Window (see Figure 3.19).

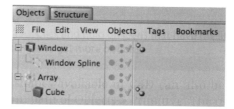

FIGURE 3.19   The Objects Manager with the renamed Extrude NURBS and linked spline.

8. In the Attributes Manager for Window, enter 400 for the Z movement (the third box over, *not* labeled with a Z). This creates a longer extrusion (see Figure 3.20).

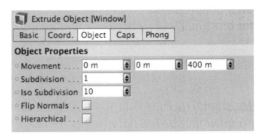

FIGURE 3.20   Enter 400 in the third box over to make the extrusion longer.

9. Switch to the Perspective view to see the results better.
10. Click the Model tool icon, or press V, and select Tools > Model from the pop-up menu (see Figure 3.21).

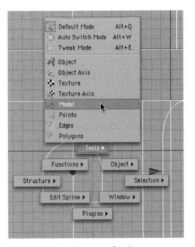

FIGURE 3.21   You can find many shortcuts on the pop-up menu.

11. In the Coordinates Manager, change the position of the Window to Y –20 and Z –200, or do it manually with the Move tool. Basically, make sure that the extrusion intersects the castle walls (see Figure 3.22). It should poke out on both sides.

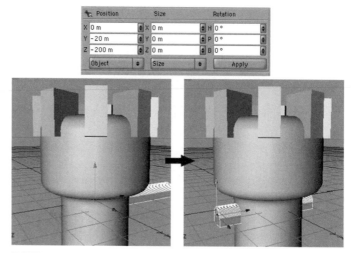

FIGURE 3.22 Input values into the Coordinates Manager or move the Window object manually.

BOOLEANS

Simply put, *Booleans* allow you to take two objects, or group of objects, and either combine them, subtract one from the other, or define their intersecting geometry.

Boolean objects are created from the top, horizontal icon palette (see Figure 3.23a) or by choosing Objects > Modeling > Boole. The Boolean object itself has no geometry but rather generates forms from other objects placed as children within it. The first object is always referenced as "A" with the second being "B." If you single-click the Boolean object in the Objects Manager, the settings of the Boolean object are displayed in the Attributes Manager. Here you can change the function of the Boolean to perform the functions shown in Figure 3.23b.

Boolean the Shapes Together

You've created all the geometry that is required for the castle. Now you need to link it all together. Here, the hierarchy will make it all work. This happens mostly in the Objects Manager.

Create the Boolean:

1. From the main menu, select Objects > Modeling > Boole or select it from the icon menu.

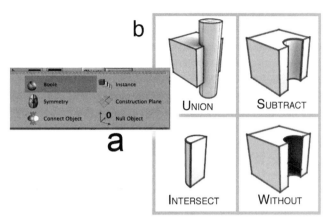

FIGURE 3.23   (a) The icon palette used to create the Boolean object.
(b) Examples of the different functions of the Boolean object, in
this case, the relationship between a cube and a cylinder.

2. With the Ctrl key, select both the Window and Array objects. You do not have to select their child objects, just the parents. Press Alt+G (Option+G for Macintosh) to group these under a Null object. Rename the Null object to *Negatives*. Grouping allows multiple objects to be used in the Boolean operation (see Figure 3.24).

 R10 has changed how objects are selected. It is now the same as selecting files in Windows. Shift now selects ranges between the first and last clicked-on object, and Ctrl selects multiple objects. In other words, use Ctrl instead of Shift for multiple selection in the Objects Manager.

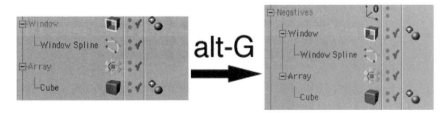

FIGURE 3.24   A group of the window and array, expanded.

3. Link the negatives group to the Boole. Then link the castle base to the Boole. Your Objects Manager should look something like Figure 3.25.
4. View the complete, expanded hierarchy in Figure 3.26.
5. From the main menu, select Edit > Deselect All. Press F1, and view the final 3D castle (see Figure 3.27). Nice work!

FIGURE 3.25   The basic hierarchy for the Boole, Castle Base, and Negatives.

FIGURE 3.26   The expanded hierarchy.

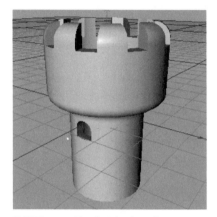

FIGURE 3.27   The finished castle.

Exploring Important Boolean Functions

There is a lot more to the Boole than just what was done here. Apart from subtraction, the Boole can also unite and create intersections of objects. You can also layer Booleans into sophisticated hierarchies to create very complicated shapes. That being said, keep in mind that Boolean modeling may not be appropriate for all situations. In fact, be careful in how much you use them as they can often bring even the most powerful computer to its knees.

Explore the Boole Object Properties:

1. Select the Boole object in the Objects Manager.
2. Explore the different options found in the Attributes Manager (see Figure 3.28).

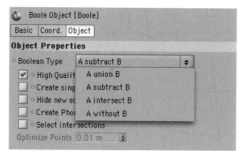

FIGURE 3.28   In the Attributes Manager, you can control the different aspects of the Boole Object Properties.

Wrap Up

You learned how to create a castle using basic shapes and the Boole object. Although C4D is known for its ultra stability, no operating system or 3D program is completely immune to crashes. Remember to save your work and often.

To save:

1. From the main menu, select File > Save As.
2. Choose a location. Enter *My Castle* for the document name, and click Save.

Be glad you saved and save often!

TUTORIAL 3.2   MODELING A DESK LAMP

Although you can model many different objects with NURBS, a lamp is a good choice because it has both organic and nonorganic features. Our lamp is of the ordinary, desk variety. It has a base, cord with plug, bendable neck, and head with various parts. Each part will be modeled separately and then combined to make the final form. You will learn how to use each NURB generator along with some of the dos and don'ts of NURBS modeling. Use the Standard interface (Window > Layout > Standard) unless directed otherwise. This tutorial also uses the Classic scheme. To begin, launch C4D, or from the main menu, select File > New.

You will learn about the following:

- Spline creation and important settings
- The relationship among splines, generator, and polygon count
- The Extrude NURB

- The Lathe NURB
- The Loft NURB
- The Sweep NURB
- Align to Spline
- Modeling with displacement maps
- Modeling parts of an object for later assembly
- Hiding and unhiding objects

Making the Base

The base has three parts: a spline, a Lathe NURBS generator, and a cylinder for detail (see Figure 3.29).

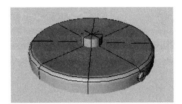

FIGURE 3.29   The base you are about to create.

Create the base spline:

1. Use the Linear Spline tool to make a spline as shown in Figure 3.30. Make sure you do so in the Front view. Stay left of the y-axis. The first and last points should have a value of 0 for their X position in the Coordinates Manager. You should have a total of 6 points.
2. Turn on Snapping, and turn off the axis in the Viewport Filter to facilitate the creation process.

You can configure the Viewport so that the modeling axis is hidden. Sometimes it can get in the way of point creation. Use Alt+D to hide/unhide the axis, or in the Front Viewport, go to Filter > Axis. to uncheck Axis. Recheck it after you are finished creating the spline, and turn off Snapping if it's on.

3. In the Structure Manager, check the positions of the 6 points to make sure that they match Figure 3.31. This will ensure that the base is exactly the size you want it to be. (The Structure Manager is the tab right next to the Objects Manager. It's very useful at examining the numerical values of each point in the spline.)

FIGURE 3.30   The basic spline for the base.

Point	X	Y	Z
0	0	0	0
1	-325	0	0
2	-325	75	0
3	-55	75	0
4	-55	120	0
5	0	120	0

FIGURE 3.31   The spline points in the Structure Manager should look like this.

4. In the Structure Manager, select point 2 by clicking on 2 (this is the equivalent of point 3 you created in Figure 3.30), or you can just select the upper-left point, and use the Chamfer tool, Structure > Edit Spline > Chamfer, to round the edge (see Figure 3.32). Remember, in order for you to edit points, you need to be using the Points tool.

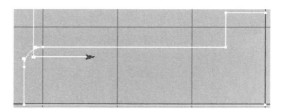

FIGURE 3.32   The finished base spline, with rounded corner.

Create the Lathe NURB:

5. From the main menu, select Objects > NURBS > Lathe NURBS. The new object appears in the Objects Manager.
6. Rename the Spline to *base spline*. Rename the Lathe NURBS to *base Lathe NURBS*.
7. Drag and drop the base spline onto base Lathe NURBS. The generator creates the shape (see Figure 3.33).

You can bring any NURBS generator into your scene and link it to your spline in one fell swoop. To do so, make sure you have the spline you want to link selected. Then, while holding down the Alt key, bring in the desired NURBS generator. Your NURBS generator is automatically made the parent of the selected spline. It works with other types of hierarchical objects too!

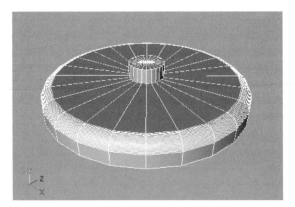

FIGURE 3.33 The base in the Perspective view. Grid and World access have been hidden for clarity.

Create the detail cylinder:

8. Create a cylinder. Rename it as *power cyl*.
9. In the Object Properties (Attributes Manager), change the following: Radius = 25, Height = 17.5. Change the Orientation to +X.
10. Activate Fillet under the Caps button. Change Segments to 5 and Radius to 6.
11. In the Coordinates Manager, change the following for the position: X = 332.5, Y = 37.5, Z = 0.
12. In the Objects Manager, click on base Lathe NURBS, and then Ctrl-click on power cyl so that both objects are selected. Press Alt+G (Option+G on Mac) to create a group under a Null object. Rename the Null object to *Base*. Your hierarchy and Perspective view should look something like Figure 3.34.

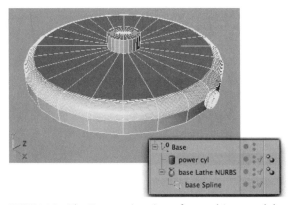

FIGURE 3.34 The Perspective view of your objects and the base hierarchy.

Save your work:

13. Save the scene to your hard drive.
14. Name it *Lamp base*. Remember where you put it because you will use it later.

Making the Neck

Modeling this part of the lamp is fairly straightforward. The Sweep NURBS is a perfect way to get this geometry. You will create a path and a profile and then link them to the NURBS generator. To get the detail in the lamp's neck, we use displacement maps. This is a material that is applied to the geometry. The surface is later deformed in the renderer.

There are many ways you could model the neck, from an Extrude NURB to a Loft NURB or even just a cylinder. However, it will be clearer later on why you are better served, in this instance, to use the Sweep NURBS and displacement mapping.

Create the path:

1. Start a new scene by choosing File > New. Maximize the Front view.
2. In the main menu, select Objects > Create Spline > B-Spline, or select it from the Spline icons palette.
3. In the Front view, create a series of nine vertical points starting near the origin and ending around four major grid lines up (see Figure 3.35). Don't worry about exactness. You'll edit in the next step.

You can configure the Viewport so that the modeling axis is hidden. Sometimes it can get in the way of point creation. In the Front Viewport, go to Filter > Axis to uncheck Axis. Recheck it after you are finished creating the spline, and turn off Snapping if it's on.

FIGURE 3.35   The neck path spline.

4. In the Structure Manager, change the point's values to the ones in Figure 3.36. You may need to zoom out slightly to see how the points have moved.

Objects	Structure	Browser	
File	Edit	View	Mode

Point	X	Y	Z
0	0	16	0
1	0	50	0
2	0	100	0
3	0	150	0
4	0	200	0
5	0	250	0
6	0	300	0
7	0	350	0
8	0	400	0

FIGURE 3.36   The Structure Manager for the spline path points.

5. In the Objects Manager, change the name of the spline to *path for neck*. In the Object Properties, change Intermediate Points from Adaptive to Uniform, and then enter a value of 40 in the Number box. This value determines the density of the final mesh. A value too low will not allow for convincing bends and displacement maps. A value too high means wasted resources on unneeded polygons.

Create the profile:

6. In the Front window, create a 2D circle (Objects > Spline Primitive > Circle).
7. Rename it as *profile for neck*.
8. In the Object Properties, change the Radius to 8.5.

 As a general rule, whenever using the Sweep NURBS, create the profile in the Front view. The generator prefers the XY plane. If you create spline primitives in other views, you can change their Plane to XY in the Object Properties.

Create Sweep NURBS:

9. In the main menu, select Objects > NURBS > Sweep NURBS, or choose it from the 3D icons palette. Rename it as *Neck*.
10. In the Objects Manager, drag and drop *path for neck* onto *Neck*.
11. In the Objects Manager, drag and drop *profile for neck* onto *Neck*.
12. Refer to the hierarchy in Figure 3.37a. It is important that the profile is above the path in the hierarchy. If not, you will get unexpected results. Done correctly, the geometry appears as a thin, elongated cylinder in the Perspective view (Figure 3.37b).

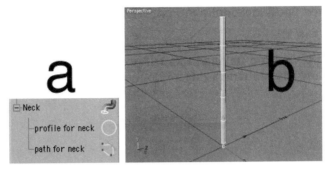

FIGURE 3.37   (a) The neck hierarchy. (b) The Perspective view of the neck should look like a thin cylinder.

Displacement Mapping

Modeling is not confined to just splines, polygons, and NURBS generators. Materials and their accompanying Displacement Maps can be used to alter geometry. The neck for the lamp has ridges that would be very time consuming to model with splines. An easier way is through displacement.

An Early Introduction to the Materials Manager

In the standard C4D interface, the Materials Manager is located near the bottom of the screen and has its own File menu (in R10, it's labeled Materials). Concerning materials, we will not go into depth until Chapter 5 "Materials and Textures." But here you will create a material, modify it, and then apply it to the neck.

Create displacement maps:

1. In the Materials Manager, select File > New Material. In the Manager, you will see a round sphere with the word *Mat* underneath it. That indicates a default material has been created (see Figure 3.38).

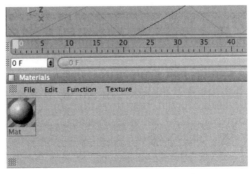

FIGURE 3.38   The Material Manager with a new material.

To create a new material quickly, double-click in the Materials Manager window.

2. Double-click on the New Material icon, and the Material Editor window appears. Change the name of the material to *Neck*. In the window, you will see a row of channels on the left. The Displacement channel is near the bottom. Activate the Displacement channel by clicking on the box next to it. After that, click on the word *Displacement* to see its properties (see Figure 3.39).

FIGURE 3.39　In the Material Editor, you can change the name of the material and turn on Displacement.

3. Locate the small, black triangle next to the word *Texture,* and then select Surfaces > Tiles (see Figure 3.40). Tiles appear next to Texture on a bar. Click on the word *Tiles* that is on that bar (see Figure 3.41).

FIGURE 3.40　Clicking on the triangle reveals a pop-up menu along with submenus. Choose Surfaces > Tiles.

FIGURE 3.41   Click on the Tiles button to see the options.

4. Change the Tile attributes to the ones in Figure 3.42a. Make sure the Grout Color and Tiles Color 1 are set to black. Tiles Color 2 should be set to white. Set the Pattern to Lines 1. Set Grout Width and Bevel Width to 1% each, and set Global Scale to 500%.
5. Click on the Displacement channel to bring back its properties, or alternatively, click on the Back button at the top of the Material Editor. Change Type to Intensity. Close the neck material window. The material should look similar to Figure 3.42b in the Material Manager.

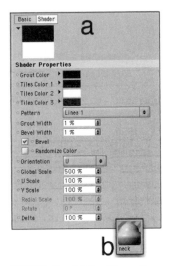

FIGURE 3.42   (a) The Tile options and (b) what the material will look like in the Materials Manager.

6. Drag and drop the neck material onto *Neck* in the Objects manager. You will see a material tag appear next to the object (see Figure 3.43).
7. Click on the material tag to see its properties. Change Tiles Y to 50 (see Figure 3.44). If you don't change the tiling of the material, you'll get 1 large groove instead of 50 little ones.

Render the neck:

8. Change to the Perspective view.

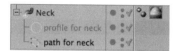

FIGURE 3.43   When you drag and drop the material onto the object, a material tag will appear next to it. Selecting it will reveal its Tag Properties in the Attributes Manager.

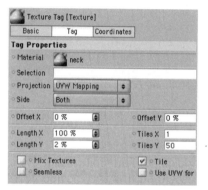

FIGURE 3.44   In the Tag Properties, change Tiles Y to 50.

9. To verify that the neck has its ridges, select Render > Render View from the main menu, or click on the Render Active View button. You can only see the displaced geometry in the rendered view, not in the editor window. You should see something similar to Figure 3.45.

FIGURE 3.45   The neck and its ridges become visible in the renderer. The ridges are not visible in the editor.

Save the neck:

10. From the main menu, select File > Save as.
11. Name the file *Lamp neck*, and save it to your hard drive (preferably in the same directory as Lamp base. You will use it later.

The Head Assembly

There are many objects to the head assembly, so naming the parts and hierarchy is very important. None of the parts is difficult to make, but keeping track of so many pieces can be a challenge. It is often useful to hide and unhide objects or groups so that you can concentrate on particular aspects of the scene.

Start by creating a new scene. In the main menu, select File > New to create a blank document.

Create the Loft NURBS and head/neck connector:

1. Maximize the Perspective view. Insert a circle primitive into the scene (Objects > Spline Primitive > Circle). In the Objects Manager, rename the circle as *Circle bottom*.
2. In the Object Properties, change the following for the circle: Radius = 11 and Plane = XZ.
3. In the Perspective view's menu, select Edit > Frame Scene (shortcut H key) and then zoom out slightly.
4. Make a copy of the circle bottom. There are several ways of doing this. A quick way is to select it in the Objects Manager, and click-drag downward while holding down the Ctrl key. You can also do a traditional copy and paste from the Object Manager's Edit menu.
5. Rename the copy as *Circle middle bottom*. For its Y position, enter 16.5. Reframe the scene so that you can see both objects.
6. Make a copy of *Circle middle bottom,* and rename it as *Ellipse middle top*. In its Object Properties, activate Ellipse. Change Radius Y to 22. In the Coordinates Manager, change the Y position to 25. Reframe the scene.
7. Make a copy of *Ellipse middle top,* and rename it to *Ellipse top*. In its Object Properties, change Radius Y to 25. In the Coordinates Manager, change the Y position to 33.5. Reframe the scene.
8. From the main menu, select Objects > NURBS > Loft NURBS. Link in the following order the circle primitives to the Loft NURBS: Circle bottom, Circle middle bottom, Ellipse middle top, and, finally, Ellipse top. Rename the Loft NURBS as *head/neck connector*. Your hierarchy and scene should look similar to Figure 3.46.

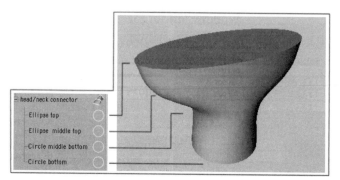

FIGURE 3.46   The circles and ellipses act as ribs for the Loft NURB to connect between. You can still edit the primitive's position and other attributes. That's why this is called *nondestructive* modeling.

Scene Management: Hiding and Unhiding

In the Objects Manager, next to each object, you will notice one large gray dot plus two smaller, gray dots. The large gray dot gives you access to the Layer Browser, but we won't worry about this now.

The other two dots consist of a top and bottom dot. The top dot corresponds to visibility in the editor, whereas the bottom dot refers to visibility in the renderer. The three conditions for the dot are gray, green, and red. Red hides the object and anything connected to it. Green displays the object, even overriding a parent's red condition. Gray is neutral. By itself, an object with a gray dot is visible. But if you link it to an object with a red dot, it will be hidden.

Hide the head/neck connector:

1. Click twice on the top dot (see Figure 3.47). The object should now be invisible, leaving nothing visible in the Viewports. Remember, however, that it would still be visible in the renderer.

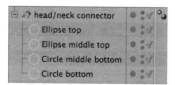

FIGURE 3.47   When the top dot next to an object is red, it will be hidden in the Editor.

2. In the Objects Manager, click on the minus symbol to the left of the head/neck connector to minimize the object (see Figure 3.48).

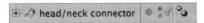

FIGURE 3.48   A plus next to the object indicates that it is minimized.

Create the head:

3. Draw a spline (see Figure 3.49) using the Bezier Spline tool, found in Objects > Create Spline > Bezier. Remember to do so in the Front view, and use the *y*-axis as the center. The point that rests nearest to the *y*-axis should have an X positional value of 0. Remember that you only need to make an approximation of this spline. Yours might be slightly different. After you are finished making and editing the spline, change to the Model tool (press V > Tools > Model).

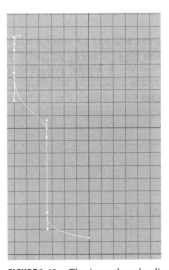

FIGURE 3.49   The Lamphead spline.

Remember, single-click to create a point with no handles, and click-drag to create a point with handles. You can then hold down the Shift key and click on a handle to break it.

4. Make sure the spline is still selected, and change its Size to X = 60 and Y = 160 in the Coordinates Manager. This may make it appear much smaller and may change its proportions a little. Rename the spline as *Lamphead spline*.
5. From the main menu, select Objects > NURBS > Lathe NURBS. In the Objects Manager, rename it as *Lamphead*. Link the Lamphead spline to Lamphead. Your hierarchy should look similar to Figure 3.50.

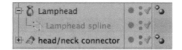

FIGURE 3.50   The Lamphead hierarchy.

6. Select the Lamphead. In the Coordinates Manager, enter 90 in the P value so that it rests upright. In the Front view, it may look like it is facing you.
7. Unhide the head/neck connector by clicking once on the red dot. Both dots should be gray.
8. In the Right view, move the Lamphead so that it sits on top of the head/neck connector. The two should intersect slightly (see Figure 3.51). If you can't see your move axis handles, make sure they are turned on in the Viewport's Filter menu.

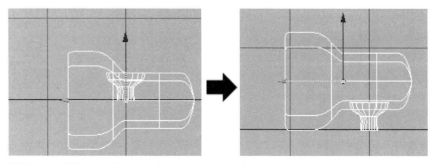

FIGURE 3.51   With the Move tool, move the Lamphead so that it sits on top and intersects slightly the head/neck connector.

9. After you have placed the groups, hide them both by clicking twice on their respective top dots, which will turn them red.

The Switch Assembly

The switch will lie at the back of the lamp head. It consists of several parts, including a Capsule primitive, an array of cylinders, an Extrude NURBS with a spline primitive, a Cube primitive, and a few Boolean operators. The capsule provides the main form for the switch. The cube cuts the capsule in half when both are linked to a Boolean. The rest adds some nice detail. After you've completed modeling the switch, you will move it into position.

Create the capsule and detail:

1. From the main menu, select Objects > Primitive > Capsule. In the Object Properties, change Radius to 9.2, Height to 33.5, and Orientation to

+Z. Change the name of the Capsule to *Switch body Capsule*. Maximize the Perspective view, and frame the scene (the object may appear small at first).

2. From the main menu, select Objects > Primitive > Cylinder (it may cover your view at first). In the Object Properties, change Radius to 1 and Height to 35. Make sure that Orientation is set to +Y. Rename it as *Cylinder cutters*.

3. From the main menu, select Objects > Modeling > Array. In the Object Properties, change Radius to 9.3. Link the Cylinder cutters to the array.

4. Select the array in the Objects Manager. In the Coordinates Manager, enter 90 for the P value.

5. From the main menu, select Objects > Modeling > Boole. Rename it as *Switch body*. First link the array and then the switch body capsule object to the switch body Boole. Your hierarchy should appear like Figure 3.52a, and the result like Figure 3.52b.

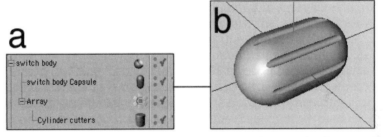

FIGURE 3.52   (a) The Boolean hierarchy. (b) The capsule is "cut" by the array of cylinders.

6. From the main menu, select Objects > Primitive > Cube (it may appear very large in the scene). Rename it to *Cube cutter*. In the Object Properties, change Size X, Y, and Z to 33. In the Coordinates Manager, change Z to −17.

7. From the main menu, select Objects > Modeling > Boole. Rename it as *switch Boole*. First link Cube cutter and then switch body to the switch Boole. This will make the Cube cutter cut the switch body in half (see Figure 3.53). You may want to deselect your objects to better see the result.

Create the switch connector:

8. From the main menu, select Object > Spline Primitive > Cogwheel. An object named Cogwheel enters the scene. You can leave it at the default name since it is fairly descriptive or change it to something more personal. In the Object Properties, change Teeth to 70, Inner

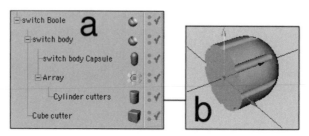

FIGURE 3.53   (a) The Boolean hierarchy. (b) The switch body group is "cut" by the Cube cutter object.

Radius to 8.5, Middle Radius to 9, and Outer Radius to 9. Make sure the Plane is set to XY.

9. From the main menu, select Objects > NURBS > Extrude NURBS. Change the name to *switch connector*. Link the Cogwheel spline to the switch connector Extrude NURBS.

10. In the Extrude NURBS (now called switch connector) Object Properties, change the Movement Z value to 1.

The Movement section does not label the boxes X, Y, or Z. However, the first box is X, second for Y, and third for Z.

11. Select switch connector in the Objects Manager, and then change its Z position to –2.

12. Select the switch Boole and switch connector groups in the Object Manager. Press Alt+G (Option+G on the Mac) to group the objects. Rename the Null object as *Switch Assembly*. Check Figure 3.54 to see your hierarchy and result.

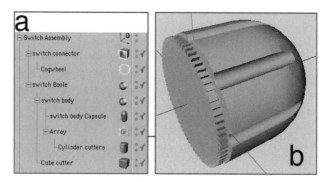

FIGURE 3.54   (a) The switch assembly hierarchy. (b) The result.

Place the switch assembly:

13. Unhide Lamphead and head/neck connector by making their dots gray.
14. Switch to the Right view. Frame the scene. Place the switch assembly at the back of the Lamphead with the Move tool (see Figure 3.55). Check the Perspective view to verify.

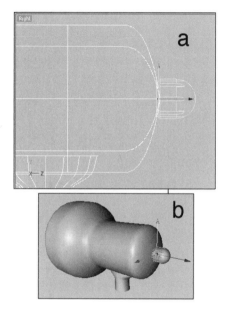

FIGURE 3.55   (a) The Right view of placement. (b) The Perspective view.

Create the light bulb:

15. From the main menu, select Objects > Primitive > Sphere. Rename it as *light bulb*. Change the Radius to 35 in the Object Properties.
16. Move it into position inside the Lamphead (see Figure 3.56). The sphere only approximates the shape of a light because the lamp is meant to be seen from the outside. You could make a more sophisticated bulb. But why? It will likely never be seen.

The Head Detail

Part of the modeling process is learning how to problem solve. You can only learn so much from a book or someone else showing you how to do something. Now is the time to figure out how to achieve a particular result. Don't worry; you'll be given enough hints to help guide you. However, don't be afraid to trek out on your own if you want to achieve

FIGURE 3.56   The light bulb is a simple sphere.

a different design goal. Remember, you can always use the example file on the companion CD-ROM.

On the back of the Lamphead, you will add seven venting holes. The front of the lamp could use some sprucing up as well.

Things to remember when problem solving include the following:

- Keep it organized. Remember in order for the Booleans and arrays to work properly, you will need the right links and hierarchy.
- Name your objects.
- Keep it simple. Use the techniques already covered.
- It doesn't have to be exact, just an approximation.
- If you can't make it work, find another solution. Be creative.

Add holes and other head detail:

1. Add holes to the back of the Lamphead (see Figure 3.57). Think about what processes you need to achieve that result. *Hint:* you can use the same method you used to add the notches on the switch, namely, an array of cylinders and a Boolean object. The cylinders should only have 1 height segment. In the Boole's Objects Properties, set Boolean Type to A without B.
2. Add detail to the front of the head (see Figure 3.58). Think about what processes you need to achieve that result. *Hint:* the new parts are marked in red. You can use Tube primitives and arrays of cubes to get this result. Don't be afraid to try something else, however.
3. When you are finished modeling the detail, group (Alt+G) everything under a single Null object, and rename it as *Lamp head* group. Look at your objects in the Objects Manager. As you can see, it can get fairly complex easily. Figure 3.59 shows one possible hierarchy.

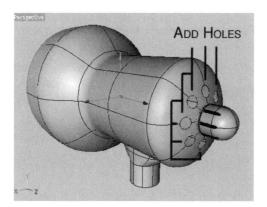

FIGURE 3.57 The holes in the back are an array of cylinders, the Lamphead, and a Boolean object.

FIGURE 3.58 The front details are Tube primitives along with cubes linked to arrays.

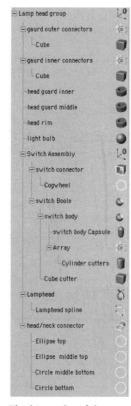

FIGURE 3.59 The hierarchy of the Lamp head group.

4. Select the Lamp head group. Press V, and then choose Tools > Object Axis (or just click its icon). In the Coordinates Manager, enter 0 for the X-, Y-, and Z positions. Make sure you are using World coordinates (see Figure 3.60). After you are finished, return to the Model tool (press V, and choose Tools > Model). This moves the model's center point without moving the object itself. You'll see why this is important when we attach the head to the neck.

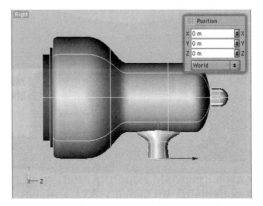

FIGURE 3.60   The axis center will move to the origin without moving the object. The axis should be right under the head/neck connector group.

Save your work:

5. Save the scene on your hard drive, preferably in the same directory where you saved Lamp base and Lamp neck.
6. Name the file *Lamphead assembly*.

Bring the Parts Together

So far you've created three different C4D document files that correspond to the creation of the lamp. By making the parts in separate environments, it is easier to focus on object making and less on scene management. That doesn't mean that you can't make multiple objects in a scene. On the contrary, being able to hide objects greatly facilitates working with a high object count. The point is that you have a choice and can mold the application to your style and needs.

Now that the major parts have been completed, let's bring them all together. There are two ways to accomplish this. You could open all the scenes and then copy and paste each part, or you could use the Merge Object command in the Objects Manager. With this command, you can import C4D files or any other supported file format, including Adobe Illustrator paths.

Merge the objects:

1. In the main menu, select File > Close All to close all the documents you may be working with. You may be prompted to save any modified work. After the operation, you will be left with a blank document.
2. In the Objects Manager File menu, select File > Merge Objects. Select the directory where you saved your lamp files. Load Lamp base. The Base group will be imported into the scene.
3. Repeat the Merge Objects command for Lamp neck and Lamphead assembly, importing those groups into the document.
4. Maximize the Perspective view, and frame the scene (Edit > Frame Scene). Your view should look something like Figure 3.61. This is, of course, not the way you want it to look. For starters, the Base group is much too large, and the Lamp head group is not in the right position. Fortunately, these are simple problems to solve.

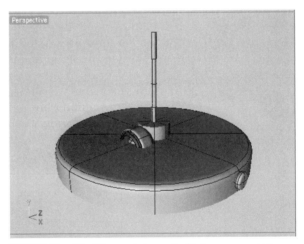

FIGURE 3.61   All of the parts imported into a new scene.

5. In the Objects Manager, select the Base group Null object. Do not select the individual objects linked to it. It's important that you select the uppermost parent in the hierarchy for this group. You may notice that its center point is not at the origin (0,0,0).
6. Switch to the Object Axis tool (press V, and choose Tools > Object Axis). Enter 0s in the Coordinates Manager for its position for all X, Y, and Z. Change back to the Model tool (press V, and choose Tools > Model).
7. In the Coordinates Manager, under Scale, change the Size pull-down menu to Scale (see Figure 3.62a). Change the 1s in each axis box to 0.2 (see Figure 3.62b), and then click Apply. The Base group will be scaled down to an appropriate size.

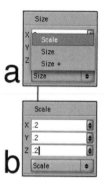

FIGURE 3.62 (a) Change Size to Scale, and (b) then enter .2 in each axis box.

Align To Spline

The lamp head is still not in the right position. Instead of just moving it there, you are going to make the head follow the neck no matter how it is bent. This is why you used a Sweep NURBS to model the neck and not another method because the Align To Spline works with path splines.

Connect the head and neck:

1. In the Objects Manager, close the Lamp head group. Select the Lamp head group, and then right-click on its name. You will see a pop-up menu appear. Select CINEMA 4D Tags > Align To Spline (see Figure 3.63a).
2. Select the Align To Spline icon that appears next to the group (see Figure 3.63b).

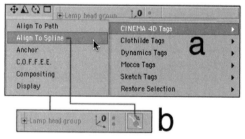

FIGURE 3.63 (a) Choose Align To Spline from the CINEMA 4D submenu in the pop-up menu, and (b) select the icon next to the object.

3. Make sure that the Neck group is open, but do not select any of the parts. Doing so will deselect the Align To Spline tag. If you do deselect, make sure you reclick it. Visually locate path for neck in the Objects Manager (see Figure 3.64a).

4. Do not single-click, instead, click-drag the path for neck down into the empty Spline Path box in the Align To Spline Tag Properties (see Figure 3.64b).

5. The Lamp head group is now aligned to the path for neck spline. In the Position box for the tag, enter 100 percent. The head will rise to the top of the neck (see Figure 3.65). Usually Align To Spline is thought of as an animation tool, but it works pretty well for modeling too.

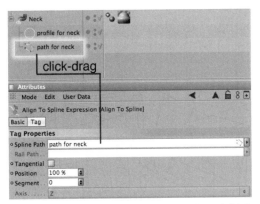

FIGURE 3.64   (a) Locate the path for neck, and (b) drag it to the empty Spline Path box.

FIGURE 3.65   The assembled lamp.

Moving the neck and head:

6. In the Objects Manager, select the path for neck spline, and switch to the Points tool. In the Right view, select the top two points, and move them around. The head will follow. The head will always remain level, but you can manually rotate it into position. Try some

different neck and head positions by changing the points of the path for neck and rotating Lamp head group.

7. Don't forget to render the scene so that you can see the ridges in the neck (see Figure 3.66).

FIGURE 3.66 When you render the lamp, you will see the ridges in the neck.

Discover More

Try to model a cord and plug-in. Use a Sweep NURBS to model the cord. HyperNURBs (you will learn more about that in the next chapter) or Loft NURBS will work well for the plug-in. Extrude NURBS will work for the prongs. Remember that problem solving is similar to learning a new language in that you have to repeat and memorize. You need to recall how to perform a particular function and the best way is through practice. If you need extra help, please refer to the file LampWcord.c4d on the CD-ROM (CD-ROM > Tutorials > Chapter03 > Chapter3-2).

ON THE CD

Save your scene:

1. After you are finished, save the scene to the hard drive.
2. Name it whatever you like.

CONCLUSION

NURBS are a powerful way to model everyday common shapes. The key is often mastering spline control, whether it be drawing or editing. In conjunction with other techniques, such as polygon modeling and HyperNURBS, there is no shape that can't be made.

Now that you've gotten your feet wet with NURBS, let's move onto other modeling techniques.

POLYGON MODELING

In This Chapter

- N-Gons and Subdividing
- The Benefits of N-Gons
- TUTORIAL 4.1   Polygon Modeling a Basic House
- A Look at the Structure Manager
- TUTORIAL 4.2   HyperNURBS: Modeling a Dolphin

There are generally two approaches to polygon modeling: box modeling and additive modeling. *Box modeling* implies that you take a primitive object, such as a cube, and modify it. *Additive modeling* means that you start from scratch with no initial geometry (see Figure 4.1). You will find, however, that as your modeling skills increase, these differences aren't that important because you will be using the exact same toolset.

FIGURE 4.1   Additive modeling.

The upcoming tutorial will show you how to build objects starting with the most elementary parts of a polygon: points (also referred to as the vertex). In addition, we will cover a range of Cinema 4D (C4D) tools, including tools that were new to R9 and are tweaked in R10. Consequently, many of the techniques learned here can be transferred to other 3D programs such as 3D Studio Max and Maya. Although the tools and methods are sometimes different, the concepts are very often the same.

It is important to remember that past versions of C4D only supported triangles and quadrangles. R9 introduced N-Gons or n-sided polygons. However, even though you can create more than four sides, there are some things you'll want to know about the consequences of N-Gons.

N-Gons and Subdividing

In Figure 4.2, notice how triangles, quads, and n-sided polygons react differently to the Subdivide command. Basically, each polyline is divided in half by a vertex (a polyline connects two vertices). New polylines are drawn from the new vertices. A triangle subdivided has 4 triangles. A quadrangle subdivided has 4 quadrangles, and an n-sided N-Gon will have n quadrangles. More importantly, each quadrangle in a newly subdivided N-Gon will share a single vertex. So, if you have a 25-sided N-Gon, and you subdivide it, the result will be 25 quads each sharing a single vertex (see Figure 4.3). This "starring" is something to avoid!

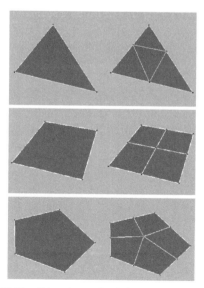

FIGURE 4.2 Triangles and subdivision, quadrangles and subdivision, and N-Gons and subdivision.

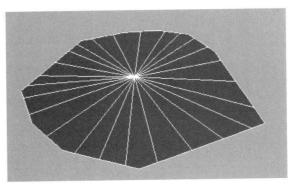

FIGURE 4.3   The evil and very ugly 25-sided N-Gon, subdivided.

THE BENEFITS OF N-GONS

Even though quadrangles are usually preferred, being able to go beyond that can be liberating. As you'll see in this next tutorial, there are times when N-Gons are clearly much easier to work with and allow more creativity with fewer restrictions. In the following tutorial, you'll learn when and how to use them.

This whole chapter uses the Classic interface. It provides better contrast for some of the screenshots. Don't worry, there's no loss of functionality. For this tutorial, it is recommended that you switch to the Classic scheme, which you can do by choosing Edit > Preferences. In the Common section, change the Scheme to Classic. For pre-R10 users, you'll feel right at home.

| **TUTORIAL 4.1** | **POLYGON MODELING A BASIC HOUSE** |

C4D has an excellent array of tools to let you create any shape imaginable. However, with so much power comes a learning curve, which is best overcome with practice, practice, and more practice. It also helps to start with the basics and work your way up. We start off by modeling a structure that isn't too complicated: a basic house (see Figure 4.4).

The objectives of this tutorial are to show you:

- Point and polygon creation from scratch
- Point, Edge, and Polygon tools
- Selection modes
- Live Selection and Rectangle Selection
- Cloning
- Basic polygon editing and manipulation
- Point management

FIGURE 4.4   The house in final form.

- Accessing modeling and display features through keystrokes
- Changing layouts

To begin:

1. Launch C4D, or open a new document (File > New).
2. Switch to the modeling layout by selecting Window > Layout > Modeling from the main menu (see Figure 4.5).

FIGURE 4.5   The Modeling layout adds a row of polygon tools near the bottom of the screen. With no active objects, the menu is grayed out (a). When you're editing a Polygon object, you'll see accessible tools there (b).

Modeling Layout

C4D has several different layouts to choose from. Each one is optimized for the major task you are about to perform. Use the Animation layout for animating, Modeling layout for modeling, and so on. You can access these from the main menu or press and hold the Revert To Default Layout icon to access the nested options (see Figure 4.6). The icon is found just below the Undo icon in the upper-left corner of the application.

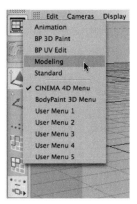

FIGURE 4.6   The Modeling layout chosen from the Default Layout icon.

Create Polygon Tool for the Floor

You will begin by creating the base of the house and then work your way up. You will use snap settings to lay down the first points. Then, you will learn how to make copies of points to help in the construction and how to make connections between those points to make polygons.

Create the floor of the house:

1. Press F2 to access a maximized Top view. In the Top view's Display menu, make sure that Lines and Isoparms are active. You can also press the N key, which will display a list of options along with the keyboard shortcuts to activate them. Pressing N and then G will select Lines. Pressing N and then I will select Isoparms (see Figure 4.7).

FIGURE 4.7   The display type of the Viewport can be modified by using the N keyboard shortcut.

2. From the main menu, select Objects > Polygon Object. Rename the new Polygon object House.
3. With the House object selected, click on the Points tool.
4. From the horizontal row of modeling icons, click the Create Polygon icon, or from the main menu, select Structure > Create Polygon. You may also press M to access the pop-up menu and then press E. A fourth option is to right-click anywhere in the Viewport to see a list of modeling options. You'll find that C4D is ready to be molded to your modeling style, whether through menu sets, icons, or keystrokes. Use the one you feel most comfortable with.
5. In the Create Polygon tool options, enable Snapping. You can alternatively use the P key and activate 2.5D snapping.
6. Observe the grid, and click to create six points (see Figure 4.8). It is important that you do this in order.

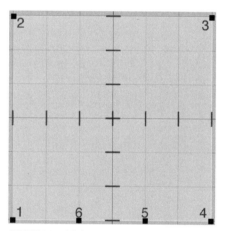

FIGURE 4.8   Make six points on the grid. Click on the first point, or double-click your last point to end the operation.

7. First point is 3 grid spaces down and 3 grid spaces to the left.
8. Second point is 3 grid spaces up and 3 grid spaces to the left.
9. Third point is 3 grid spaces up and 3 grid spaces to the right.
10. Fourth point is 3 grid spaces down and 3 grid spaces to the right.
11. Fifth point is 3 grid spaces down and 1 grid space to the right.
12. Sixth point is 3 grid spaces down and 1 grid space to the left.
13. To finish, click on the very first point, or double-click your last point. You should see blue lines connecting the points to form a square. This is the first polygon that makes the floor (see Figure 4.9).

While using the Create Polygon tool, click to make points. To finish the operation, click on the very first point created, or double-click the last point you want to create. To delete points during creation, hold down the Shift key and click on that point. To create intermediary points, hold down the Ctrl key and click.

By default, each major grid line represents 100 meters. But this is not an important factor for this tutorial.

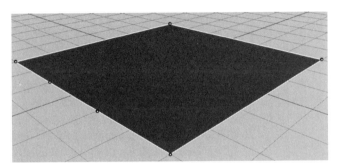

FIGURE 4.9   Perspective view (F1) of the floor, which resembles a simple plane. This figure has been enhanced to more clearly show the points.

A LOOK AT THE STRUCTURE MANAGER

Because each polygon object is an arrangement of points, it is sometimes beneficial to see and edit these points numerically in a list. The Structure Manager allows you to do just that.

Edit points using the Structure Manager:

1. Click on the Structure Manager tab.
2. Make sure you are in Points mode (not to be confused with the Points tool) by selecting Mode > Points from the Structure Manager's File menu (the default setting).
3. Check to see if there are points whose values have strayed from the grid. Double-click inside a box to make changes. Press Enter when finished. Your points should look like Figure 4.10 when finished.

Point	X	Y	Z
0	-300	0	-300
1	-300	0	300
2	300	0	300
3	300	0	-300
4	100	0	-300
5	-100	0	-300

Objects | Structure | Browser
File Edit View Mode

FIGURE 4.10   Your point's XYZ values should look like this.

Create Groups of Points Using Clone

Now that there are points for the floor and the beginnings of a door, you will add a group of points for the top of the door and wall. Even though you could create new points using the tools we just covered, you would have to do so one at a time. The Clone command will let you select a group of points and duplicate them.

To clone points:

1. Select the four corner points that form the square but not the two noncorner points. In the Structure Manager window, this would be the first four points labeled 0-3. You can select points in the Structure Manager or do so manually with the Live Selection tool.
2. From the main menu, select Functions > Clone. Look at the Attributes Manager for its settings. Make sure that both the Options and Tool settings are visible by shift-clicking the buttons with those titles. Enter 1 for Clones, set Offset to 600, and set Rotation to 0 (see Figure 4.11).

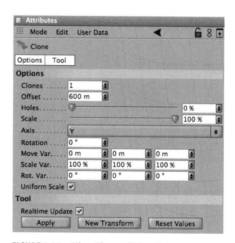

FIGURE 4.11   The Clone dialog box.

3. Click Apply to finish the command.
4. In the Structure Manager, select the points labeled 4 and 5 by clicking on them while pressing the Shift key. These are the points that represent the bottom of the door.
5. Notice that the Attributes Manager still has the Clone tool active. This means that you can continue cloning. If necessary, reactivate the Clone tool by selecting Functions > Clone.
6. Change the Offset value to 300, and click New Transform. Your Structure Manager will now have 12 points (0-11) and should look like Figure 4.12. To see the house, change to the Perspective view (F1).

From the Perspective view's menu, select Edit > Frame Scene (H key) to ensure you can see everything. Your object appears to have a floor with a series of unconnected dots (see Figure 4.13).

Point	X	Y	Z
0	−300	0	−300
1	−300	0	300
2	300	0	300
3	300	0	−300
4	100	0	−300
5	−100	0	−300
6	−300	600	−300
7	−300	600	300
8	300	600	300
9	300	600	−300
10	100	300	−300
11	−100	300	−300

FIGURE 4.12   The Structure Manager shows 12 points so far.

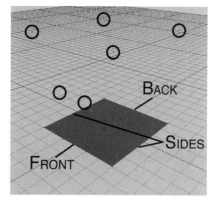

FIGURE 4.13   A Perspective view of the floor and points. Make sure you frame the scene. Imagine the front, back, and sides of the soon-to-be house. Circles have been drawn around the floating points.

Connect the Dots With the Bridge Tool

So far, you have points for the floor, walls, and door opening. Only the floor has been filled, and now it's time to build the walls. The Bridge tool is a quick way to do that. This tool creates a polygon between either three or four points. Since the walls are comprised of four points each, this will work well here.

To create the polygons for the side and back walls using the Bridge tool:

1. Make sure that you are still using the Perspective view and that you can see all your points. If you need to, select Edit > Frame Scene from the Perspective view's menu set.
2. Make sure you are using the Points tool and that you have House selected in the Objects Manager.
3. Press B to invoke the Bridge tool, right-click and choose Bridge, or select it from the Modeling icons on the bottom palette.
4. In the Perspective view, click and drag from bottom to top, clicking on the first point, dragging to the second point, and then letting go. Then click-drag on the third point to the fourth point and let go, again from bottom to top (see Figure 4.14).

Make sure you can see your object well in the Perspective view. If you need to, very slightly rotate the view so you can see where your points are.

The Polygon Normals may be pointing in the wrong direction. Instructions will follow on how to fix this later.

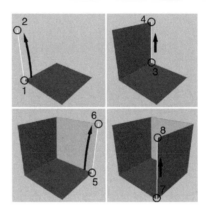

FIGURE 4.14 As you click-drag, you'll notice the polygons created to form each wall. This is a fast way to make polygons.

Create Polygon Tool for the Front Wall

The side and back walls are done, and now it's time for the front wall. This will involve making an n-sided polygon using the Create Polygon tool.

Make the front wall:

1. Select the Create Polygon tool by pressing M and then E from the pop-up menu.
2. Click on the points in order from 1 to 8 (see Figure 4.15). Double-click on the last point (number 8) or click on the first point to end the operation. As you create the polygon by clicking on the points, it will start to fill in. A yellow line and a filled yellow polygon indicate this. When you finish, the polygon will turn gray and indicate the operation is over and was successful.

Edge Cut and Bridge Tools for the Roof

The roof will eventually be sloped. That means you need two extra points along the tops of the front and back walls. You could try and add points manually with other tools. However, in this case, the Edge Cut tool will work just fine. After that, you'll add a roof with the Bridge tool and then slope it using the Move tool.

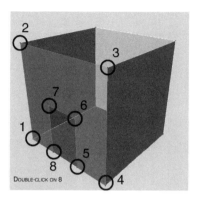

FIGURE 4.15   Double-click on number 8, or click the first point you started with to end the Create Polygon operation.

Make points for the sloping roof:

1. Select the Edge tool or press V and select Tools > Edges from the pop-up menu.
2. With the Live Selection tool, select the top edges for the front and back walls. Make sure that those are the only two edges selected (see Figure 4.16).

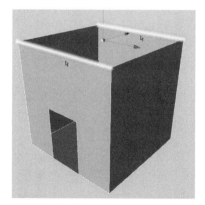

FIGURE 4.16   Select the top two edges with the Live Selection tool. Make sure that you have no other edges selected.

3. Click the icon for the Edge Cut tool (see Figure 4.17a), or press M and then F from the pop-up menu.
4. Find the Edge Cut tool settings (see Figure 4.17b). Leave the settings at their default, and click Apply. Something very important happened here, but you won't be able to see the results until you switch tools.

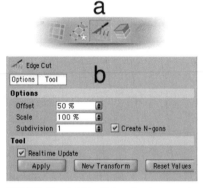

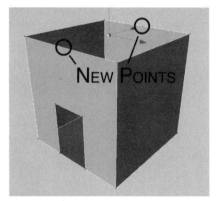

FIGURE 4.17   (a) The Edge Cut icon and (b) the Edge Cut options.

5. Select the Points tool to see the results, or press V and then choose Tools > Points from the pop-up menu. You now have two more points (see Figure 4.18) sitting right in the middle of the roof edges.

FIGURE 4.18   The Edge Cut tool adds extra vertices on the selection.

Use the Bridge tool to make a roof:

6. Press M and then B to invoke the Bridge tool.
7. In order, from points 1 to 2, click-drag and then release the mouse button; from 3 to 4, click-drag and then release the mouse button; and then from 5 to 6, do the same (see Figure 4.19).

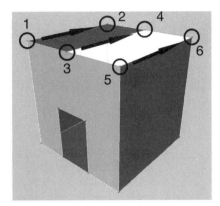

FIGURE 4.19   The Bridge tool connects points to make polygons for the roof.

Using Auto Switch

Until now, you've been changing among points, edges, and polygons manually. The handy Auto Switch mode will give you access to all three. When your mouse rolls over a polygon, edge, or point, it will light up, indicating you can select or edit it.

When to Use Auto Switch, Default and Tweak Mode

There are three modes to choose from when making changes to your polygon model: Auto Switch mode, Default mode, and Tweak mode. Use Auto Switch mode when you need quick access to all three polygon elements. It is useful for steps that require small selections and limited operations. Do not use Auto Switch if you need to do extensive cutting of faces and extrusions, and you want to select large parts of a model. For that, it is best to use Default mode.

Tweak mode removes the need to select and then edit the elements of the polygons object. For example, using the Move tool, you can just click a point and move it all in one motion, instead of having to select it first and then move it second. Be aware that many of the editing functions are disabled in this mode.

Use Auto Switch to select an edge and raise the roof:

1. Press V and then from the pop-up menu, select Tools > Auto Switch Mode (see Figure 4.20).
2. Select the middle top edge with the Live selection tool. Notice how elements light up when you put your mouse over them. This indicates when to select the element you want.

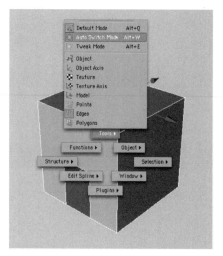

FIGURE 4.20 Auto Switch gives you access to points, edges, and polygons without changing tools.

3. In the Coordinates Manager, enter 850 for the Y position value. If you decide to do it manually, turn off the Snap Settings. Jerky movement can result with it on while using the Move tool. If you want an exact value, use the Coordinates Manager.

4. Frame the scene. The result is a sloped roof (see Figure 4.21).

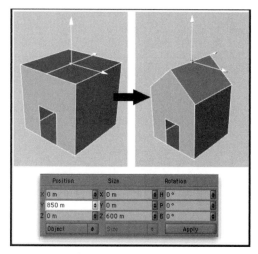

FIGURE 4.21 After you select the middle edge, enter 850 for the Y position to raise it.

Knife Tool for the Window Hole

The Knife tool in R9 was updated with several enhancements. Most notably you can now choose among different cutting modes (see Figure 4.22). To cut out a window, the Hole option will work best. Knifing is a good way of adding complexity to the entire model or to just selections of polygons. If you want to, open a new scene, create a cube, make it editable, and try the different Knife tool modes on it. You can also refer to Help > Help for more information.

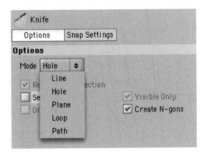

FIGURE 4.22   The Knife tool options.

Cut out the window:

1. Change modes to Default by pressing V and then choosing Tools > Default Mode from the pop-up menu. Press V again, and choose Tools > Polygons. By changing to Default mode and Polygons mode, you ensure that you will only select polygons for this operation.
2. Press F4 for a maximized Front view. Press H to center the house. Make sure the house is selected in the Objects Manager.
3. Press N and then G to switch to Lines. Press N and then H to switch to Wireframe. You can also do this through the Front window's Display menu.
4. Using the Live selection tool, select the front polygon. Quickly switch back to the Perspective view (F1) if you need to verify that you have selected only the front polygon. Press F4 to return to the Front view (see Figure 4.23).
5. It is important that you only select the front polygon and no others. The knife operation will affect any polygons you have selected. Since you only want to cut a window out above the door, you should only select that front polygon.
6. Select the Knife tool from the Modeling tool palette, or press K.
7. In the Knife Options, change the Mode to Hole. Turn on Enable Snapping in the Snap Settings.

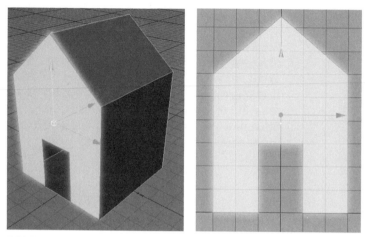

FIGURE 4.23   Select only the front polygon.

8. In the Front window, click on the grid lines above the door four times to make a square (see Figure 4.24). Click on the first point to end the operation (see Figure 4.25).

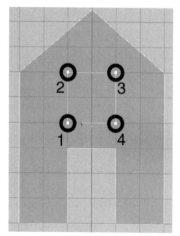

FIGURE 4.24   Using the Knife tool, cut a hole in the selected polygon. Click on positions 1, 2, 3, and 4. Click on 1 again to end the operation.

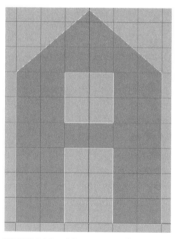

FIGURE 4.25   After you make your last click, a hole will appear. The dimensions of the hole should match the grid because you enabled snapping.

Shrink the window hole:

1. Select the Edge tool by pressing V and then choosing Tools > Edges from the pop-up menu. Select the Live Selection tool.

You can toggle the Live Selection tool with the last used Move, Scale, or Rotate tools using the spacebar. Press E for Move, R for Rotate, and T for Scale.

2. Select the edges that represent the window.
3. Select the Scale tool.
4. Scale by clicking and dragging in the window, or in the Coordinates Manager, enter 115 for both the Size X and Y.
5. Press F1 to see the result in the Perspective view (see Figure 4.26).

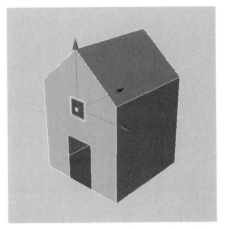

FIGURE 4.26   The result of the window hole after you scale.

Create the Sides of the Roof with Extrude

One of the most-used tools in polygon modeling is Extrude. This tool makes a connected copy of points, edges, or polygons and extends it either outward or inward. In other words, you can "pull out" faces, edges, or points. You will do just that on the roof. First, you will select the tops. Then, using Extrude, you will pull out new polygons for thickness.

Extend the roof:

1. Make sure you are in Default mode. Select the Polygon and Live Selection tools. You should have the Perspective view maximized (F1).
2. Select the top two polygons that represent the roof. When selected, they turn red, indicating their selected state.
3. Press D to invoke Extrude, or select its icon. In the tool's options, enter 25 for the Offset value and click Apply (see Figure 4.27).

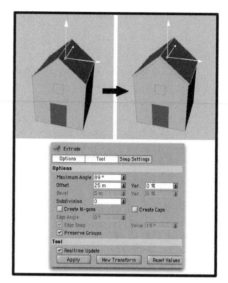

FIGURE 4.27   The result of Extrude is a thicker roof.

Selection: Only Select Visible Elements and Radius

When working with a polygon object, it is helpful to both select elements on the surface of the object and/or select elements through the object. Imagine you want to select faces on the front and the back of the object without having to rotate the image to see the other side. In the Selection tool options, you can tell the Live Selection tool which behavior you want using the Only Select Visible Elements preference. It is on by default, which means you can only select surface elements. Turning if off means you can select both surface and elements behind the surface. Be careful to remember which option you are using. When in doubt, check. Unwanted behavior might result if you don't know if this option is on or off.

In this case, you want to select the newly created sides of the roof for further extrusion. One way to do that is to turn off Only Select Visible Elements for the Live Selection tool.

There are times when the selection radius is too big or too small. If, for example, you wanted to select a face that is very small, then your radius should be set to a low value. On the other hand, if you need to select a large number of elements, then a larger value would be more appropriate.

Understanding Only Select Visible Elements and Display

Learning how to pick both surface and back elements is very important. You need to also understand the different ways to view your model and how those might make things easier for you. A default shaded view makes things simple to see and understand, but it often is nice to see a wireframe of the model so that you know what you're selecting. You need to always be aware what mode your selection tool is in; that is, is it selecting back faces or not.

Turn on/off only select visible elements and change the radius:

1. Select the Live Selection tool.
2. In the options window, note the status of Only Select Visible Elements. Change the radius to 1 (see Figure 4.28a). As you progress through this tutorial, be very aware of the status of this tool.

At some point, it might be necessary to change the Radius value back to 10. Otherwise, you may find it more difficult to select elements. The number 10 is a reasonable value because it is usually not too small or too large.

Holding the left mouse button down and rotating the mouse scroll wheel can also change the Live Selection tool's Radius.

3. In the Viewport's menu, open Display to see the list of options (see Figure 4.28b). You'll notice different settings such as Quick Shade, Lines, and Wireframe. While we won't go into depth on each of these here (see Help > Help for that), you should know how to switch Viewport to these settings. You can do that here, or through the N pop-up menu. For example, you can switch to a Lines view by pressing N and then G.

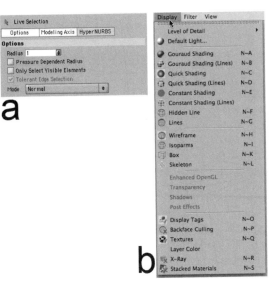

FIGURE 4.28   (a) The Live Selection tool options. (b) The Viewport's Display options.

Loop Selection

The Live Selection tool is very useful. However, there are times when you want to use other selection methods. In our next steps, we want to be able to select the rim of the newly created roof polygons, so that we can extrude them. We could use the Live Selection tool to do this, but there is a quicker method, Loop Selection.

Loop select and extrude faces:

1. Press F1 to see a maximized Perspective view. Frame the scene if you need to.
2. Hide the grid. Go to the Filter menu in the Viewport, and unselect Grid. This just helps to unclutter your view of things. You can bring it back at any time by the same method.
3. Change your display to Wireframe (N and then H) and Lines (N and then G). This helps you see your model, and what you are about to select, more clearly.
4. Activate the Loop Selection. You can get to the Loop Selection by going to Selection > Loop Selection in the main menu. Or you can press U and then L (see Figure 4.29b). You'll see a pop-up window when you press U, and it will go away as soon as you hit L, indicating that you're ready to use the Loop Selection tool.
5. The Loop Selection tool works not by selecting a single polygon but a loop or series of polygons. To get the selection you want, it's important to know how the tool chooses what loop to select. It does so according to the edge you put your mouse over. Look at the front side of your roof. Put your mouse over the edge shown in Figure 4.29a. You'll

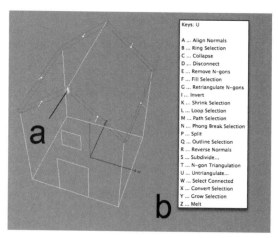

FIGURE 4.29   (a) Put your mouse over this edge to select those loops. (b) The U selection pop-up window. Use U and then L to get to the Loop Selection.

notice that the polygons will light up, showing what is about to be selected. Go ahead and make that selection as indicated by Figure 4.30.

In the end, it doesn't matter how you select these elements. If you can't get the Loop Selection to work, try the Live Selection instead.

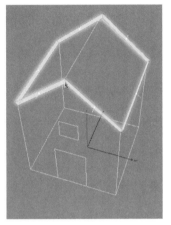

FIGURE 4.30   The Perspective view of your selection. The figure has been exaggerated for clarity.

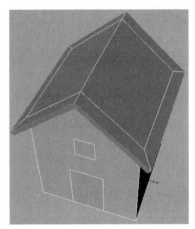

FIGURE 4.31   The result of Extrude.

6. Press D to extrude. In the tool options, change Maximum Angle to 360 and Offset to 75, and then click Apply. Change the Viewport's display to Quick Shading (N and then C). The result will look like Figure 4.31, with the roof sides extended outward.

Do It Again for a Double Roof

If one roof is good, two are better. You will use the exact same tools and techniques to make a double roof. Practice makes perfect!

Make a double roof:

1. In the Perspective view, select (use the Live Selection tool) the middle top roof polygons (see Figure 4.32a). Make sure that Only Select Visible Elements is on in the Live Selection tool options. Double-check the selection by rotating the view around the object or changing your Display to Lines as discussed earlier. You do not want any other elements selected.

2. To extrude, press the D key. Click on Reset Values to set the tool to its default setting. Use 25 for the Offset value. Click Apply to extrude the roof (see Figure 4.32b).

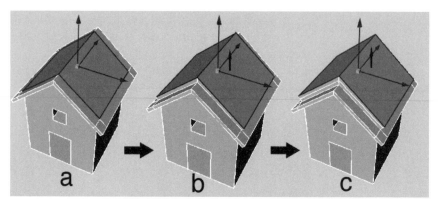

FIGURE 4.32   (a) Roof selection. (b) Extrude once. (c) Extrude twice.

3. Repeat this, extruding the roof once more (see Figure 4.32c). You can do this by clicking New Transform in the tool's Options.
4. Using the Loop Selection tool (U and then L). Select the top roof side faces. Remember to put your mouse over the little center edge, look for the polygons to light up, and then click to select (see Figure 4.33).
5. After you've made sure that you've selected no other polygons, extrude the faces with Maximum Angle set to 360 and an Offset value of 100. The result is a double roof (see Figure 4.34).

FIGURE 4.33   Select the sides using the Loop Selection tool. The selection goes all the way around the top, side polygons.

FIGURE 4.34   The double roof.

Make an Attic Using Extrude Inner and Extrude

There are a couple of ways you could go about adding an attic to the house. However, another popular tool is Extrude Inner. This function makes a copy of the face either shrink or grow parallel with the polygon's plane. The combination of Extrude and Extrude Inner provides lots of flexibility.

Start the attic:

1. With Live Selection, select the middle part of the top roof. Make sure you select no other faces (Only Select Visible Elements on).
2. Press the I key, or select the Extrude Inner icon from the modeling toolset. In the tool's options, change the Offset value to 200 and click Apply. The face has now been pulled inward and forms the base of the attic (see Figure 4.35).

 Instead of entering values for the Extrude and Extrude Inner, you can just click and drag inside the Viewport (not on the axis handles though!) to get an interactive extrude. For this exercise, it doesn't matter which way you do it.

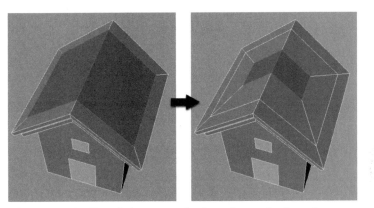

FIGURE 4.35   Use Extrude Inner to make the polygons for the attic.

Create the attic extrusions:

3. Press D to perform an Extrude on the attic selection. Click the Reset Values button. In the tool's options, change Offset to 0. Click Apply. The reason you extrude with a 0 setting is that a larger value would make the attic grow outward too much. A 0 setting lets you create an overlapping, connected face that you can later move upward. That will make the walls straight up and down instead of slanted.
4. Enter 1100 for the face's Y Position. The results are the walls of the attic (see Figure 4.36).
5. Perform another Extrude. Click Reset Values before entering 25 for Offset, and then click Apply (see Figure 4.37).
6. Select the small side polygons you just created of the new attic roof. Use the Loop Selection tool, just like before. Make sure you have no other faces selected.

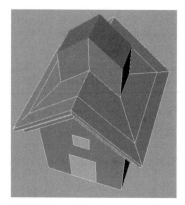

FIGURE 4.36   Raise the attic walls.

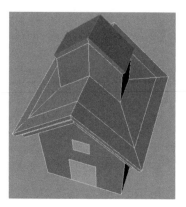

FIGURE 4.37   The beginnings of the attic roof.

7. Extrude the faces. Set the Maximum Angle to 360 and Offset to 75 (see Figure 4.38).

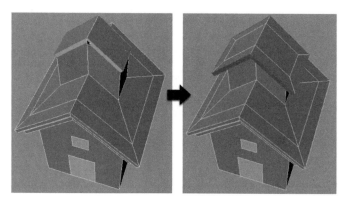

FIGURE 4.38   The attic. Select the side attic polygons, and then extrude them.

The Attic Window

The house is almost complete, but the attic needs a window. There are no additional tools you need to know to complete this. If you need to, refer to the section where you created the first window.

Create the attic window:

1. Press F3 for the Right Viewport, and press H to center it.
2. Turn the grid back on in the Viewport's Filter menu. Change the Display to Quick Shade (N and then C) so that you can better see which face to select.

3. With Live Selection, select the polygon that corresponds to the attic wall (see Figure 4.39). Make sure that Only Select Visible Elements is on. You only want to select this face.

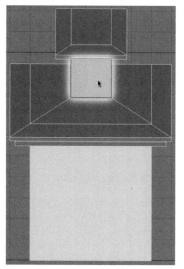

FIGURE 4.39   The face you need to select for the attic window is highlighted.

4. Change the Display to Lines (N and then G) so that you can see the grid behind your selection. Use S to maximize your selection, or choose Edit > Frame Selected Elements in the Viewport's menu.

5. Use the Knife tool (K) to cut out a hole for the window (it doesn't matter how big or small). Make sure Snapping is on for a perfectly rectangular opening. Make sure that the Knife tool is configured to Hole in the Mode section in the Attributes Manager (see Figure 4.40). See the results in the Perspective view with Quick Shading turned on (see Figure 4.41).

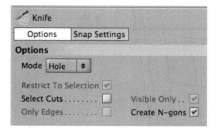

FIGURE 4.40   The Knife tool options.

FIGURE 4.41   The attic window in Perspective view.

A Frame for the Window

Apart from extruding faces, you can also extrude edges. For the windows and doors, this will be useful for making frames. To do so, you will need to use the Edge tool.

Make the frame for the attic window:

1. Select the Edge tool, or press V and then choose Tools > Edges from the pop-up menu.
2. Using the Live Selection tool, click on the edges that make up the inside of the window. Make sure Only Select Visible Elements is on and that the Radius is large enough. Make sure you have no other edges selected (see Figure 4.42a).

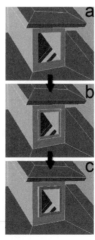

FIGURE 4.42   (a) Select the edges of the window. (b) Extrude the edges inward manually. (c) Switch to polygons and extrude to make the frame.

3. Press D to Extrude. Instead of using an Offset value, click and drag in the view and manually pull in new edges so that you create enough space for the frame (see Figure 4.42b).

4. Switch from edges to polygons, and select the newly created faces (Loop Selection works well here). Press D to extrude those faces outward. Instead of using the Offset, do it manually by click-dragging in the view (see Figure 4.42c).

Polygon Normals

During the creation of any polygon model, it is common for you to get reversed faces. Every polygon face has a front face and a back face. To see which direction a polygon is pointing, select it. A red (orange for Light scheme) polygon is facing toward you. A blue (light blue for Light scheme) polygon is facing away from you. You want all the polygons on the house to be red on the outside (facing outwards).

Two tools to use for this are Functions > Align Normals and Functions > Reverse Normals in the main menu (you can also right-click on the model when in Polygon mode).

When you are finished modeling the house, select all of the polygons and then choose the Align Normals command. This will make all the polygons either red or blue. Then choose Reverse Normals if the polygons are blue to make them red. You can also choose individual polygons and reverse them.

Discover More

To finish the tutorial, make frames for the other window and door opening. Use the techniques you just used for the attic window frame (see Figure 4.43). Have some fun, and practice the tools you've learned.

FIGURE 4.43   The finished house—with a little stylish Sketch & Toon rendering.

Wrap Up

Polygon modeling is powerful because you are working directly with the most basic elements in 3D. Master it, and you will find that you can create any shape imaginable. This tutorial covered just the basics, and there is still much to learn. In the next tutorial you will discover how to combine polygons and HyperNURBS for organic modeling.

Save your scene:

1. From the main menu, choose File > Save as, and save your scene.
2. Back up your work too.

TUTORIAL 4.2

HYPERNURBS: MODELING A DOLPHIN

HyperNURBS are MAXON's fancy way of saying subdivision modeling. C4D supports two main types of geometry: NURBS and polygons. Hyper-NURBS will try to affect any geometry connected to it, but you will find that it is most effectively used in conjunction with polygons. The easiest way to do this is through *box modeling*, which means starting with a primitive, usually a cube; converting it to a polygon object; and then adding geometry where necessary (see Figure 4.44).

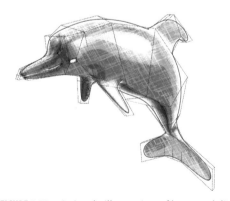

FIGURE 4.44   A simple illustration of box modeling.

What Do HyperNURBS Do?

HyperNURBS subdivide and round linked objects. So, a polygon cube will become subdivided and rounded (see Figure 4.45).

Keep in mind that the number of polygons in a scene will always go up when you use HyperNURBS, sometimes dramatically. Higher polygon numbers mean slower render times. It is usually *not* necessary or prudent

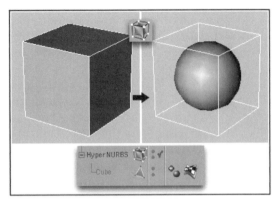

FIGURE 4.45   Polygon cube, cube, HyperNURB, and basic HyperNURBS hierarchy.

to use HyperNURBS with NURBS (there are exceptions to every rule!). Use polygons instead. Very creative, organic, and exciting shapes can be realized by learning the power of polygon modeling and HyperNURBS (see Figure 4.46).

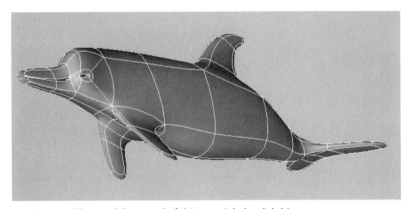

FIGURE 4.46   The modeling goal of this tutorial: the dolphin.

Modeling the Dolphin

The goal of this tutorial is to teach you basic polygon primitive modeling (box modeling) in conjunction with HyperNURBS.

You will learn about the following:

- Basic HyperNURBS hierarchy
- The Symmetry tool
- Configuring Viewports to display images to be used as modeling guides

- Configuring Viewport options
- HyperNURBS settings and keystrokes
- Polygon modeling from a cube primitive

To begin:

1. Launch C4D, or from the main menu, select File > New.
2. Change to the Modeling layout by selecting Window > Layout > Modeling from the main menu.

ON THE CD

3. Make sure the CD-ROM is loaded, locate the files Dolphin_front, Dolphin_side, and Dolphin_top (CD-ROM > Tutorials > Chapter04 > Chapter4-2), and copy them to your hard drive. Place them in the same folder you will be saving this C4D document.

Configuring the Viewports

In real life, you would be lucky to have a finished model to use as a reference because that's not usually the norm. Instead, either drawn or photo images are used as modeling guides to help you create your object. The files you copied to the hard drive are for this very purpose. You will import images into the Top, Right, and Front views. You will then resize the images so that the proportions are correct. These images are of the rough polygon shape before the HyperNURB is applied. This is done for clarity and to show you how to construct the polygon cage. If you were to do this from scratch, you would make your own drawings or photographs.

Configure the Viewports:

1. Press F5 for a four-window layout. Each view has a menu set, which is referred to as the Viewport menu. Locate the Viewport menu for the Perspective view, and select Edit > Configure All (see Figure 4.47). The other three views are highlighted in green, and the Viewport options appear. Examine the options and note that there are buttons for Display, Filter, View, Back, and HUD. Clicking any one of these will bring up different preferences. Make sure that you are in the Display options (see Figure 4.48).
2. Change Shading to Lines.
3. Change Wire to Isoparms.
4. Make sure that Isoline Editing is not check marked. Having this unchecked will allow you to see the polygon cage on top of the rounded form.
5. Click the HUD button. Make sure that Total Polygons and Projection are check marked.
6. Click the Filter button. Make sure all are check marked *except* Axis Bands and N-Gon Lines and Grid. This helps to keep the Viewports uncluttered.

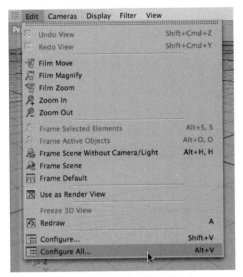

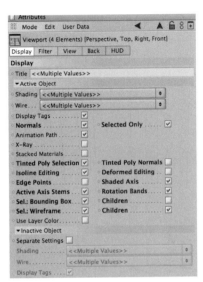

FIGURE 4.47   Configure All will make changes to all the Viewports.

FIGURE 4.48   The Display options.

In the Filter checklist, you will find options for Grid, Axis, Horizon, HUD, and many others. It is often useful to turn these on or off, depending on your preferences. Remember that you can also configure each window separately. To do so, choose the Viewport's Edit > Configure option. Now only that particular view will be affected.

The HUD can be configured to give feedback on polygon count, an important aspect of polygon modeling. For more information on the HUD, refer to Chapter 13 "Customizing the C4D Interface."

7. It would be a good idea to change the Perspective window's Display to a shaded view instead of lines in order to better see your object in that view.

Import images into the Viewports:

8. Press F2. From the Viewport's menu, select Edit > Configure. In the Viewport attributes, click the Back button. Click on the ellipsis button (. . .), which is next to a blank text field titled Image. Locate on your hard drive the images you copied from the CD-ROM at the beginning of this lesson. Load Dolphin_top. Resize the Size X to 283. You will see Size Y change automatically if Keep Aspect Ratio is on (it is on by default) as shown in Figure 4.49.

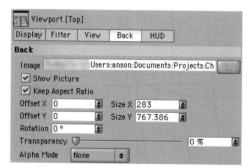

FIGURE 4.49   Click on the Back button, and then import the image.

9. Press F3 to access the Right view. The Viewport's attributes will show this view's options, but the image field will appear blank because you have not yet loaded an image for this view.
10. Load Dolphin_side into the Viewport, and change its Size X to 772.
11. Press F4 to access the Front view. Load Dolphin_front, and then change its Size X to 271.

Turning off the grid simplifies the workspace visually. You can turn it back on at any time.

In the Viewport's Back options, you can change the transparency of the image. It can aid in viewing if you find it difficult to see your object and the guides. Alternatively, you can turn the image off by deselecting Show Picture.

If you were doing your own images, you could find the right image proportions by lining up the images to a cube or other object.

Start with a cube:

12. Bring a cube into the scene. Locate the cube's Objects Properties. Change Size X to 110. This makes it slightly smaller in the Front Viewport.
13. Convert the cube into a Polygon object by selecting Functions > Make Editable from the main menu, clicking the Make Editable button, or using the C shortcut. Rename *cube* to *Dolphin Cage*.

The HyperNURB

1. Select Objects > NURBS > HyperNURBS from the main menu, or click the HyperNURB button in the icon palette. If you select the Dolphin Cage object first, then select your HyperNURB object while

holding down the Alt key, this will automatically link your objects, and you can skip step 2.

2. Drag and drop the Dolphin Cage onto the HyperNURB. You will now notice that the cube has become rounded.

3. Select Dolphin Cage in the Objects Manager. Press the Q key. This key toggles on and off the HyperNURBS object and can be used at any time during the modeling process. Make sure that the HyperNURBS is off. The red X next to the HyperNURBS in the Objects Manager verifies this. The cube will also no longer be rounded.

You may not be able to see your object clearly yet because it is represented by a white outline, and the white from the image is covering it. If that is the case, increase the image's transparency setting in the Viewport's Edit > Configure options.

Modeling the Dolphin's Cage

You are set up and ready to start modeling the dolphin. You will modify points, edges, and polygons to manipulate the shape. First, you will line up the points, and then extrude the cube to create more.

Line up the points:

1. Click on the Points tool and the Live Selection tool. Make sure that Only Select Visible Elements is off because you will need to be able to select points behind surfaces.

2. Press F3 to access the Right view. Using the Live Selection tool and the Move tool, rearrange the points so that they match the guide (see Figure 4.50).

For every point you see in the Right view, there is a corresponding point right behind it. So, while it appears you are selecting only one point, you are really selecting two. That's why you made the changes to the Live Selection tool.

Remember that to edit the Dolphin Cage, you must have it selected in the Objects Manager. It is common to deselect it doing other tasks. You cannot edit points, polygons, or edges if you have the HyperNURBS selected.

It is better to select with the Live Selection tool than with the Move tool because you need to be selecting doubled-up points. You cannot select doubled-up points with the Move, Scale, or Rotate tools.

3. Now switch to the Top view (F2). Instead of using the Move tool, use the Scale tool, and select any of the points on the right side of the model. Hold down the Shift key, and select the corresponding point

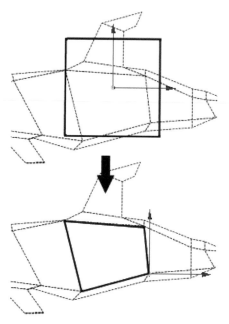

FIGURE 4.50 Select and then rearrange the points in the Right view. Try to match the guides.

on the left side. Now using the Scale tool, match the points up with the drawing. Move on to the rest of the points, selecting at least two at a time (one on the right side and the corresponding left side). Don't worry about being overly exact (see Figure 4.51). Use other selection tools, like the Rectangle Selection tool, if need be.

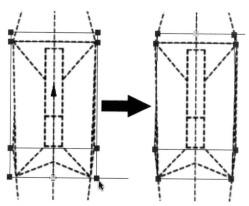

FIGURE 4.51 Use the Scale tool to reposition points symmetrically.

Extruding the front:

4. Press F1 to see the object in the Perspective view. Change to the Polygon tool.
5. In the Live Selection's tool options, make sure Only Select Visible Elements is on.
6. Select the front polygon (the one closer to the dolphin's head). Make sure you have no other polygons selected (see Figure 4.52). You can verify this by pressing N and then G for a line view, and then return to a shaded view by pressing N and then C.

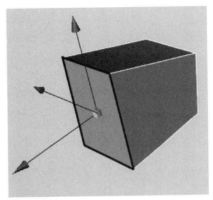

FIGURE 4.52   Select the polygon that is closest to the dolphin's head.

7. Switch to the Right view (F3). Press the D key (Extrude). *Without* clicking on the axis arrows, click-drag from left to right in the Viewport (see Figure 4.53).

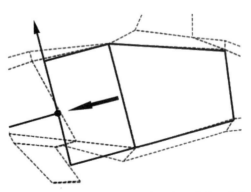

FIGURE 4.53   When you click-drag from left to right, the face will move outward.

8. Change to the Points tool and the Live Selection tool. Make sure Only Select Visible Elements is off. Rearrange the points to match the guide (see Figure 4.54).

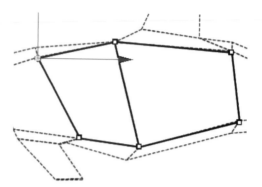

FIGURE 4.54 Align the points to the guide.

 If you have invoked the Extrude tool (or Extrude Inner), and you accidentally click, chances are you have created an extrusion so small you don't even know it's there. This is undesirable but can be remedied through the Undo command. If in doubt, double-check through undoing and redoing. You can undo multiple times.

9. The spacebar toggles between the Selection tool and the last tool used. In the case of editing the cage, you can toggle between the Live Selection tool and the Move tool quickly this way.
10. Change to the Top view. Use the Scale tool to line up the new points (see Figure 4.55). Don't worry about being overly exact.

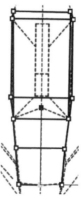

FIGURE 4.55 Align the points to the guide using the Scale tool.

Keep extruding and aligning:

11. Switch to the Right view (F3). Make sure you are using the Polygon tool. Do not deselect the polygon. If you do, reselect the front polygon in the Perspective view, and then return to the Right view. Press D, and extrude. Switch to points and align the vertices just as you have been doing. Remember to align in the Top view also (see Figure 4.56).

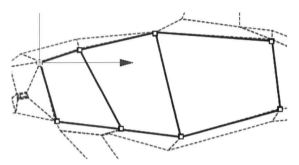

FIGURE 4.56   Extrude and align the points.

12. Using the same techniques, extrude and align once more (see Figure 4.57).

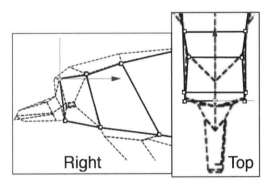

FIGURE 4.57   Extrude and align the points in the Right- and Top views.

13. Check the model in the Perspective view. It should appear similar to Figure 4.58. It looks nothing like a dolphin! Be patient, we are just getting warmed up.

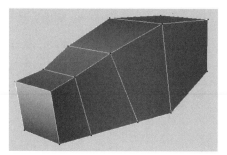

FIGURE 4.58 A Perspective view of the model so far.

The Dolphin's Mouth

So far, you have been using Extrude to create more points. For the mouth, you will use the Knife tool to slice a line in order to give you enough geometry to work with. You will do so with only the front polygon selected so that the cut is limited to that surface and not the whole model.

Use the Knife tool to slice:

1. Press F4 to switch to the Front view. In the Viewport's Display menu, select Quick Shade, or press N and then C. Switch to the Polygon tool. Make sure that the front polygon is selected. By selecting this polygon, you ensure that the Knife tool will be limited to that surface (see Figure 4.59). Zoom in so that you can better see the selected polygon.

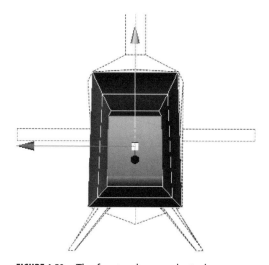

FIGURE 4.59 The front polygon selected.

2. Press K to invoke the Knife tool. In the tool's options, make sure that the Mode is set to Line. Leave the other options to their default setting. Hold down the Shift key while you make your knife cut. This will ensure perfectly horizontal lines. Starting outside the geometry, make two horizontal cuts so that the polygon is divided into roughly three equal parts (see Figure 4.60).

Extrude and modify the mouth:

3. With the Live Selection tool, click on the middle polygon of the ones you just made (see Figure 4.61). Make sure Only Select Visible Elements is on and that no other polygons are selected (verify this in the Perspective view).

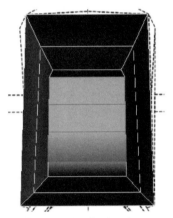

FIGURE 4.60   Cut the face into roughly three equal parts.

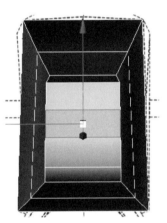

FIGURE 4.61   Select the middle polygon.

4. Switch to the Right view (F3). Move and then rotate the polygon so that it lines up with the guide (see Figure 4.62). Alternatively, you can edit the point positions to get the same result.

5. Switch to the Front view (F4). Select both the middle and bottom polygons. In the Viewport's Display menu, activate X-Ray. This will let you see both your model and the guides (see Figure 4.63).

6. Use the Scale and Move tools to shrink the selection so that it matches the guides. Don't worry if the polygon cage is not exactly like the image. Remember that this exercise is only an approximation (see Figure 4.64).

7. Return to the Right view. With the same polygons selected, press D for Extrude. In the tool's options, uncheck Preserve Groups to allow you to pull out faces as separate extrusions (which you want because the top and bottom of the mouth are not connected). Click-drag from left to right, and pull out new faces. You should also switch to Points and

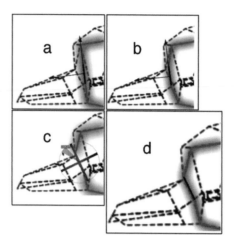

FIGURE 4.62 (a) Select. (b) Move. (c) Rotate. (d) Align to the guide.

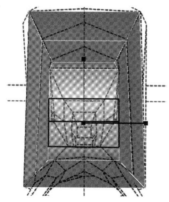

FIGURE 4.63 The bottom two polygons selected. X-Ray lets you see through the model.

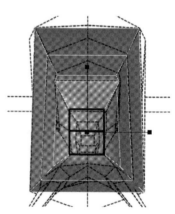

FIGURE 4.64 Move and scale the polygons into place following the guide.

Live Selection (with Only Select Visible Elements off) and align (see Figure 4.65). Repeat again until you're at the end of the nose (see Figure 4.66). You should rotate the end polygons to match the guide.

8. Double-check the Top and Front views to make sure they are lined up. The ends of the mouth will overlap. Change to the Perspective view to see the results (see Figure 4.67). Some tweaking of the points and polygons may be needed.

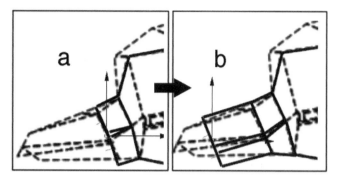

FIGURE 4.65 (a) Extrude with the Preserve Groups turned off. (b) Repeated.

FIGURE 4.66 You should rotate the end polygons to match the guide.

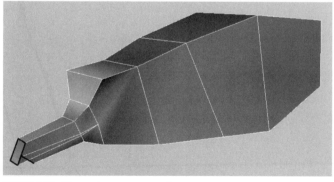

FIGURE 4.67 The polygon cage so far.

The Tail

The mouth is mostly finished. You will now select the back polygon and extrude it to make the tail.

Select and extrude:

1. In the Perspective view, select the back polygon (make sure no other polygons are selected). Then switch to the Right view. Extrude the face, and line it up with the guide (see Figure 4.68). Check the Top view, and modify with the Scale tool.

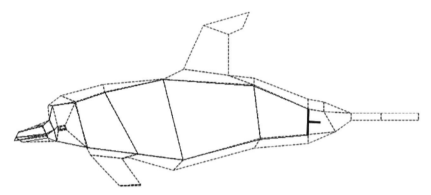

FIGURE 4.68 Lining up your points to the guide. Also verify for the Top view (not shown).

2. Continue extruding and editing elements in the Right and Top views (see Figure 4.69).

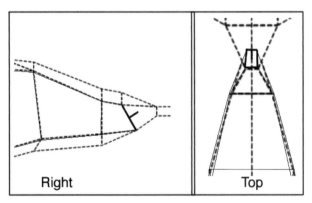

FIGURE 4.69 Right view and Top view.

3. Continue extruding and editing in the Right view and Top view (see Figure 4.70).
4. Change to a four-view layout (F5). In the Perspective view, extrude for the beginnings of the tailfin (see Figure 4.71). Verify in the Top view that the cage is lining up with the guide.

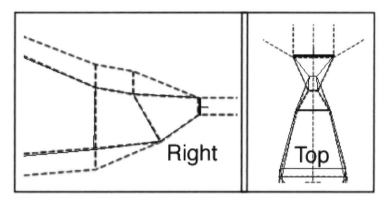

FIGURE 4.70   Right view and Top view.

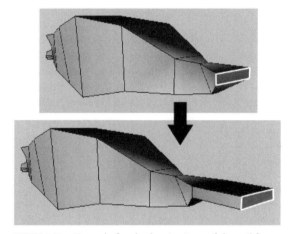

FIGURE 4.71   Extrude for the beginnings of the tail fin.

5. Change to the Right view. Click on the Live Selection tool, and in the tool's options, change Radius to 1. Make sure Only Select Visible Elements is off. Select the polygons that correspond to the sides of the tail. Verify in the Perspective view that you have only those polygons selected (see Figure 4.72).

6. In a four-view layout (F5) (see Figure 4.73), extrude the sides to make the fins. Then pull them back a little to make them line up with the guide. Verify the correct position in the Top view and Right view.

The Dorsal Fin

This fin resides on the top of the dolphin. It can be made first with an Extrude Inner and then a series of Extrudes.

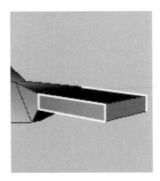

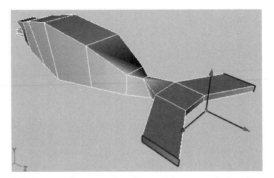

FIGURE 4.72   Make sure you only have the side polygons selected.

FIGURE 4.73   Perspective view of the extruded and positioned tail fins.

Make the dorsal fin:

1. Select the polygon on top of the dolphin cage that is closest to the dorsal fin on the drawing. You must be using the Polygon tool and the Live Selection tool, and have Only Select Visible Elements on (see Figure 4.74a).
2. Perform an Extrude Inner (I shortcut key) (see Figure 4.74b).

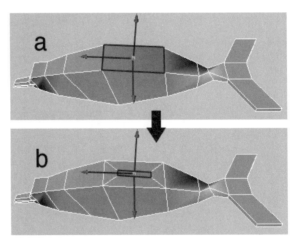

FIGURE 4.74   (a) Select the top polygon and (b) perform an Extrude Inner.

3. Change to the Right view (F3). Raise the selected polygon up slightly. Change to the points and the Live Selection tool. Make sure Only Select Visible Elements is off so that you can select hidden points. Increase the selection tool's Radius if you need to. Match the points up to the guide (see Figure 4.75).

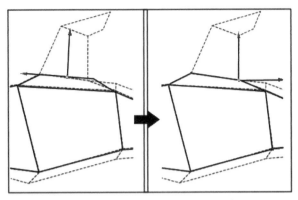

FIGURE 4.75   Raise the polygon, and then switch to points.
Align to the guide.

4. Continue to extrude and match the points with the guide. Check the Right, Top, and Perspective views (see Figure 4.76).

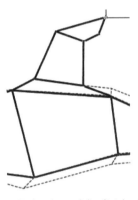

FIGURE 4.76   A Right view of the finished dorsal fin.

Extrude the flippers:

5. On the bottom of the Dolphin Cage, select the polygon nearest the flippers on the drawing (see Figure 4.77). Make sure Only Select Visible Elements is on.

6. Press I for Extrude Inner, and in the tool settings, enter 15 for the Offset value. Click Apply. Change to the Front view, and move the new polygon down slightly using the guides as a reference (see Figure 4.78).

7. Switch to the Perspective view. When you created the inner extrusion, you made a polygon that can be used for the flipper. Select the polygon that matches Figure 4.79.

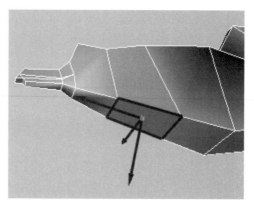

FIGURE 4.77 A Perspective view of the polygon that will make the flippers. Make sure you have no other polygons selected.

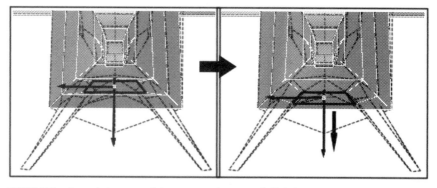

FIGURE 4.78 Extrude Inner and then move downward slightly.

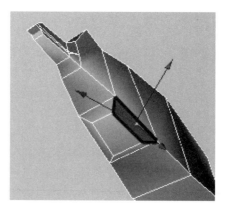

FIGURE 4.79 Select the side polygon that will be the flipper.

8. Change to the Right view. Press D to invoke the Extrude tool. In the options, enter 15 for the Offset value. Change to points, and align them to the guide (see Figure 4.80). Don't worry about being overly exact.

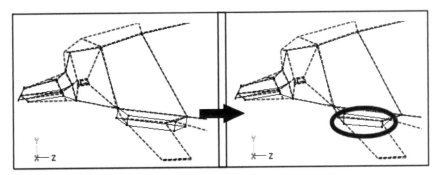

FIGURE 4.80   Align the points to the guide.

9. Return to the Polygon tool, and extrude again. Align to the guide using points (see Figure 4.81) in both the Right view and Front view.

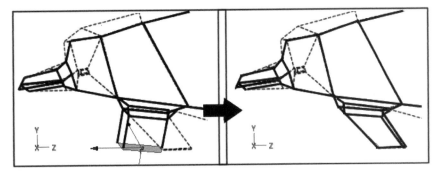

FIGURE 4.81   Align the points to the guide.

Splitting the Cage

There's no sense in modeling the other flipper because you can cut the Dolphin Cage down the middle, delete one side, and then mirror the other half.

Using the Knife tool:

1. In the Front view, make sure you have no polygons selected. In the Viewport's Filter menu, reactivate the grid. Press K for the Knife tool. Make sure it is set to Line, that Visible Only is off, and that Restrict To Selection is unchecked. Enable Snapping (see Figure 4.82).

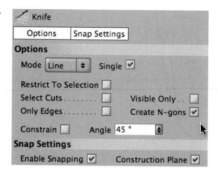

FIGURE 4.82   In the Knife Options; turn off Visible Only so that you can cut through the entire model.

2. Draw a line down the center of the cage. It is important that it be exactly in the middle (see Figure 4.83). Use the green *y*-axis as your guide. After you finish, switch to the Points tool.

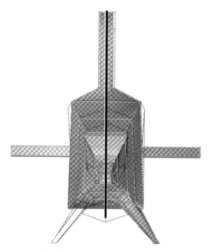

FIGURE 4.83   Draw a vertical, cutting line through the center of the object.

3. Change to the Rectangle Selection tool (under the nested options for the Live Selection tool) and in the tool's options, make sure Only Select Visible Elements is off. Select the left half of the points on the cage. Make sure that you don't select the very center row of vertical points (see Figure 4.84).
4. Press the Delete key to delete half of the model (see Figure 4.85).

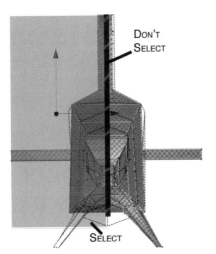
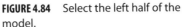
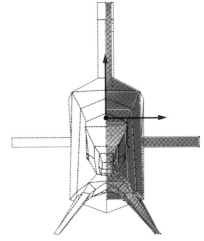

FIGURE 4.84   Select the left half of the model.

FIGURE 4.85   The deleted half of your model.

The Symmetry Object

A useful way to mirror geometry is to use the Symmetry object. It takes any geometry and mirrors it along a specific axis. In this case, we want the Dolphin Cage to be mirrored exactly on the *x*-axis. It is important that the center points have a 0 value for their X positions.

After you mirror the geometry, you will see a seam on the object if the center points aren't set to 0 for the World x-axis. In the Front view, using the Rectangle Selection tool and with Only Select Visible Elements set to off, Marquis select all the points that hug the vertical y-axis (the ones that will be the center points). Go to the Structure tab in the Objects Manager, and make sure all the entries highlighted in blue have an X value of 0.

Alternatively, you can use Structure > Set Point Value, and set all the point's X values to 0.

Use the Symmetry object:

1. From the main menu, select Objects > Modeling > Symmetry. Doing so while you having the Dolphin Cage selected and holding down the Alt key will arrange your hierarchy automatically, and you can skip step 2.
2. Link the Dolphin Cage to the Symmetry, and then link the Symmetry to the HyperNURBS. The Dolphin Cage will now be reflected. Whatever changes you make on the original will be transferred to the mirror (see Figure 4.86).

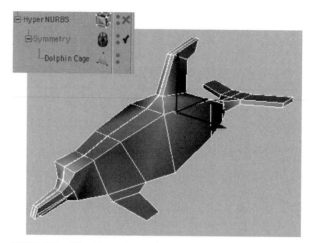

FIGURE 4.86 The hierarchy and Symmetry results.

Discover More

The model is mostly finished. It could use some eyes, and the centerline needs to be adjusted to the guides. Continue tweaking the points, and use the Knife tool to make eyes. After you are finished, turn the HyperNURB on.

Create eyes:

1. Make a hole for the eye with the Knife tool. Make sure that the Knife tool's options are set correctly for this.
2. Fill the hole with the Close Polygon Hole tool (Structure > Close Polygon Hole). This tool works by putting your mouse over the hole. The tool will let you know when it's found a hole it can fill by lighting up. You can then click to fill the hole.
3. Extrude it inwards a few times (see Figure 4.87).

For the eyes, you are creating an N-Gon. You must watch N-Gons closely because they sometimes misbehave (especially with HyperNURBS). It is highly advisable that you select the N-Gon and convert it to regular polygons. You can do this by selecting it and then choose Functions > Remove N-Gons. This will help it interact more cleanly with the HyperNURB (see Figure 4.88).

Tweak the centerline:

4. Adjust the centerline with the Points, Live Selection, and Move tools (see Figure 4.89).

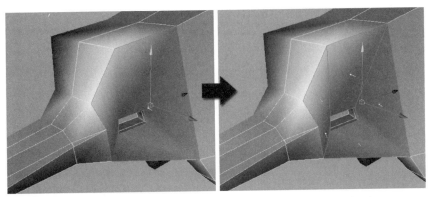

FIGURE 4.87   Use the Knife, Close Polygon Hole, and Extrude tools to make the eye.

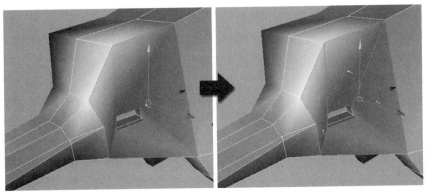

FIGURE 4.88   Remove the N-Gon surrounding the eye. It will help the HyperNURB to deal with that area better.

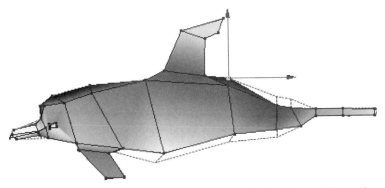

FIGURE 4.89   The centerline was created when you knifed the model in half. Adjust it to the guides.

5. Turn on the HyperNURB (see Figure 4.90).

FIGURE 4.90   The final model: A happy dolphin.

Save your work:

6. From the main menu, select File > Save.
7. Give the file a name, and save it.

CONCLUSION

HyperNURBS and polygon modeling are powerful ways to create a variety of shapes. Practice and the knowledge will serve you well. This is a primary technique for creating the human figure or parts of the human body, such as facial modeling. It can also be used for low polygon character modeling for games. Whatever you want to model, HyperNURBS and polygon modeling will be a serious part of your toolset and workflow.

MATERIALS AND TEXTURES

In This Chapter

- Materials
- Procedural Shaders
- TUTORIAL 5.1   Applying Materials
- TUTORIAL 5.2   Layered Shaders and the Banged-Up Old Robot
- TUTORIAL 5.3   Basic BodyPaint

When they are not in motion, very little visually differentiates a bowling ball from a tennis ball, a pea from a beach ball, or a golf ball from a wicker ball. One distinguishing factor is material. *Materials* are the visual clues that reference the tactile and visual qualities of a surface. Material, or sometimes also referred to as *texture*, is everywhere, and, without it, our real world would be a drab existence.

3D is no different. If you've been following the tutorials, you're probably tired of looking at the same gray, plastic-looking models. In this chapter, we're going to examine ways to spruce up our models, to give them color, dimension, tactile surfaces, and reflective qualities; we'll even define the geometry of objects through texturing.

MATERIALS

An important thing to note before we get started is that although "texture" is the general catchphrase for surface qualities in 3D, each program handles the actual nomenclature a little differently. C4D uses the term *material*, which is a collection of properties that defines a surface. These materials are kept track of in the Materials Manager at the bottom of the interface. A new material can be created by selecting File > New Material within this Materials Manager (see Figure 5.1). This new material will be represented by a little swatch that shows a sphere with an approximation of the material in its currently defined state. The Materials Manager stores all of the materials you have created for a given project.

 This entire chapter uses the Classic interface because it provides better contrast for some of the screenshots. Don't worry, there's no loss of functionality. For this tutorial, you should switch to the Classic scheme, which you can do by choosing Edit > Preferences. In the Common section, change the Scheme to Classic. For pre-R10 users, you'll feel right at home.

FIGURE 5.1   The Materials Manager with a newly created material swatch.

Each of the instructions that define the material is called a *channel*. When you double-click a material swatch within the Materials Manager, a window called the Materials Editor will open, allowing you to alter these parameters (see Figure 5.2). The materials also appear in the Attributes Manager by single-clicking on them (see Figure 5.3). This is really a nice function because it leaves you plenty of screen real estate and is generally easier to access. Similarly, you can have the Attributes Manager show you more than one channel at a time, which makes for quick editing of a material's channels.

Let's look again at Figure 5.2. Along the left hand side are located the list of channels, along with a little checkbox that indicates if that particular parameter is active or not. So, for example, the *Color* channel is active, but *Diffusion* is not. To edit a channel, you click on its name and its properties appear in the right side of the Material Editor window. Most channels have both a Color and a Texture space where you can reference image files. The idea here is that you can define a flat color in the Color section, or you can import a bit-mapped image or a procedural shader into the Texture section. The images brought into the Texture input fields are often referred to as *texture maps*.

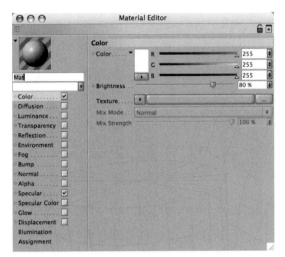

FIGURE 5.2   Double-clicking a material swatch in the Materials Manager opens the Material Editor.

FIGURE 5.3   Single-click to see the material properties in the Attributes Manager.

Looking again at Figure 5.3, in the Attributes Editor, you can activate certain channels in the Basic section and jump to each activated channel by clicking (Shift-click to add to your selection, Ctrl-click to remove) its name at the top of the Attributes Manager.

Each channel can be defined separately from other channels. However, a material takes into account all *active* channels to create a final surface quality.

PROCEDURAL SHADERS

Procedural shaders are mathematically derived and thus are independent of pixel-based images. There are two different types of shaders.

The first kind are volume shaders, which are found in the File menu in the Material Manager under File > Shader (see Figure 5.4a). These shaders have their own unique properties and should be used depending on what look and feel you are trying to get. For example, the Banji shader is especially designed to emulate glass and other transparent surfaces, whereas Danel is good for metals.

The second kind is found inside the material channels. When you click on the Color channel, for example, you will see its properties displayed on the right side of the Material Editor window. There are Color and Brightness settings along with Texture. Next to the word "Texture" is a little triangle (see Figure 5.4b). Clicking and holding on this button will reveal the different shaders and effects. For convenience, we'll call this the *Texture Triangle* button.

R10 has moved all of the Basics materials to the Content Browser. The Content Browser can be found in the main menu by choosing Window > Content Browser. This browser also contains many other shaders and presets.

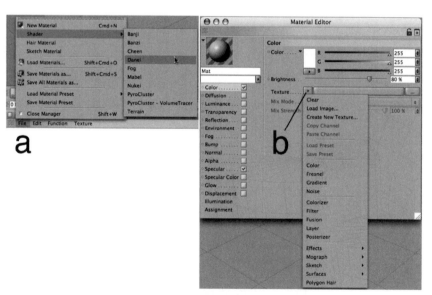

FIGURE 5.4   (a) The different volume shaders. (b) In the Material Editor window, for each channel, there is a Texture Triangle button. Click-hold to see the different shaders and effects available.

Effects

Available to each channel in the materials are some built-in *effects*. There's not enough room in this book to cover all of them, so refer to Help > Help or the manual for questions on what an individual effect does. But, we'll cover a few here so you'll feel comfortable using them.

TUTORIAL 5.1   APPLYING MATERIALS

This tutorial teaches you to navigate through the Materials Manager and the Material Editor windows, along with applying a material to an object. You'll also learn about the effects you can add to materials and how materials relate to lighting. Lighting is covered in more detail in the next chapter, but you'll soon see that there is a deep connection between materials and lighting.

You will learn about the following:

- The Materials Manager
- The Material Editor
- Channels
- Effects
- How to apply materials to objects
- The relationship between materials and lighting
- Checking materials in the renderer

To begin:

ON THE CD

1. From the CD-ROM, choose Tutorials > Chapter05 > Chapter5-1 > robotbegin.c4d. A prepared file with a robot object will open.
2. In the Materials Manager, create a new material (File > New Material) (see Figure 5.5).

You can also create a new material by double-clicking on empty space anywhere in the Manager.

3. Double-Click on the swatch to open the Material Editor (see Figure 5.6).

Channels

Notice in the Material Editor a list of names on the left side: Color, Diffusion, Luminance, Transparency, and Reflection to name a few. These are the different properties of the material. Notice that some are check marked, indicating an active channel, and others are not.

FIGURE 5.5 Choose File > New Material.

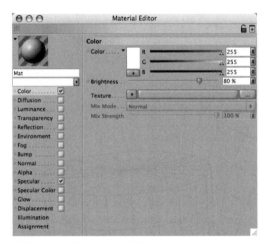

FIGURE 5.6 The Material Editor.

Activate channels:

1. Check the box next to Luminance to activate it. This channel lets you simulate light emitting properties for an object (by default, however, an object with Luminance does not become a light, in the sense that it does not light up objects around it).

2. Single-click on the word Luminance to see its properties. Be aware that just because you check mark a channel doesn't mean that you are actually looking at its properties. Only a channel that is highlighted will display its properties, and you must click on the word to highlight it.

Use effects:

3. In the Luminance properties, next to the word Texture, is the Texture Triangle button. Click it, and from the pull-down menu, select Effects > Subsurface Scattering (see Figure 5.7). After you do so, you'll see the empty space next to Texture replaced with the effect's name.
4. Click on the name Subsurface Scattering to see its properties (see Figure 5.8). Change Strength to 100 percent. This effect mimics how light passes through objects and is one of the many effects available to you in C4D.

 If you do not have the Advanced Render module, use any of the Surface options also found under the Texture Triangle.

FIGURE 5.7   Each channel has a triangle where you can access shaders and effects. Select Subsurface Scattering for the Luminance channel.

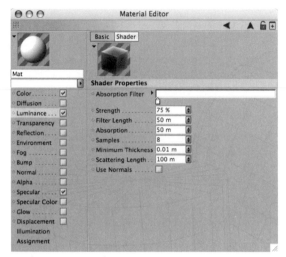

FIGURE 5.8   The properties for Subsurface Scattering. Change the Strength to 100%.

Name the material:

5. In the Material Editor window find the word Mat in the upper left hand corner. In the text box change the name to *Glow*. That will be reflected in the Materials Manager. Naming your materials is just as important as naming your objects. Too many unnamed materials can create confusion.
6. Close the Material Editor window.

Link the Glow material to the robot:

7. In the Materials Manager, click-drag the swatch Glow (see Figure 5.9a), and drop it onto the word *Robot* in the Objects Manager (see Figure 5.9b). You can also drop materials directly onto the objects in the Editor window. However, when a scene is full of objects, this can be problematic, so use the Objects Manager instead. It is also important that you drop the material onto the *actual word* in the Objects Manager and not other parts as it might have an undesirable effect.

Rendering

After you assign the material to the object, you can see its effects by rendering an image. This particular scene has been preset so that you don't have to worry about render settings. For now, you can just sit back and watch it render, but you'll learn more about rendering in later chapters.

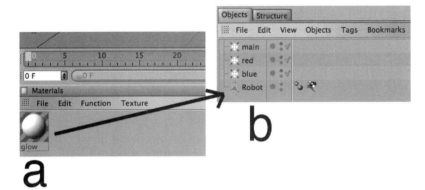

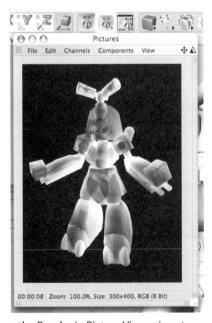

FIGURE 5.9   (a) Drag Glow from the Materials Manager over to (b) Robot in the Objects Manager, and drop it over its name. This applies the material to the object.

Render:

1. Click on the Render in Picture Viewer icon (see Figure 5.10). Do not click and hold, as this will bring up the nested options. Rather, single-click to cause a Pictures window to appear and the scene to render.
2. You can also use the shortcut Shift + R to render to the Picture Viewer.

FIGURE 5.10   Click on the Render in Picture Viewer icon to see what the robot looks like with the Glow material. (Robot model by Matthew Swinehart.)

Save the rendered image:

3. From the Picture Viewer's File menu, select File > Save Picture As.
4. Choose a file format, and then click OK.
5. Name and save the file in a directory of your choice.

Materials and Lighting

As you can see from the rendered image, the robot appears to glow with parts of it appearing semitransparent. This is the Subsurface Scattering effect you applied earlier. This effect simulates what happens to objects as light penetrates beneath their surface. Just because you apply a material to an object, however, don't expect it to look the way you want right away. Lighting affects greatly how materials will look. That's why this scene had lights prepared for you; otherwise, it would look quite different. To see this in action, delete or hide all the lights from the scene and re-render. It looks drastically different!

Wrap Up

You've learned the basics of how materials work, how to apply them to objects, and how to edit them in the Material Editor. Now let's move to the next tutorial on how to build sophisticated material systems.

TUTORIAL 5.2   **LAYERED SHADERS AND THE BANGED-UP OLD ROBOT**

The material system in C4D is truly remarkable. This tutorial will teach you how to build a network of materials and apply them in layers to an object. Again, a prepared scene with lights is already set up and ready to go. After the tutorial you will be encouraged to play with the materials you create so that you can better understand what's going on. Also note that the prepared scene is meant to be viewed from a particular camera angle, so there's no need to use your Viewport camera.

ON THE CD

No texture tutorial is complete without some explanation of texture mapping. On the CD-ROM, you will find prepared image files for this tutorial.

Note that this tutorial is moderately difficult. You'll be asked to activate a lot of different features, and it may not be apparent *why* you're doing it. Although great care will be taken to try and explain as best possible all the whys, feel free to choose Help > Help for more on some of the different terms you're bound to run into. Following are some terms you should flag for study.

You will learn about the following:

- Layer shader
- Fusion shader
- Noise shader
- Fresnel shader
- Dirt effect and the Diffusion channel
- Bump channel
- Reflection and Environment channel
- Alpha channel
- Specular channel and Color
- Displacement channel
- Importing images to use as textures
- Texture mapping
- Texture tag editing
- Material layering

ON THE CD

The files you need are on the CD-ROM. Copy the whole folder CD-ROM > Tutorials > Chapter05 > Chapter5-2 over to your hard drive. You will need all the files in this folder, and the tutorial will not be complete without these.

A Word About File Structure

Open the newly copied folder that is on your hard drive, and take a look at its file structure. On the first level in the folder, you'll see two C4D project files: a render folder and another called "tex." This last folder contains all of your texture files. This structure is very important because C4D project files look for their texture image files in the folder with this name. So, whenever you make image files for your projects, make sure you place them in a folder called tex in the same directory as your project files. If you do not, C4D may not be able to render properly.

From the newly copied folder on your hard drive, open the file robot-shade_begin.c4d. The file contains a robot, along with a background, camera, and a few lights. You will notice that you cannot modify the camera. This is by design. The only object you need to worry about is the robot. That is where the texture magic will occur.

Create a material:

1. From the Materials Manager's File menu, select File > New Material.
2. Double-click on the newly created swatch in the Materials Manager. The Material Editor will open.
3. Rename the material to *Roughmetal*.

The Color Channel and the Layer Shader

The Color Channel is where you will apply the primary color for the material. You will apply a Layer shader and then add multiple layers of shaders for just this channel. The Layer shader works similarly to Photoshop where you can add layers and then change how they affect each other. It means there will be a lot of subcomponents that will have to be dealt with in the Layer Shader.

Add the Layer shader to the Color channel:

1. In the Material Editor, click on the Color channel (not the check mark, just the name) to see its properties. Click-hold on the Texture Triangle, and from the pull-down menu, select Layer (see Figure 5.11). After this step, you will see the Layer shader occupy the texture space (see Figure 5.12a).
2. Click on the word *Layer* to see its properties (see Figure 5.12b).

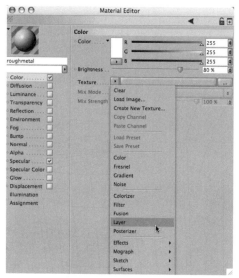

FIGURE 5.11   All of the shaders are found in the Texture Triangle's pull-down menu. Select the Layer shader.

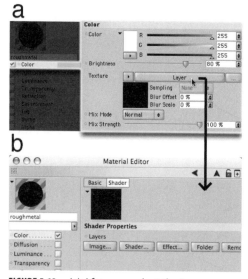

FIGURE 5.12   (a) After you select the Layer shader, it will appear in the Texture space. (b) Clicking on the Layer button in the Texture space will reveal its properties.

Add a Fusion Shader to the Layer Shader

The Layer shader by itself doesn't do anything. It has to contain other elements to produce results. You will add a Fusion shader to the Layer shader. The Fusion shader takes two images, colors, or other shaders and then combines them to form one resulting shader. It is similar to the Layer shader in that you'll have access to Photoshop-like layering effects. The difference is that the Layer shader can have many different *layers*, but Fusion is limited to two layers with a few more options.

Add a Fusion shader:

1. In the Shader Properties for the Layer shader is a horizontal row of buttons for Image, Shader, Effect, and so on. Click on the Shader button, and choose Fusion from the pull-down menu (see Figure 5.13a). After doing so, you will see the Fusion shader appear as a layer in the Layer shader (see Figure 5.13b)

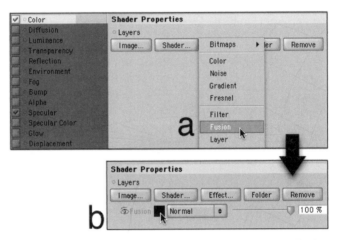

FIGURE 5.13   (a) The Layer shader is empty. Add the Fusion shader, and then you will see Fusion in the Layer list (b). Click on the black box next to the word *Fusion* to see the Fusion shader's properties.

2. Next to the word *Fusion* is a black box (see Figure 5.13b). Click on it to see the Fusion shader's properties. Right now, there is nothing in this shader. Fusion takes two channels and blends them together using blend modes. The two channels are labeled Blend Channel and Base Channel. From the Texture Triangle next to Base Channel, load Effects > Lumas (see Figure 5.14). This will load the Lumas shader into the Base Channel.

3. Click on the word *Lumas* to see its properties. The Lumas shader is specifically designed to help you achieve metal-like surfaces.

4. In the Lumas Shader properties you will see the Color option. The default color is red, which is indicated by the red box. Just left of that box is a little triangle. Click on it to see the RGB color options (see Figure 5.15). Change the red value to 128, green to 64, and blue to 18 (see Figure 5.15). You should see a dull orange color appear in the color box.

FIGURE 5.14 The Fusion Shader properties. Load the Lumas Shader into the Base Channel. Then click on Lumas to see its properties.

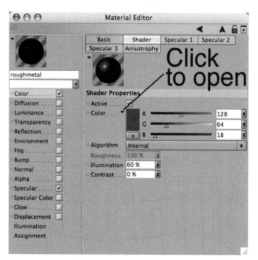

FIGURE 5.15 Click on the Color triangle to see the color RGB values. Change them to 128, 64, and 18 for a dull orange color.

5. Notice the three Specular tabs at the top. Click on each one, and set their values to that of Figure 5.16. You will need to open each color box option to see the RGB numbers. Verify Intensity, Size, Contrast, Glare, and Falloff for each one. Specularity is similar to a reflection but only reacts to the lights in your scene. It shows up as bright spots on the objects that have Specular properties.

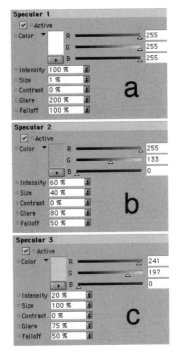

FIGURE 5.16   (a) Click on the Specular 1 tab to change its colors and settings. Do the same for (b) Specular 2 and (c) Specular 3.

6. Click on the Anisotrophy tab. Click on the Activate button, and then change Amplitude to 100%. Anisotrophy changes how bright spots that reflect on the material appear. It also makes it more metallic looking.

7. At the top of the Material Editor window are some arrows that act like browser buttons. Click on the Back button to go back to the Fusion shader (see Figure 5.17). For the Blend Channel, click on the Texture Triangle, and then choose Noise (see Figure 5.18).

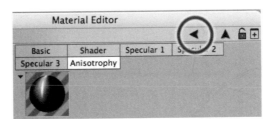

FIGURE 5.17   Click on the Back button to go back to the Fusion shader.

FIGURE 5.18 Select Noise for the Blend channel. Then click on the word *Noise* to edit its properties.

8. Click on the word *Noise* to see its properties. Change the following values: Color 1 to 115, 175, 255, and Color 2 to 0, 51, 186. Both colors should now be a shade of blue. Set Global Scale to 300% and Contrast to 56%. Click on the Back button to go back to the Fusion shader, and change the mode to Overlay (see Figure 5.19b). You'll see the round preview sphere update to show the material's current status (see Figure 5.19a). Noise is one of the most useful shaders in the bunch. In this case, it varies the color value over the surface of the material, making it more interesting to look at.

9. Click on the Back button again to take you back to the Layer shader. You'll see the updated Fusion shader in the list.

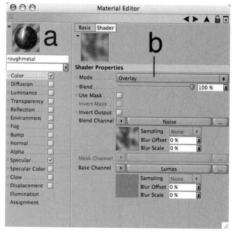

FIGURE 5.19 (a) The preview sphere will update after you change the mode to (b) Overlay.

Add more layers:

10. In the Layer shader, click on the Shader button, and then select Fresnel (see Figure 5.20a). Change the mode to Overlay and the percent-

age to 50% (see Figure 5.20b). Fresnel changes the color of the texture depending on the angle of the surface to the camera. In this case, the more perpendicular the angle, the more black is the texture, and the more parallel the angle, the more white is the texture. By changing the mode to Overlay, you now tell it to interact with the Fusion shader below it.

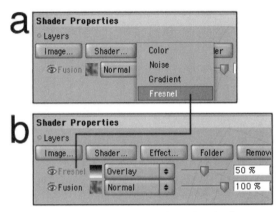

FIGURE 5.20   (a) Choose Fresnel from the Shader button. (b) It will appear in the Layers list. Change the mode to Overlay and the percentage slider to 50%.

11. In the Layer shader, click on the Shader button, and then select Noise. Change the mode to Overlay and the percentage to 24% (see Figure 5.21).

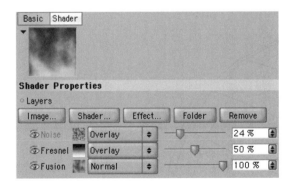

FIGURE 5.21   Click on the Shader button and add Noise. Change the mode to Overlay, and move the slider to 24%.

12. Click on the box next to the word *Noise* to edit its properties. Change Color 1 to 4, 0, 167, and Color 2 to 0, 91, 255. Both Color channels should have a slightly different blue value. Change Noise to Stupl, Octaves to 10, Global Scale to 200%, and Contrast to 57% (see Figure 5.22). After you are finished, click on the Back button to see all of the layers (see Figure 5.23).

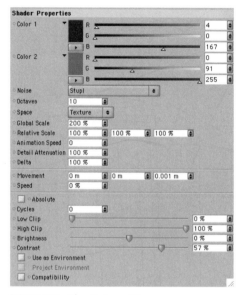

FIGURE 5.22   The Noise settings.

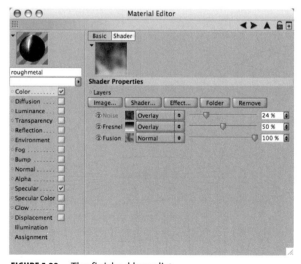

FIGURE 5.23   The finished layer list.

The Color channel is now complete. You have three different shaders in the Layer shader. Think of this like Photoshop, where you have three different layers that all interact to make one image. Something very similar is happening here.

Moving on, there is more to this material than just its color.

The Diffusion Channel

The Diffusion channel is similar to the Color channel except it should be thought of in terms of grayscale. If you add color to this channel, only its grayscale value will affect the material. The model is supposed to look old, so you need to add an effect that will make it look dirty. This channel will serve nicely for that.

This next section requires the Advanced Render module. If you don't have it, just skip this step and move to "The Reflection Channel" section.

Use ambient occlusion:

1. To activate the Diffusion channel, check the box and then click on the word *Diffusion* to see its properties. Load the Ambient Occlusion effect into the Texture space by clicking on the Texture Triangle and choosing Effects > Ambient Occlusion. Affect Specular and Affect Reflection should be checked in the Diffusion settings (see Figure 5.24).
2. Click on the words *Ambient Occlusion* in the Texture space to see its properties. Change Maximum Ray Length to 10,000, Accuracy to 1%, Minimum Samples to 1, Maximum Samples to 16, and Contrast to 100% (see Figure 5.25).

FIGURE 5.24   Add the Ambient Occlusion effect to the Diffusion channel.

FIGURE 5.25   The Ambient Occlusion settings.

Ambient Occlusion is an effect that shades an object's area of intersections or corners (for example, where a wall meets a floor). This effect is often used for lighting but works great here as a "dirt" effect too.

The Reflection Channel

Because the robot is inherently made out of metal, even old metal, it is somewhat reflective. The Reflective channel is also good for helping objects react to simulated light. A Sky object with a color linked to it is already in the scene and will be, partially, what the robot will reflect. However, because the Diffusion channel was set to affect the Reflection channel, this reflecting of the sky will be less noticeable (it will be partially covered by the dirt).

Activate the Reflection channel:

1. Check the box next to Reflection to activate it.
2. In the Texture space, load in Fresnel from the Texture Triangle (see Figure 5.26). Click on the word *Fresnel* to edit its properties. Fresnel in the Reflection channel will affect the amount an object will reflect from edge to center (that is to say, less in the center, more on the edges).

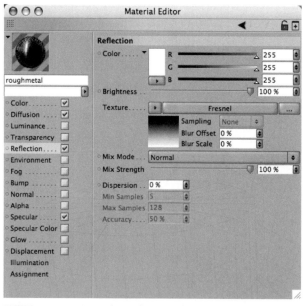

FIGURE 5.26   Activate the Reflection channel, and then click on the Texture Triangle. Select Fresnel from the pull-down menu. Click on the Fresnel button to edit its Shader properties.

3. In the Shader Properties, click the triangle next to Gradient to see the color options.
4. Click on the first white color marker, and enter 159, 167, and 255 for the RGB values for a bluish color (see Figure 5.27a). This will make any edge reflection seen on the object bias towards blue.
5. Click on the second black color marker. Change its position (labeled Pos) to 60% (see Figure 5.27b). Moving this over increases the area of nonreflectivity in the center.

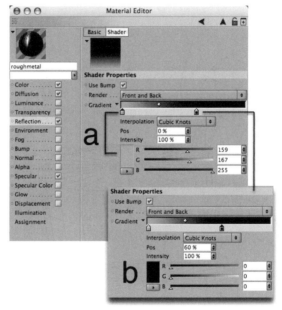

FIGURE 5.27   (a) The color options for the first color marker. Notice the RGB values. (b) Change the black color marker's position to 60%.

Rendering

It's time to see what the object looks like so far (no more drab, plastic gray!). You need to apply the Roughmetal material to the Robot object. A material tag will appear next to the robot after the link is made. You will edit this tag to change how the material is wrapped around the object. Then you will render the scene to see the progress of the texturing. It is common for artists to render many times while experimenting. For that reason, the antialiasing has been turned off to speed up the rendering times. The results, however, are jagged lines around the object in the render. Ignore this for now; you can change that later.

Apply the material:

1. Close the Material Editor window.
2. Click-drag the Roughmetal material in the Materials Manager to the Robot object in the Objects Manager. This applies the material to the robot, and you should see the robot change color in the Editor. You can also apply materials directly to objects in the Viewport.
3. Click on the new material tag next to the Robot object in the Objects Manager. It will be highlighted in red (see Figure 5.28a). You will see the Tag Properties in the Attributes Manager.
4. In the Tag Properties, change the Projections from UVW to Cubic (see Figure 5.28b). This changes how the material is *wrapped* around the object.

For a more detailed explanation of the different types of Projection types, go to Help > Help. In the Search field, type in Tag Properties Projection. In the results list, find Tag Properties (Texture Tag). Here you'll find information about projections and the texture tag in general.

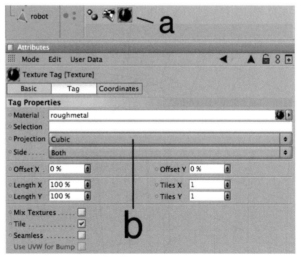

FIGURE 5.28   (a) A texture tag appears next to the Robot object in the Objects Manager after you apply it. (b) Change the Projection from UVW to Cubic under the Tag Properties.

Render:

5. Click on the Render in Picture Viewer icon to see the robot render (see Figure 5.29).
6. After you are done reviewing, close the Pictures window.

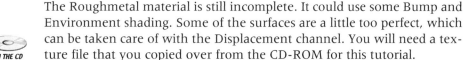

FIGURE 5.29   The robot now has the material
properties in the render. Not too shabby either.

7. Save your project file. Go to File > Save. Make sure you save it in the
folder that you copied over at the beginning of the tutorial.

Environment, Bump, and Displacement Channels

ON THE CD

The Roughmetal material is still incomplete. It could use some Bump and
Environment shading. Some of the surfaces are a little too perfect, which
can be taken care of with the Displacement channel. You will need a texture file that you copied over from the CD-ROM for this tutorial.

The Environment channel is a Reflection channel. But unlike Reflection, which reflects other objects in the scene, Environment reflects
image maps. So activating this channel by itself won't do anything. You
must also insert a map or shader into the channel.

The Bump channel is used to simulate roughness or unevenness on a
surface. For example, paint on a wall often has a noticeable bumpy texture to it. Although this method is good for simulated bumpiness, its limitation is that it does not actually change the geometry. So a very cratered
asteroid texture in the Bump channel applied to a sphere will still be
spherical. The edges won't look any different.

This is where the Displacement channel comes in, which actually
does deform the geometry. Both Displacement and Bump channels work
by raising and/or lowering a surface based on the black, gray, and white
values of a texture map.

Use the Environment channel:

1. In the Materials Manager, double-click on the Roughmetal swatch to open the Material Editor.
2. Activate the Environment channel.
3. In the Texture space, click on the ellipsis button (with three dots) (see Figure 5.30a). Using your operating system's file browser, locate the folder Chapter5-2 that you copied to your hard drive, and open the file Chapter5-2 > tex > snowfield2.hdr. Wait until you see the texture appear in the Material Editor. (This may take a few moments, depending on the speed of your computer.)

If you get a message that reads "This image is not in the document search path. Do you want to create a copy at the document location?" this means that your file organization needs some work. Remember, C4D project files look for texture files that are placed in a folder called tex. That tex folder needs to be in the same directory as your project file. If you're getting this message, it is because that is not the case. To remedy this, either click Yes to copy the file to your document location (it will not put it in the tex folder, but rather in the same directory, which is also part of the document search path) or click No, reorganize your files, and then try again.

4. After it has loaded, change Mix Mode to Multiply, the Brightness setting to 20%, and the Mix Strength to 60% (see Figure 5.30b). This

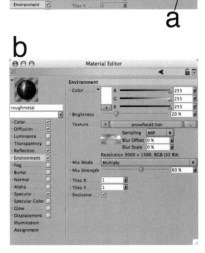

FIGURE 5.30 (a) Click this button to load the texture file. (b) Change the Brightness and Mix Strength settings.

will lessen the map's effects on the material. Your material is now reflecting the map that you just loaded. Remember, the difference between the Reflection and Environment channels is that Reflection reflects the objects that are in the scene, whereas Environment reflects image maps, like the one you just loaded.

Use the Bump channel:

5. Activate the Bump channel.
6. Click on the Texture Triangle, and from the pull-down menu, select Noise. Click on the word *Noise* to edit its properties.
7. In the Noise Shader Properties, change the Noise type to Wavy Turbulence, Low Clip to 27%, and Contrast to 32% (see Figure 5.31a).
8. Click on the Back button near the top of the Material Editor window to take you back to the Bump settings.
9. Change the Strength of the bump to 77% (see Figure 5.31b).

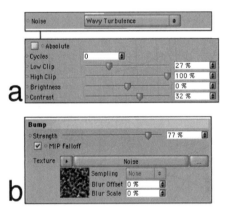

FIGURE 5.31 (a) After you've loaded the Noise shader for the Bump channel, change the Noise settings. (b) Change the Bump Strength to 77%.

Use the Displacement channel:

10. Activate the Displacement channel.
11. Click on the Texture Triangle, and from the pull-down menu, select Noise. Click on the word *Noise* to edit its properties.
12. In the Noise Shader Properties, change the Noise type to Dents. Change Color 1 to 127, 127, 127 (gray); Color 2 to Black; Global Scale to 550%; and Contrast to 46% (see Figure 5.32).
13. Click on the Back button near the top of the Material Editor window to take you back to the Displacement settings.

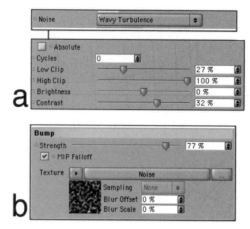

FIGURE 5.32 The Noise settings.

14. Change the Height to 10, and make sure the Strength slider is set to 100% (see Figure 5.33).

For a displacement effect that is more rounded, you can use Sub-Polygon Displacement. When activated, it subdivides the geometry before rendering, allowing you to use displacement mapping on low polygon surfaces. Be forewarned that using subdivision levels that are too high can greatly increase render times. You will need the Advanced Render module for Sub-Polygon Displacement.

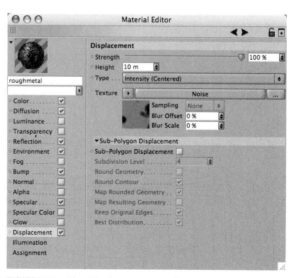

FIGURE 5.33 The Displacement settings.

Deactivate the Specular channel:

15. In the Material Editor channel list, click the check mark next to Specular to deactivate it (see Figure 5.34). The Lumas shader in the Color channel already provides specularity.
16. Close the Material Editor window.

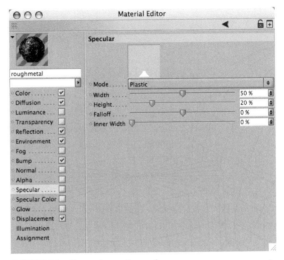

FIGURE 5.34   Deactivate Specular.

Render Settings

The Roughmetal material is finished, so render the image again in the Pictures Viewer to see the updated material. You will see that the image appears very rough for several reasons: high bump settings, the Ambient Occlusion effect, and the lack of antialiasing. Let's turn antialiasing on now.

Render settings:

1. Click on the Render Settings button (or Render > Render Settings), and change the Antialiasing settings to Geometry (see Figure 5.35).
2. Re-render the image. The image still has areas that are fairly rough because the Geometry setting doesn't smooth reflections (or transparencies) and because most of the robot is reflecting something, which is a problem.
3. Change the Antialiasing in the Render Settings to Best.
4. Re-render the image. It looks much better, but render times took a pretty big hit. On a Dual G5, this took about a 90 seconds to render, and 34 seconds on a Core 2 Duo processor (see Figure 5.36).

5. Change the Antialiasing back to None in the Render Settings. This will speed rendering up for previews.

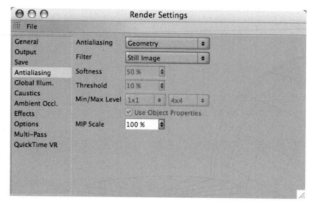

FIGURE 5.35   Render Settings.

FIGURE 5.36   At best antialiasing, this image took 34 seconds to render.

Texture Mapping and an Alien Symbol of Doom

The robot isn't from this planet and thus uses a different language altogether. In the folder you copied are texture files that will help illustrate this a little better. It will also teach you how to texture map an image onto the surface of the robot along with layering shaders on objects.

Create a new material:

1. From the Materials Manager, select File > New Material. Double-click on its swatch to open the Material Editor window.

2. Change the material name to *Aliensymbol*.
3. Click on the Color channel (the word *Color*) to see its properties (not on the check mark as that will turn it off).
4. Load the file Chapter5-2 > tex > aliensymbol.jpg that you copied over to your hard drive into the Texture space.
5. Activate the Bump channel.
6. From the Bump Texture Triangle, load Noise. Change the Noise type to Wavy Turbulence. Make sure the Bump Strength is set to 100%.
7. Activate the Alpha channel. This channel uses grayscale values, which tell the material where to be solid and where to be transparent. It uses white for solid and black for transparent.
8. Load the file Chapter5-2 > tex > aliensymbolBW.jpg that you copied over to your hard drive into the Texture space. You will see the material sphere update the preview (see Figure 5.37). This black-and-white map tells the material where to be solid and transparent.
9. Close the Material Editor window.

FIGURE 5.37   The Alien symbol for doom material preview.

Texture mapping the leg:

10. Apply the Aliensymbol material to the robot in the Objects Manager (onto its name). Make sure you do not drop the new material onto the other texture tag that is already there, as that will override it. When you apply it, you'll see the symbol applied all over. You need to change its projection. Click on the new material tag that was just created.
11. In the Attributes Manager, shift-click on the Coordinates button so that you can see both the tag properties and the coordinates. Change Projection to Flat, and uncheck Tile. Enter 44.4 for the X and −273.8

for the Y position values (see Figure 5.38) to place the symbol on the robot's legs (see Figure 5.39).

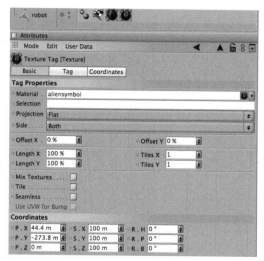

FIGURE 5.38 The Aliensymbol tag settings.

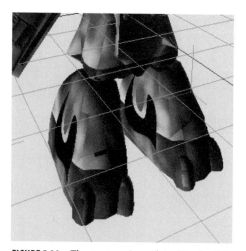

FIGURE 5.39 The texture is updated in the Editor.

Duplicate the Aliensymbol tag for the belly:

12. In the Objects Manager, make sure that the Aliensymbol tag is selected (it will be highlighted in red). Ctrl-click-drag on that tag to the right, and drop a duplicate next to it (see Figure 5.40). Ctrl-click-dragging and dropping is a quick way to copy things throughout C4D.

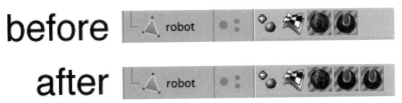

before after

FIGURE 5.40   Hold down the Ctrl key and click-drag to the right of the selected tag to copy it.

Edit the duplicated tag:

13. Make sure that the new tag is selected.
14. In the Tag Properties, change Side to Front. The Coordinates should be 44.4, −38.9, and 20 for the position X, Y, and Z. Enter 49 for the three Size X, Y, and Z values. Change the R. H value to 90 (see Figure 5.41). This will place the duplicate symbol onto roughly the center of the robot.

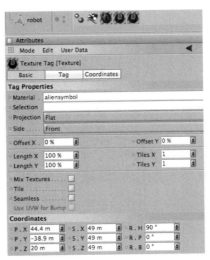

FIGURE 5.41   The duplicated Tag Properties and Coordinates.

Duplicate and edit the Aliensymbol tag again for the right shoulder:

15. In the Objects Manager, make sure that the rightmost tag is selected. Ctrl-click-drag to the right, and drop another duplicate. Make sure the new tag is selected (see Figure 5.42).
16. In the Coordinates for the tag, change the Position to 44.4, 172, and −102 for X, Y, and Z. For Size, change X, Y, and Z to 37 (see Figure 5.42).

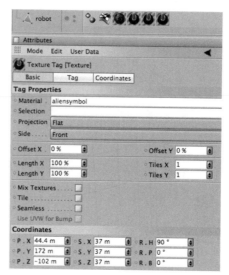

FIGURE 5.42 The duplicated Tag Properties and Coordinates.

The Texture Tool

Until now, you have been entering in coordinate values for the Aliensymbol tags. There is a more interactive way to do this, which may help you understand better what is happening. The Texture tool, in conjunction with the Move, Scale, and Rotate tools, lets you manually place the texture in the Editor. For the left shoulder, you will duplicate the Right Shoulder tag and move it manually.

Duplicate the tag:

1. At this point, you have three Aliensymbol texture tags. Select the far right tag, Ctrl-click-drag to the right, and drop a new tag. You will now have four Aliensymbol texture tags.
2. Make sure that you click on the robot inside the Objects Manager, and then click on the rightmost tag to reselect it. It is important that you have both the robot and the far right texture tag selected for this operation to work (see Figure 5.43).

FIGURE 5.43 Click on the robot and then the far-right texture tag inside the Objects Manager.

3. Select the Texture tool, or press V and choose Tools > Texture from the pop up menu.
4. Select the Move tool.
5. Using the red move arrow, slide the texture (which is indicated by a blue grid with the move handles inside) over to the right about 240, which is indicated in a box after you start moving it (see Figure 5.44). If you like, you can check in the coordinates for the tag. The Z position value should be close to 138. Either way, the texture is now on the left shoulder.
6. Render the image to see the Aliensymbol textures on the robot (see Figure 5.45).

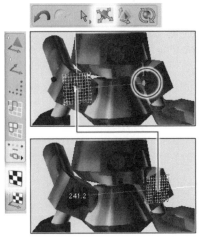

FIGURE 5.44   Using the Texture tool and the Move tool, slide the texture over to the left shoulder (as in the robot's left shoulder).

FIGURE 5.45   The rendered robot now has the Alien Symbol of Doom textures. Notice how they blend nicely with the underlying metal.

More Dents

This alien robot just isn't roughed up enough. (He's been known to scramble across faraway battlefields, stretching hundreds of miles, just to get to his favorite food, sushi.) Our adventurous little buddy needs some more pockmarks, both large and small. Keep in mind he's been shot at (and hit) many times. These materials have already been prepared for you and were copied over from the CD-ROM.

ON THE CD

Load materials:

1. From the Materials Manager, select File > Load Materials. Open Chapter5-2 > Dents.c4d from the copied folder (see Figure 5.46).

FIGURE 5.46 Load Dents.c4d into the Materials Manager.

Two new materials named Big Marks and Small Marks will appear in the Materials Manager (see Figure 5.47).

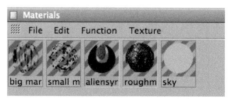

FIGURE 5.47 The new materials will appear as Big Marks and Small Marks. Apply both to the robot.

2. Drag and drop both of them onto the Robot model in the Objects Manager. Change both of their projections to Cubic in their Tag Properties.
3. Render the image to see the results. The image is rather small.
4. From the main menu, select Window > Picture Viewer.
5. From the Picture Viewer's File menu, select File > Open. Go to the Chapter5-2 folder and load Renders > RobotFinaltexture.tif into the Picture Viewer. This is what the image looks like when rendered at 600 × 800 with best antialiasing (see Figure 5.48).

FIGURE 5.48   The final render: a battered-up, old robot.

Wrap Up

The alien, risk-taking, sushi-loving robot is looking quite beat up (which is what we wanted!). C4D takes a backseat to no one when it comes to textures and materials. Remember that good texturing makes a good model look great. There's a lot to learn about materials and texturing—enough to fill many volumes. One thing that needs to be addressed is how to unwrap and use the digital 3D painting aspects of C4D.

TUTORIAL 5.3   **BASIC BODYPAINT**

BodyPaint is now included in MAXON's basic distribution of C4D, regardless of which bundles you buy. BodyPaint (BP) is a module that allows you to *unwrap* your models and apply texture to them. It is a powerful application that has a vast feature set. To give it due justice, volumes would need to be written about it. Because we don't have that luxury here, only the most important features to get you up and running have been chosen for this next tutorial.

ON THE CD

You'll work from a file off the CD-ROM. The file includes a basic head that needs to be prepared for texturing. We'll walk you through the basic steps of UV unwrapping and how to do basic coloring and brush work using BP.

This tutorial uses the Classic scheme. You can switch to this in Edit > Preferences. Under the Common section, change Scheme options to Classic.

This tutorial will teach you about the following:

- Unwrapping UVs
- BP layout
- BodyPaint 3D Setup Wizard
- Selection tags
- Canvas and show UV mesh
- UV mapping
- Relax UV
- Removing and adding image files to channels
- Layers
- Selections and Fill
- Fill Polygons
- 3D painting
- Saving textures

If you are new to 3D or to BP, it's important to note that we deal with some concepts that are sometimes difficult to understand. Great care will be taken to explain to you the *whys* along the way. Don't be discouraged if you have a hard time. A second go at the tutorial can do wonders in gaining understanding. Also, refer to Help > Help, and under Content, explore the BodyPaint 3D section for a greater understanding of what this program will do.

ON THE CD
To get started, navigate to Tutorials > Chapter05 > Chapter5-3 located on your CD-ROM. Copy the whole folder Chapter5-3 over to your hard drive, and then open the file BP_head_start.c4d. After it loads, move on to the next section. Remember not to just load the file directly off the CD-ROM as you'll get texture errors when you render if you do.

Selection Tags

Selection tags are very useful at isolating polygons for later editing in BP. They allow you to make selections of polygons, edges, or points that you can later recall and edit, without having to redo the selection. For example, our model has one edge selection set followed by four polygon selection sets. You can see this by the little triangles that are located to the right of the Maiden object in the Objects Manager. Figure 5.49 shows the selection sets.

Because this model already has selection sets done for you, most of the work for that is finished. However, to get you more acquainted with selection sets, you will create one more before heading off to BP. Our model has all the geometry in sets except the polygons that make up the front hair strands. To see that better, you'll hide all the polygons that are in sets to reveal what is left over.

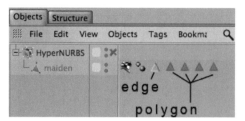

FIGURE 5.49   Selection sets.

Create a selection tag:

1. Make sure that the Perspective view is maximized. In the Viewport's menu, choose Filter > Grid to hide it. This is done for clarity only.
2. Make sure you have the Maiden object selected and you are in Polygon mode (also referred to as the Polygon tool; press V and select Tools > Polygons or its icon). You need to be in Polygon mode so that you can see the selection tags in action.
3. Locate and select the second selection tag (first tag begins on the left, last tag is on the far right) on the Maiden object. The tag has been called Hair. Notice the Attributes Manager options for this tag (see Figure 5.50a).

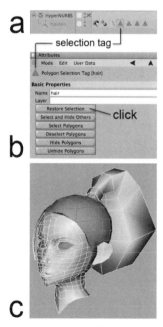

FIGURE 5.50   (a) Click on the second selection tag. (b) Click on Restore Selection. (c) The resulting selection.

4. Click on the Restore Selection button in the Attributes Manager (see Figure 5.50b). You'll see the hair section of the model turn red. This is because this selection set was created when those polygons were first selected (see Figure 5.50c).

A quick way to restore the selection is to double-click the selection tag.

5. Hide the selection by clicking Hide Polygons in the Attributes Manager. This will hide those polygons in the Viewport.
6. Select each of the polygon selection tags, and hide their geometry until you see just the geometry for the hair strands remaining in the Viewport.
7. Deselect any selection tags you may have selected by Ctrl-clicking on them. A selected selection tag has a red box around it. A deselected tag has no box around it. Make sure none of your tags are selected; otherwise, any new selection sets you make will override a selected selection tag, which is not what you want for the next step (see Figure 5.51).

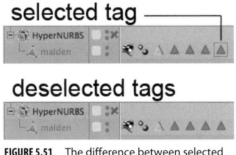

FIGURE 5.51 The difference between selected selection tags and deselected selection tags. Deselected tags have no red box around them.

8. Using either the Live Selection tool or the Rectangle Selection tool, with Only Select Visible Elements turned off, select the remaining hair strand polygons in the Viewport.
9. In the main menu, choose Selection > Set Selection. This creates a new selection tag that is placed rightmost with the other tags. This new tag pertains to the hair strands. Make sure the new tag is highlighted, and change its name in the Attributes Manager to *Hair Strands* (see Figure 5.52).
10. In the main menu, choose Selection > Unhide All to unhide all of the polygons. You should now be able to see the entire head, and now your selection sets are complete. The model is ready to be moved to BP for unwrapping.

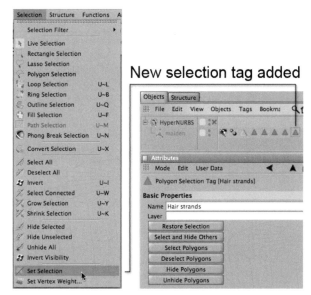

FIGURE 5.52   When you create a new selection tag, it will appear rightmost with the other tags. After you highlight it, you'll be able to rename it in the Attributes Manager.

BodyPaint 3D

BP is where you do all your texture magic, but to get there, you need to change layouts. There are so many tools in C4D that they can't be shown at the same time, either with icons or menu sets. To change to the BP layout, either use the Layout button and choose BP UV Edit (see Figure 5.53), or choose Window > Layout > BP UV Edit from the main menu. After doing so, you'll see the BP user interface (see Figure 5.54).

FIGURE 5.53   Use the Layout button to change to the BP layout.

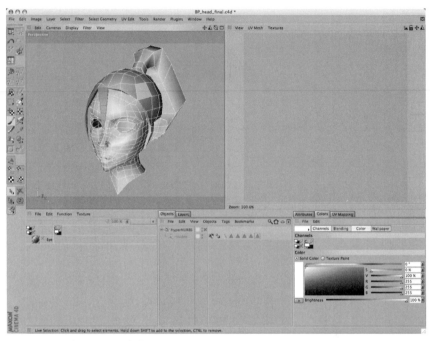

FIGURE 5.54 The BP UV Edit layout.

BodyPaint 3D Setup Wizard

Now that you've switched to the BP layout, you are ready to run the model through the BodyPaint Setup Wizard. This wizard will take a model, with no texture maps, and unwrap it and apply an image map. In other words, its does a lot of the work for you.

Use the Paint Setup Wizard:

1. Either use the Wizard icon in the upper-left corner of the interface, or from the main menu, choose Tools > Paint Setup Wizard. A dialog box will appear with green check marks next to all your objects.
2. Click on the green check mark next to Eyes. It turns into to a red X indicating that the wizard will ignore this object. We do this because the eyes in the scene already have a material. We only need to use the wizard for the Maiden object (you can leave the green check mark for both the Maiden and HyperNURBS objects untouched). After doing so, your wizard will look something like Figure 5.55.
3. Click the Next button a few times, until you see it turn into a Finish button. Click that as well and then close the wizard. The maiden model is now ready for 3D painting. However, there are still several steps to do before we get to this.

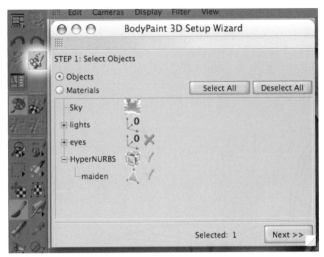

FIGURE 5.55   The BodyPaint 3D Setup Wizard.

What just happened? The model was unwrapped, and a new material along with a gray texture map in the Color channel was created and applied. The model now appears a darker gray and you'll see a new material in the Material Manager called Mat. A new material tag is also present on the Maiden object.

The Canvas and Show UV Mesh

When the wizard is done, it makes a 2D representation of the 3D polygons of the model. This 3D to 2D conversion is called *unwrapping*. The 2D polygons in the representation are referred to as *UV polygons*. It's very important to understand the difference. Polygons are not UV polygons, and as such, we use different tools to edit them. However, in BP, you can see the UV polygons in both the Viewport and on the Canvas, which is the gray space next to the Viewport. Right now, they are not being shown. Let's see them.

Show the UV mesh:

1. In the Canvas's menu set, choose UV Mesh > Show UV Mesh (see Figure 5.56a). You will then see the UV polygons over the canvas space (see Figure 5.56b).

A quick method to show the UV Mesh is to drag the UVW tag into the 2D Canvas window.

2. Click on the UV Polygons icon, or from the main menu, choose Tools > UV Tools > UV Polgyons (see Figure 5.57). When in UV Polygon mode, you can select and edit these elements.

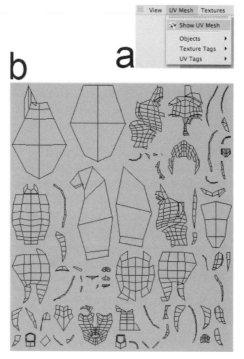

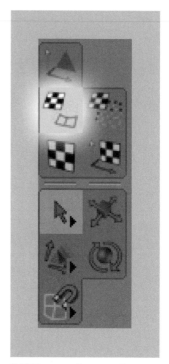

FIGURE 5.56 (a) Show UV mesh. (b) The Canvas with the UV polygons overlaid.

FIGURE 5.57 The UV Polygons icon.

UV Mapping

When you are using the UV Polygon tool, you'll notice that the UVs are no longer black but have turned a blue color. Selected UVs are shown in red (Classic scheme). Now that we can see and edit the UV polygons, we need to do some better grouping as the wizard only does basic unwrapping and is often not sufficient. For this, we'll use extensively what's found under the UV Mapping tab in the lower-right corner of the layout.

Remember, selection sets allow you to quickly select a group of polygons and their UV counterparts, and remap them using the UV Mapping tools. If you don't have selection sets, you'll have to go through the laborious process of reselecting the groups of polygons and unwrapping them. In the next few steps, it will be even clearer how selection sets are very useful in the mapping processes.

The purpose of the next section is to teach you how to remap the polygons, grouping them by selection set, and then fit them onto the canvas. This should be done before any digital paint process.

Selection sets and remapping:

1. Make sure you have the Maiden object selected in the Objects Manager. Click on the second selection tag (first tag being the leftmost edge selection tag, last tag being the rightmost polygon selection tag). Make sure that the Attributes Manager's tab is also selected. You'll see the Hair selection tag's properties there.
2. Click on Restore Selection. You'll see the selection in the Viewport and Canvas change (see Figure 5.58). You'll notice that the Hair UVs are all over the place. This is why we are going to remap them.

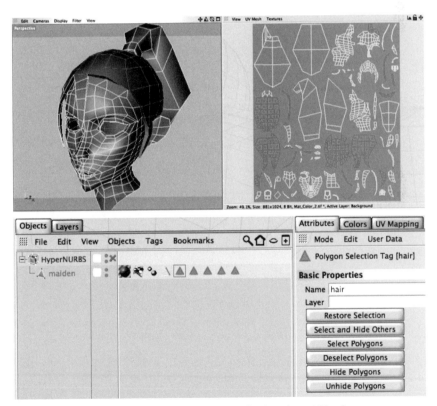

FIGURE 5.58   Restore Selection for the Hair tag will select those UV polygons.

3. Click on the UV Mapping tab, click on the Projection button, and click Sphere (see Figure 5.59). This remaps the Hair UV polygons using a spherical projection. More importantly, it groups all the UV polygons

together. This will simplify the painting you'll do later on (see Figure 5.60).

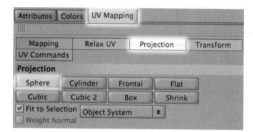

FIGURE 5.59 The UV Mapping tab. Choose the Projection button, and then the Sphere button.

FIGURE 5.60 The hair UVs will be remapped to a spherical projection.

4. Zoom the Canvas out slightly so you can see the space around it (you use the same mouse buttons + Alt key actions as you do in the Viewport). Using the Move tool, move the selected UVs off the Canvas entirely (see Figure 5.61). You'll use this method—select, remap, and move them off—with all the selection sets. Later, you'll shrink them and move them back on.

The mouse wheel or the keyboard "+" and "-" keys can also be used for zooming in and out.

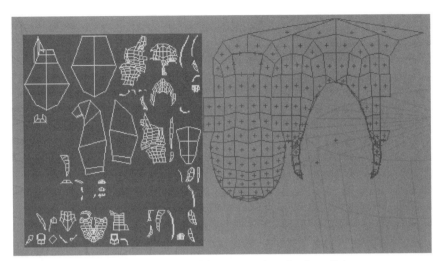

FIGURE 5.61   Zoom out the Canvas, and then move the selection off the canvas.

Select, Remap, and Move

The rest of the unwrapping is very similar. You've already done the hair polygons, so we'll move on to the ears, face, ponytail, and hair strand selection sets. This tutorial is just getting to the basics, so we won't spend a lot of time unwrapping. That being said, you will learn a few tricks to help unwrap tricky geometry.

Ears, ponytail and hair strands:

1. Select the ear selection tag on the Maiden object (the third one over from left to right). Click on the Attributes tab to see the tag's Basic Properties options.
2. Click Restore Selection. You will see the ears highlighted in the Viewport and on the Canvas. Restore Selection is different from Select Polygons in that it will deselect anything else first (see Figure 5.62). This is important, otherwise, you might remap the hair polygons along with the ear, and that is not desirable since we just finished that operation. Remember, in order for you to see the polygon selections in the Viewport and Canvas, you must be using the UV Polygons tool (Tools > UV Tools > UV Polygons).
3. Now that you have the UVs for the ears selected, click on the UV Mapping tab. Click on Mapping, and then click on Optimal (Cubic). Enter 100 for Maximum Area Factor, and then click Apply (see Figure 5.63). This will group the polygons together.
4. With the Move tool, move the selected ear UV polygons off the Canvas. An exact location is not too important since this position is temporary (see Figure 5.64).

FIGURE 5.62 Select the ear selection tag. In the Attributes Manager, click on Restore Selection.

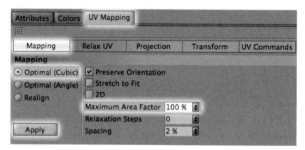

FIGURE 5.63 Click on the UV Mapping tab, then Mapping, Optimal (Cubic), Maximum Area Factor to 100, and finally Apply.

FIGURE 5.64 Move the remapped UVs off the Canvas.

5. Skip the face selection tag. We'll do that one later. Click on the ponytail selection tag instead. Click on the Attributes Manager to see its properties. Click on Restore Selection to highlight the ponytail UVs (see Figure 5.65).

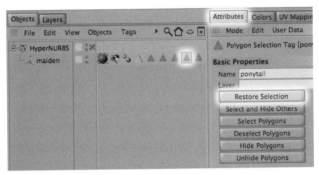

FIGURE 5.65   Click on the Ponytail selection tag, then Attributes Manager, and then Restore Selection.

6. Click on the UV Mapping tab and then the Mapping tab. Click on the Projection button, and then click Sphere (see Figure 5.66). This remaps the ponytail UV polygons using a spherical projection. This, again, groups all the ponytail UV polygons together. It's important to note that there are overlapping UVs in this arrangement. If we had to do serious painting on this part of the model, then we'd have to unwrap much more thoroughly than this. However, in this exercise, all we're going to do is a basic color application. So, grouping them is more important than having a fully unwrapped model.

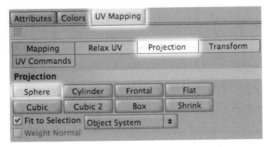

FIGURE 5.66   The UV Mapping tab. Choose the Projection button, and then choose the Sphere button for a spherical projection of the ponytail UV polygons.

7. With the Move tool, move the ponytail UVs off the Canvas (see Figure 5.67).

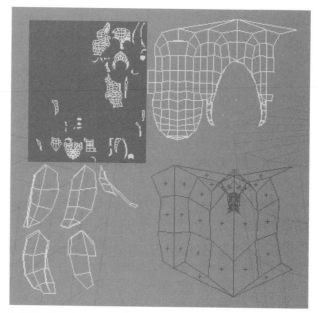

FIGURE 5.67 The ponytail UV polygons are moved off the Canvas.

8. Select the last selection tag, Hair Strands. Click on the Attributes tab, and click on Restore Selection (see Figure 5.68).

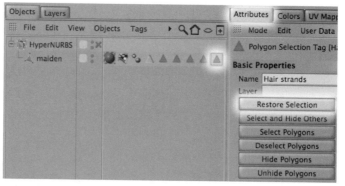

FIGURE 5.68 Click on the Hair Strands tag, Attributes tab, and then on Restore Selection.

9. Click on the UV Mapping tab, and then click the Mapping tab. Make sure that the Optimal (Cubic) is active. Make sure Maximum Area Factor is set to 0. Click Apply (see Figure 5.69).
10. Move the hair strands UVs off the Canvas (see Figure 5.70).

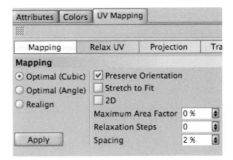

FIGURE 5.69   The UV Mapping tab settings.

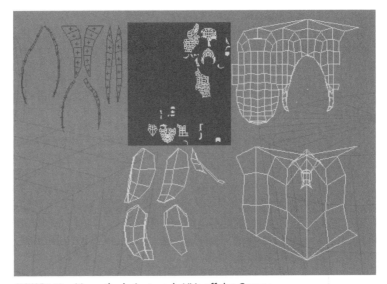

FIGURE 5.70   Move the hair strands UVs off the Canvas.

Relax UV

We've left the face UV polygons for last because there is another technique for unwrapping tricky geometry. This method would work well for the ears and the ponytail too. To keep this tutorial simple, however, we'll only do it to the face UV polygons.

Relax UV is used to help with overlapping UV polygons in a variety of ways. We'll explore a few of these methods in the next few steps. You are now going to unwrap the face with a spherical projection and then apply Relax UV to further unwrap.

Unwrap the face:

1. Click on the Face selection tag, click on the Attributes tab, and click on Restore Selection button. The UV polygons for the face have now been selected.
2. Click on the UV Mapping tab, click on Projection, uncheck Fit to Selection, and click on Sphere to give it a spherical projection (see Figure 5.71).

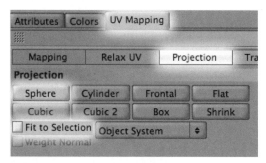

FIGURE 5.71   UV Mapping settings.

3. Zoom the Canvas so you can see the face a little better. Switch to the UV Points tool either by its icon or by choosing Tools > UV Tools > UV Points. Click on the Rectangle Selection tool either by its nested icon or by choosing Tools > C4D Tools > Rectangle Selection.
4. In the Canvas window, rectangle select the points around the eye (see Figure 5.72). The exact point selection is not important.

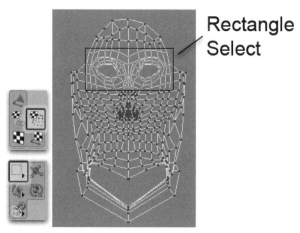

FIGURE 5.72   Using the UV Points and Rectangle Selection tools, select the eye UV points on the face.

5. In the UV Mapping tag, click on Relax UV. Activate Pin Point Selection so that when it is remapped, those points you just selected will stay put. Deactivate Pin Border Points (also Deactivate Pin to Neighbors if it is active). This will allow the borders to move and be affected. Otherwise, the overall shape would pretty much stay the same.

6. Activate Cut Selected Edges and the Use Tag option right below it. Visually locate the Edge selection tag for the Maiden object in the Objects Manager. It is the first selection tag and looks different than the other polygon selection tags. Click-drag and drop that Face Edge selection tag into the empty field box that sits left of Use Tag (don't click on the tag, just click-drag). As you do this, Face Edge will appear in the field box, as this is the name of the tag. Click Apply. See Figures 5.73 and 5.74.

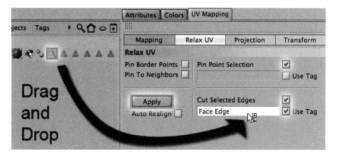

FIGURE 5.73   The Relax UV options, plus the dragging and dropping action of the Edge selection tag into the empty field below Cut Selected Edges.

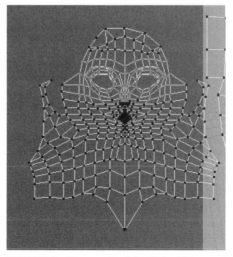

FIGURE 5.74   The result of the Relax UV operation.

Relax UV and Edge Selection

When you added the Face Edge selection tag to the Relax UV, along with the Point selection tag on the eyes, and applied it to the face, you made a better spacing of the UV polygons. We could have done this to the pony-tail and ears too, but is not necessary in this introduction to BP. However, you'll find it very useful in your own projects.

The Face Edge selection tag was an edge selection of the center edges on the back of the neck (not the hair or other parts though). The Relax UV option uses that selection as a ripping point to unwrap the UVs when Cut Selected Edges is active and the tag has been placed in the corresponding field.

 This last action of relaxing with the Pin Point Selection option and Cut Selected Edges can only be done in BodyPaint 3D. With these options activated, a new un-wrapping algorithm is used called LSCM (Least Square Conformal Mapping). This unwrapping technique is superb at unwrapping and mapping characters.

BP unfortunately doesn't have a UV edge selection so you cannot see the edge selection when working with UVs. However, you can switch to the regular C4D tools through the V shortcut (or main menu, under Tools) and then select edges. However, to see and apply the selection in the Relax UV option, you must later switch back to the UV Polygons or Points tools.

 New to R10 is the Path Selection tool, which makes selecting paths of edges or points much easier.

Return Selections to the Canvas

Now its time to put all those selections back onto the canvas. To do so, we'll move and scale them down. The exact arrangement is not important, only that all of the UV polygons are on the Canvas. No UVs should be left off.

Restore Selection, Move and Scale

 For this next set of instructions, ignore the Edge selection tag as it was only useful for the Relax UV operation.

Go through all your polygon selection tags (Hair, Ear, Face, Ponytail, Hair Strands) and follow this sequence:

1. In the Objects Manager, select a polygon selection tag by clicking on its corresponding triangle.
2. In the Attributes Manager, click on Restore Selection.
3. Use the Move tool to move the set back onto the Canvas. Try and group sets by skin and color type. For example, place the Face and Ear groups next to each other. Do the same for the Hair, Ponytail, and Hair Strands, as they'll have the same color too.
4. Use the Scale tool to shrink the set so that all the sets can be on the Canvas at the same time. Try to use up as much Canvas as possible within reason. There might be plenty of space not covered by UV polygons and that is okay.

After you are finished, your arrangement might look something like Figure 5.75. This is a fluid process, so it doesn't matter if you scale first and then move or use any combination of those tools.

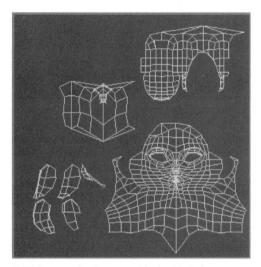

FIGURE 5.75   The Canvas with the UV Polygon selection groups moved and scaled. All the groups must be on the Canvas.

UV Size and Image Maps

It's a good habit to make your UV groups roughly the same size. You can't tell just by looking at the Canvas how big or small you should make each group so these next instructions will show you how to compare them and then make adjustments.

At the moment, the Color map we created when we first ran the wizard is active. It's what gives the Canvas its slightly dark gray color. To better understand this; let's take a look at the Material Manager (see Figure 5.76).

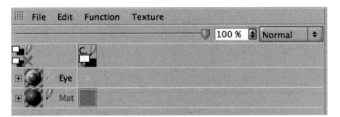

FIGURE 5.76   The Material Manager in the BodyPaint layout.

The BP layout alters the way the Material Manager looks, but it's still the same Manager. In Figure 5.76, you see two materials, Eye and Mat. Eye was a prebuilt material included in the scene file. Mat, along with an image file in the Color channel, was created when you ran the Paint Setup Wizard. If you don't see the plus (+) symbol next to the material swatches, choose Edit > Layer Manager (Expanded/Compact) from the Material Manager's File menu.

Expand the Mat material by clicking on the plus sign next to it. You'll see Color : Mat_Color_x.tif along with a little black triangle to the right of the image file text. Click on the little black triangle to expand the information about the texture file in the Color channel. You'll see an eye along with a gray square and the word Background (see Figure 5.77).

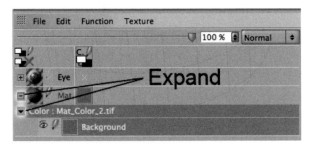

FIGURE 5.77   The Material and Color channels expanded.

If you don't see an image file in the Color channel, don't worry; we'll cover how to add one in the next section.

Deleting and Adding image Files

Mat_Color_x and Mat aren't descriptive enough. Remember, its important for you to get into the habit of naming all your items, such as models, materials, textures, files, and tags. If you are serious about doing 3D, you'll probably work in a team. Your team members won't appreciate having a project file full of Matx and Mat_Color_x filenames.

You are going to rename the Mat material. You can't just rename the texture file, so you'll delete the one you have and make a new one, renaming it along the way.

Rename Mat, and create a new image map:

1. Double-click on the word *Mat* and rename it to *Maiden Mat*.
2. Make sure the *Maiden Mat* material is selected. In the Material Manager's menu, select Texture > Texture Channels > Color to deactivate the map in the Color channel (see Figure 5.78). When you do so, you'll notice a check mark next to Color. Selecting it will remove the check mark along with deactivating it.

FIGURE 5.78   Deactivating the Color map.

3. You'll see that the Maiden Mat has no Color map linked to it now. Repeat the last action, Texture > Texture Channels > Color, to reassign a Color map. You'll see a dialog box appear as shown in Figure 5.79.
4. You can leave the New Texture settings at their default. Because you renamed your material to Maiden Mat, the new texture will assume that name, and there's no need to edit it further. Click OK.

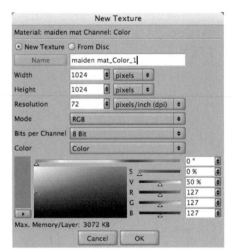

FIGURE 5.79 The New Texture dialog box.

5. Expand the Maiden Mat's Color information. Click on the eye to hide the background. This is a layer, which works exactly like Photoshop layers. You'll add more layers later.

Resizing UV Polygons Using the Checker Pattern

You may have noticed that hiding the background layer made a checker pattern appear on the Canvas. This is a good thing because the Checker pattern allows you to compare the sizes of the UV groups you've made. You can also see the checker pattern in the 3D Viewport. This is especially important as the size differences will be much more apparent here.

You might not be able to see the checker pattern yet in the Perspective view. If so, go up to the Viewport's menu, and choose Edit > Redraw. You should now see the checker pattern in the Perspective view. Notice the sizes of the checker pattern vary from the hair to the face to the ponytail, and so on (see Figure 5.80). For example, the hair checkers are much larger than the face checkers. The next few steps will resize them.

A quick way of redrawing/refreshing the Viewport is to press the A key.

Resize:

1. Go through your Polygon selection tags found in the Objects Manager. Use Restore Selection found in the Attributes Manager for each Polygon selection tag to select them.

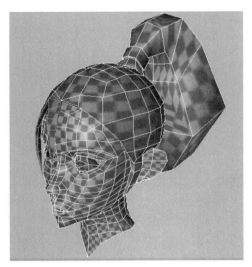

FIGURE 5.80   The checker pattern on the Maiden object in the Perspective view.

2. Move and scale each group until the checker pattern is mostly the same size in the 3D Perspective view (see Figure 5.81). They do not have to be exactly the same size for this tutorial. Some distortion will occur.

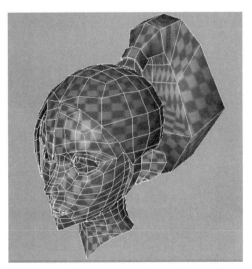

FIGURE 5.81   The pattern resizes as you rescale and remove the groups of UV polygons on the Canvas.

Layering and Selection Fill

It's almost time to paint! Setup can be tedious, but it's extremely important. Good UV preparation will make for better results later, and we've only done minimal UV editing.

You are going to use the selection tools to mark off an area on the canvas you want to paint. You'll choose a color and fill that selection for the different groups on the Canvas. Before we proceed any further, let's save our texture that we've placed in the Color channel.

Save the textures:

1. Save the texture file by choosing File > Save Texture As in the main menu.
2. Save it as a Tiff file in the same directory as this project file. This project file is not complete without the textures it references.

Layers

If you've ever used Photoshop, you're already aware of how handy layers are. BP uses layers in very much the same way. Layers make painting and editing much easier, so use them often.

Add layers:

1. Make sure your Maiden Mat material is selected. In the Material Manager, choose Texture > New Layer. A new layer called Layer will appear above the Background layer. Double-click on the word *layer,* and rename it to *Base Color Skin*.
2. Add another layer, and call it *Base Hair Color* (see Figure 5.82).

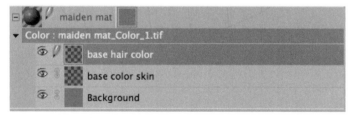

FIGURE 5.82   Layering in BodyPaint.

Selection and Color Fill

You are now going to select the areas of skin, namely the Face and Ear groups, and apply a skin color to them using the Fill tool. You do the selecting on the Canvas.

Select polylines:

1. From the main menu, choose Select > Select Polylines, or choose the icon in the nested Selection icons in the side icon tool palette (see Figure 5.83a).

 Sometimes when switching tools, you'll see your UV polygons disappear on the Canvas. If that happens, just redo the Show UV Mesh option under UV Mesh > Show UV Mesh in the Canvas menu. They should reappear.

2. On the Canvas, select the face and ears by clicking various times around it. As you click, you'll see click points. To finish the selection, double-click, or click on the first click point (see Figure 5.83b).

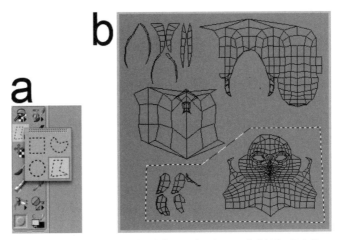

FIGURE 5.83   (a) The nested Polyline Selection tool. (b) The Polyline selection around the face and ear UV polygons.

Use color fill:

3. Click on the Colors tab. Choose a skin-like color. The exact color does not matter (see Figure 5.84).
4. Click on the Base Color Skin layer in the Material Manager.
5. Using the Fill tool (the Paint Bucket icon) either in the Tools icon palette or under the main menu Tools > Paint Tools > Fill Bitmap, click inside the polyline selection to fill that area with the skin color (See Figure 8.85).
6. Select the Base Hair Color layer in the Material Manager. Using the same technique in the previous steps, create a very dark gray polyline selection color fill for the Hair, Ponytail, and Hair Strands groups.

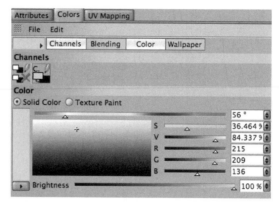

FIGURE 5.84   The Colors tab.

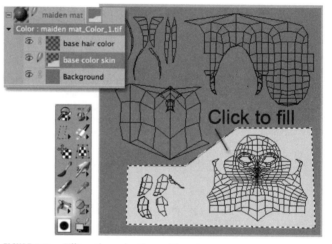

FIGURE 5.85   Filling the selection with color.

You'll see the hair polygons change color not only on the Canvas but in the Perspective view as well (see Figure 5.86).

Fill Polygons

Sometimes, you may want to fill based on your polygon selection. It is a similar process in that you choose a color, a polygon selection, and then fill it.

Fill the Polygon selection:

1. Create a new layer, and call it Lips.

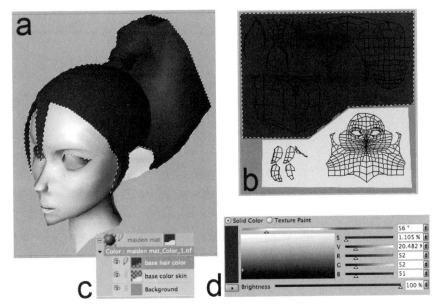

FIGURE 5.86   (a) Perspective view result. (b) Canvas. (c) Base Hair Color layer. (d) Colors tab.

2. In the main menu, Select > Deselect All. This will ensure you have no other selections, which could prevent this operation from working.
3. From the Canvas, zoom into the UV polygons that form the lips area on the face.
4. Select the UV Polygons tool.
5. Select the Live Selection tool, and change its radius to 2 in the Attributes Manager.
6. In the Canvas, select the UV polygons that form the lip.
7. Choose a color from the Colors tab.
8. In the main menu, choose Layer > Fill Polygons. The selection will now be filled with that color and be visible in both the Canvas and Viewport.
9. Render the Perspective view by choosing Render > Render View (see Figure 5.87).

3D Painting

You use the Paintbrush in the 3D Perspective view or on the Canvas. The brush is found with the other tools in the Tools icon palette. It can also be found under Tools > Paint Tools > Brush.

Paint:

1. Select the Brush tool.
2. Create another layer. Name it *Eyebrows*.
3. Choose a color.
4. Try painting some eyebrows in the 3D view. You can also paint on the Canvas (see Figure 5.88). ♣

FIGURE 5.87   A render of the Perspective view showing colors added to the different parts of the maiden. *Note: Background color has been changed from black to white for clarity.*

FIGURE 5.88   Final render. *Note: Background color has been changed from black to white for clarity.*

CONCLUSION

Save your work. When you do, you'll be asked if you want to save the texture. It's important to know where you are saving your files. Remember, texture files must either be in the same directory as your project file or in a subdirectory called tex.

BodyPaint, as you can see, is extremely powerful. Major studios all over the world have used it in their workflows. It plays nice with many other well-known 3D applications such as Maya, 3D Studio Max™, and Softimage®. This tutorial only scratched the surface of this vast, powerful application.

6

LIGHTING

In This Chapter

- Light Object
- Materials and Lighting
- TUTORIAL 6.1   Three-Point Lighting
- TUTORIAL 6.2   Area Lighting
- TUTORIAL 6.3   Global Illumination
- TUTORIAL 6.4   HDRI Lighting and Shadow Catching

In Chapter 3 "NURBS" and Chapter 4 "Polygon Modeling," you learned basic modeling skills. In the previous chapter, you learned about materials, textures, and unwrapping. Now it's time to learn about the key role lighting plays in bringing life and realism to your creations.

In the common phrase, "Lights, Camera, Action!," there is a very good reason why *light* comes first. There would be no point in animation with great models and materials if we can't see it, and if the lighting is bad, we might wish we hadn't.

This chapter will focus slightly less on the technical aspects of C4D's lighting system and focus more on certain techniques used in computer lighting. All of these can be mirrored in any major 3D program and are not limited to C4D. However, as with previous chapters, you'll be given a detailed list of technical instructions, along with their explanations, in order to complete the lighting tutorials. We will also talk about some of the theory along the way.

There are four tutorials in this chapter: "Three-Point Lighting"; "Area Lights, Radiosity, and HDRI Lighting"; and "Shadow Catching." All of them have prepared scene files and associated texture files located on the CD-ROM.

ON THE CD

This chapter uses the new R10 Icon scheme. It is different from the previous chapters that used the Classic scheme. To change to the new scheme, go to Edit > Preferences, and in the Common options, choose Light for the Scheme.

LIGHT OBJECT

Since we can't stuff all the information about C4D's lighting system into this chapter, you should know where to find the basic information about lights. Although you do not need to use this to complete the tutorials, we want you to have access to as much information as possible.

For more information about C4D's basic lighting system, choose Help > Help in the main menu. In the Content tab, choose Reference > Objects > Scene Objects > Light Object. Here you'll find a wealth of information for every little button and slider available to you in C4D's basic lighting system, including types of lights, types of shadows, and so on (see Figure 6.1).

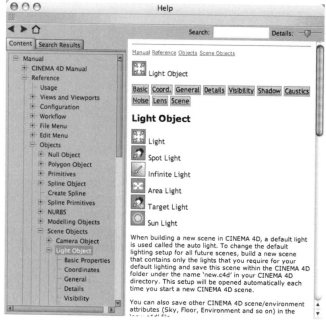

FIGURE 6.1   The C4D Help system has a wealth of information on its lighting system.

MATERIALS AND LIGHTING

You may have found yourself texturing a model, and after deciding it looks good, moved on to lighting only to find it looked completely different and had to go back to modify the material. This is because the computer mimics real light by separating it into materials and lights. In other words, you give an object a surface quality and then light it. In the real world, there is no difference between the light bulb and the material of, say, an apple. It's all just light rays that enter our eyes, hit our retina, and register information to our brain.

The computer separates, both for conceptual and practical reasons, objects that emit light from objects that receive light. So, after you've textured, of course it's going to change when you light it. Some people like to light first and then texture. Either way, at some point, you'll stop thinking about these things as two separate subjects and start treating them as one whole lighting process with materials and lights as a sub-component of the larger lighting process. They are intricately interlinked.

In the tutorials that follow, you'll see this philosophy very much in practice as we edit *both* lights and materials. However, you will not be asked to model or create complex textures. We want to get to the meat as soon as possible. So let's begin.

TUTORIAL 6.1   THREE-POINT LIGHTING

Three-point lighting is pretty self-explanatory and is one of the most commonly used because of its directness and simplicity. It is often used in stage lighting and other real world lighting situations. Three-point lighting is best used for lighting objects and less so for lighting environments. It consists of three categories of light. First is the *Key* light, which is the main, shadow-casting light in the scene. Second is the *Fill* light, which fills in the areas of darkness not reached by the Key. The third type is called the *Backlight* (sometimes called the *Rim* light). It provides an outline or silhouette of your object(s).

Despite its name, you are not limited to three lights. For example, you might have two Key lights, one Fill light, and eight Rim lights. But there are still just three categories of lights in the scene: Key, Fill, and Backlight (Rim).

Also keep in mind that you can't just keep all the lights to their default 100 percent intensity. Key and Fill lights usually follow some prescribed ratios of intensity to achieve *Low Key* lighting and *High Key* lighting. Low Key lighting means there is a smaller difference in the Key and Fill intensities. High Key lighting means there is a greater difference in there intensities. These lead to different lighting situations and thus different mood settings.

In this tutorial, you will learn about the following:

- Key light
- Fill light
- Backlight (Rim)

- Light types
- Light color
- Shadow
- Negative Intensity
- Include/Exclude
- Array of lights
- Viewport lighting
- Visible light

ON THE CD

To begin, open the file Tutorials > Chapter06 > Chapter6-1 > 3-point_ start.c4d from the CD-ROM. This is a prepared scene file with a statue and base along with a single material.

Camera Angle and Lighting

When you are setting up your lights for a scene that is to be still rendered, its important to consider *camera angle*. You might light a scene to your satisfaction only to find it completely unacceptable as soon as you change camera angles. This is because when you modify the camera, you are changing the angle of incidence for the lights, which is a key component in calculating surface intensities. So, realize that your final still renderings will be the composite relationship among *materials/textures*, *lights*, and *camera angle*.

Because of this, the 3-point_start.c4d scene file's camera is locked into position. The tutorial is based on that camera angle, and changing it will produce unknown results, so there's no need to rotate, pan, or zoom the camera. To avoid problems, in all the tutorials in this chapter, *don't change the camera angle* by panning, zooming, rotating, and so on.

Key Light

The Key light is the main light in the scene. You add it first so that there is no doubt where the principal light will be coming from. The key light will be a Spot light, which is a light that does not emit in all directions but is limited to a cone of light. The cone will later be adjusted to light up more of the statue.

Add a Spot light:

1. Add a Spot light to the scene by clicking on the nested light icon, or choose Objects > Scene > Spot light. A new light will appear in the scene. The statue may go dark because an auto light is disabled whenever you import new lights. When there are no lights in the scene, the auto light is reactivated.
2. Name the light *Key—yellow.*
3. Observe the Attributes Manager for the light. Make sure you are looking at the General tab.

4. Change the Color RGB values to 255, 248, and 196 (for a yellow color), and set Intensity to 100%. In the Shadow setting, activate Raytraced (Hard).

5. In the Coordinates Manager, change the Position for the light to 151, 268, and −64. Change the Rotation to 66, −38, and 0 for H, P, and B, respectively. Click Apply. See Figure 6.2. This will put the light up and to the right of the statue.

6. Render the scene (see Figure 6.3).

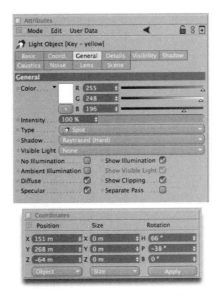

FIGURE 6.2   The Attribute Settings for the Key light along with the coordinates.

FIGURE 6.3   A rendered view of the Key light.

As you can see, the light is only lighting up half of the statue. This is because it is a Spot light, and these light types have a cone of light. The cone is too small, so you need to increase it.

Setting the inner and outer angle:

7. Make sure you have the Key—Yellow light selected.
8. In the Attributes Manager, click on the Details tab. Change the Outer Angle to 66 and the Inner Angle to 54 to widen the cone.
9. Render the view again. Now you'll see that the entire statue from head to base is lit by the Key light (see Figure 6.4).

FIGURE 6.4 Increasing the inner and outer angle for the Spot light settings increases the area it will light.

Fill Light

Notice how you can tell exactly where the Key light is coming from when you render. It's important if you've never done three-point lighting to make the Key light obvious at first; it makes things easier later on.

Also notice how much of the statue remains in darkness. That's where the Fill light comes to play. For this statue, you'll use an Omni light, which is a light that shines in all directions, along with Soft Shadows. Soft Shadows use shadow maps instead of raytracing and so are generally fast and can give a nice, soft edge. This is better for the Fill light as it will make it seam more diffuse. Remember, you don't want your Fill lights to overtake your Key light as the main light. Think of them as a hero's sidekick.

Add an Omni light:

1. Click on the Light icon or choose Objects > Scene > Light to import an Omni light.
2. Rename the Light to *Fill—Blue*. Notice that lights are named using not just the category but also the color in the description.
3. In the Attributes Manager, in the General tab, change the Color to 174, 199, and 255 for a bluish color. Change the Intensity to 50%. In the Shadow setting, switch to Shadow Maps (Soft).
4. In the Coordinates Manager, change the Position to –127, 69, and –135 for X, Y, and Z, respectively. We won't enter rotation values like we did for the Spot light because there would be no noticeable effect of rotating an Omni light. Click Apply. See Figure 6.5. This places the Fill light left of the statue, opposite of the Key light.
5. Re-render (see Figure 6.6).

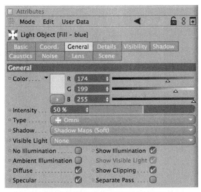

FIGURE 6.5   The Fill light Attribute Manager settings.

FIGURE 6.6   The render shows both the yellow Key light and blue Fill light.

You'll notice that by coloring the lights it makes it easier to tell them apart. It also makes the render more interesting as pure white lights are rare in nature.

Enhanced OpenGL, found in the Display menu in the Viewport, can display various visual settings such as Transparency and Shadow within the Editor. This will help speed up previews. Note that you'll need a supported video card for Enhanced OpenGL. You can check if your card is supported in the Preferences.

Low Key versus High Key

We are going to add another Fill light to help fill in more of the darkness. It is common to use more than one light in any given category in three-point lighting, and you shouldn't feel constrained to use a particular number or style of lights. In the end, we all use what works. Results are what matter.

You will use this extra Fill light to control whether the final image is Low Key or High Key. To simplify, this can be determined by what the second fill light's Intensity is set to. If the Intensity ratio between the Key and Fill is large (for example 100% Key, 10% Fill) then it will be High Key. There will be a lot of contrast in the scene, and the mood will be dark, mysterious, intense, uncomfortable, and so on. If the Intensity ratio between the Key and Fill is low (for example 100% Key, 80% Fill), then it will be Low Key, and the mood will be light, cheery, easy going, and so on. This is somewhat an oversimplification, but hopefully the point is made.

The other thing our second Fill light will do is provide some color balance. Because we have one blue and one yellow light, the statue is either shades of blue or yellow. Our second Fill light will be just white, which will help balance them out.

Add a second Fill light:

1. Choose Objects > Scene > Light, or click on the Light icon. Another Omni light will enter the scene.
2. Name it *Fill—Key Control*.
3. In the Attributes Manager, change Shadow to Shadow Maps (Soft) and Intensity to 10%.
4. Change the Position to 0, 69, and –135 in the Coordinates Manager for X, Y, and Z, respectively. This will place the light just in front of the statue. Click Apply.
5. Re-render. Now both fills work together (see Figure 6.7).

One fill has an Intensity of 50%, and the other has an Intensity of 10%, so combined they are 60%. However, because they are not in the same position, their total value is not completely cumulative. The value is still roughly 50%. This means that the ratio between our Key and Fill is about 2 to 1.

Backlighting

One of the things about real objects is that they often have a silhouette. Backlighting helps to make that apparent. Backlighting either makes an object stand out from the background, as will be the case here, or blend into the background, depending on what your needs are.

FIGURE 6.7   Results with the second Fill light.

One of the difficult things to do in achieving backlighting is to make it seem as if the light is coming from all around the object. We'll use an array of lights to achieve this.

Add a light for the Backlight:

1. Add an Omni light by choosing Objects > Scene > Light, or click on the Light icon.
2. Name it *Backlight*.
3. In the Attributes Manager, change its Intensity to 20%. Activate Shadow Maps (Soft).

Add an array:

4. Make sure you have Backlight selected in the Objects Manager.
5. While holding down the Alt key (Option for Macintosh) choose the Array icon or Objects > Modeling > Array from the main menu. This will bring an array into the scene with the Backlight linked to it. If for some reason the Backlight is not linked to the array do so manually in the Objects Manager by dragging and dropping Backlight onto the Array object. Figure 6.8 to shows what the Objects Manager looks like so far.
6. Rename the Array object to *Array Backlight*. Make sure it is selected in the Objects Manager.
7. In the Attributes Manager, change the Radius to 400. This will make the array of lights larger. The larger the array, the more light will be able to reach the sides and front of the statue.

8. In the Coordinates Manager, change the Position of Array Backlight to 0, 71, and 278 for X, Y, and Z. Rotate it 90 degrees in the P. Click Apply. This will rotate the array and move it behind the statue.
9. Re-render (see Figure 6.9).

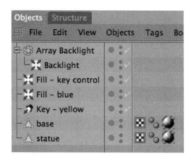

FIGURE 6.8   The Objects Manager so far.

FIGURE 6.9   A render showing the results of the array lighting.

Include/Exclude

We now have a basic three-point lighting setup. The statue's form is very understandable because of the lighting. There are, however, a few outstanding issues. For one, the light coming off the base and feet is a little overexposed. This makes perfect sense because of their angle to both the lights and the camera. Computer-generated lights, however, allow us to "cheat." That is, we can alter reality a little to get the image we want.

Color Plate 1 "Detail" © Fredi Voss

Color Plate 2 "Lost Moments" © Fredi Voss

Color Plate 3 "Schacht" © Oliver Becker

Color Plate 4 "Whirling" © Oliver Becker

Color Plate 5 "Carnivorbot" © Peter Hofmann, www.peXeL.de

Color Plate 6 "Highway to Heaven" © Peter Hofmann, www.peXeL.de

Color Plate 7 "Deep Well" © Peter Hofmann, www.peXeL.de

Color Plate 8 "Elixier" © Peter Hofmann, www.peXeL.de

Color Plate 9 "Train Flashlight 2" © D. Davidson- www.maxed.org

Color Plate 10 "Ganesh" © Matthieu Roussel

Color Plate 11 "Last Elephant" © Matthieu Roussel

Color Plate 12 "Sew" © Matthieu Roussel

Color Plate 13 "Gaucho" © Anson Call

Color Plate 14 "Bureaucratic Combine 3000" © Anson Call

Color Plate 15 "Ville" © Matthieu Roussel

Color Plate 16 "Abs" © Oliver Becker

We are going to tell the Backlight not to light up the base. C4D allows the user to do this through its Include/Exclude feature in the Scene tab. It's a powerful ability.

Exclude the base:

1. In the Objects Manager, select the Backlight light.
2. Click on the Scene tab in the Attributes Manager.
3. Do not single-click on the base as that will deselect the Backlight. Rather, click-drag and drop the base from the Objects Manager into the Objects list in the Scene tab (see Figure 6.10).
4. Re-render. Notice how the brightness on the base has dropped since Backlight is no longer lighting it (see Figure 6.11).

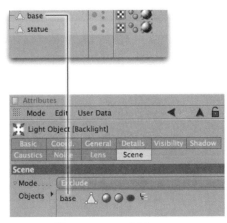

Drag and Drop

FIGURE 6.10   Drag and drop the base into the Backlight Scene tab's Objects list.

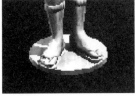 

Before   **After**

FIGURE 6.11   A before-and-after comparison of excluding the base from the Backlight.

Negative Intensity

Notice how the feet are still overexposed. We could lower the intensity of our Key, Fill, or Backlight lights, but we would have to sacrifice the rest of the statue's intensity to do so. If this was a real-world situation, you might just have to live with it. But 3D lighting can do things that would make Einstein do a double take. We can use negative values in the intensity setting and essentially throw black light onto our statue.

We'll use three Spot lights with negative intensity and shine them on the feet to lower their brightness. To not take away too much light from the base, we'll exclude the base from these new lights.

Add a Spot light for negative intensity:

1. Add a Spot light (Objects > Scene > Spot Light). Change its name to *Right Foot Negative.*
2. Change its Intensity to –50. You can do this in the text box next to the Intensity slider in the Attributes Manager.
3. In the Coordinates Manager, change Position to –11, 39, and –37 for X, Y, and Z. Change Rotation to –10, –48, and –7 for H, P, and B. Click Apply.
4. Re-render (see Figure 6.12). Notice how the right foot is now less bright. Also notice how there is a black spot on the base. That is because the Spot light is taking away light not only from the foot but also the base.
5. Make sure you have the Right Foot Negative light selected in the Objects Manager. Click on its Scene tab, and click-drag and drop the base into the Objects list to exclude it.
6. Re-render to see that the Right Foot Negative light will now ignore the base (see Figure 6.13).

FIGURE 6.12   The bright spot on right foot is gone, but there is now a dark spot on the base.

FIGURE 6.13   Using the Exclude in the Scene tab gets rid of the dark spot.

Duplicate the negative intensity Spot lights:

7. In the Objects Manager, select Right Foot Negative, and in the Manager's menu, select Edit > Copy, and then Edit > Paste. An exact copy

of Right Foot Negative will appear in the hierarchy. Rename the copy to *Left Foot Negative* (see Figure 6.14).

You can also copy objects in the Objects Manager by a combination of click-drag and drop while holding down the Ctrl key.

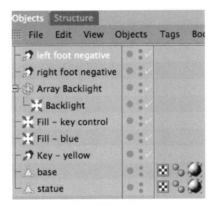

FIGURE 6.14   The Objects Manager hierarchy so far.

8. Make sure you have Left Foot Negative selected. In the Coordinates Manager, change Position to 24, 48, and –32 for X, Y, and Z. For Rotation enter 25, –53, and 19 for H, P, and B. Click Apply. This will place the light over the left foot.

9. Change Left Foot Negative*'s* Intensity to –40 in the Attributes Manager under the General tab.

10. Re-render (see Figure 6.15). The left foot is now less bright, but it could be reduced even further. The problem is that the angle of the light can only reduce the front of the foot and not the side. If we reduce too much, it will just get too dark, with the side staying too bright. The answer is another copy.

11. Make a copy of Left Foot Negative and name it *Left Foot Side Negative*. You should now have a total of three negative Spot lights (see Figure 6.16a).

12. In the Coordinates Manager, change Left Foot Side Negative's Position to 38, 48, and 8 in the X, Y, and Z. Change Rotation to 97, –54, and 95 for H, P, and B. Click Apply.

13. Change Left Foot Side Negative's Intensity to –30.

14. Re-render. The difference is subtle, but both feet now look much better (see Figure 6.16b).

FIGURE 6.15 Left foot is less bright but needs further work.

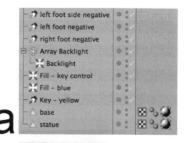

a

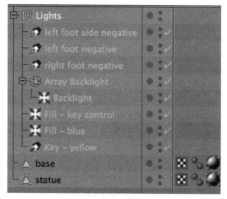

b

FIGURE 6.16 (a) The Objects Manager hierarchy. (b) With another negative light repositioned, both feet are done.

Hierarchy and the Viewport

Hierarchy is very important in C4D. You may have noticed that how the statue is being lit in the Viewport isn't necessarily related with the final render. Some of this has to do with how they are linked and which one is at the top of the list. Let's do a little grouping and organizing.

Group the lights:

1. Select all of the lights, including the Array Backlight, and then press Alt+G to group them under a Null object. Rename the Null object to *Lights,* and expand the hierarchy (see Figure 6.17).

FIGURE 6.17 Group the lights, and then rename Null object to *Lights*. Expand the group.

2. Make sure the Viewport is set to Gouraud Shading by selecting Display > Gouraud Shading in the Perspective Viewport menu. Make sure the Perspective view is maximized.
3. Hide the lights in the Viewport by selecting Filter > Lights in the Viewport menu. This will hide the lights, but their influence will still be visible. This is done for clarity.

Viewing Lighting in the Viewport

Notice how the statue seems dark with a blue outline. This is coming from the Array Backlight light group. Because it is higher up in the list (in the Objects Manager), it overrides the lights below it, so we can't see what the Key or Fill lights are doing.

Reorder the hierarchy:

1. Drag and drop the Key—Yellow light to the top of the Lights list, as shown in Figure 6.18a. The lighting on the statue updates, giving a better understanding of what Key—Yellow is doing (see Figure 6.18b).
2. Drag and drop the Fill—Blue right below Key—Yellow in the hierarchy.
3. Drag and drop the Fill—Key Control right below Fill—Blue in the hierarchy.
4. Drag and drop the Array Backlight group right below Fill—Key Control in the hierarchy.
5. Deselect all your objects, Edit > Deselect All. Your hierarchy should look like Figure 6.19.

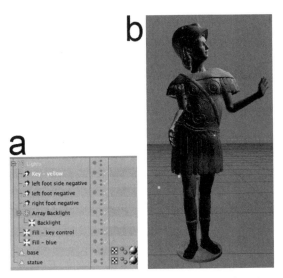

FIGURE 6.18   (a) Reordered Key-Yellow in the Object's Manager hierarchy and (b) the Viewport result.

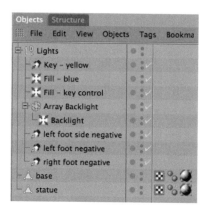

FIGURE 6.19   Final reorder of the hierarchy.

Looking at the Viewport (see Figure 6.20), you'll see that it is now a much closer representation of the renderer. You can reorder, as you like, isolating lights and groups. You can also use the Layer Browser or just the Visible in Editor and Visible in Renderer gray buttons to accomplish much the same thing. For more information on this, look in Help > Help, then in the Content tab, Manual > Reference > Object Manager > Objects Menu.

FIGURE 6.20   The Viewport now looks similar to the renderer.

Volumetric Lights

Volumetric lights cast visible rays. We are going to set up the Key light to be volumetric. With this option, it will appear that the statue is bathed in light rays.

Before we do this, there are some important things you should know about volumetric light, namely that it can slow render times down significantly. However, we have a relatively simple scene, so that is not a major worry in this case.

Setting up Volumetric light:

1. Select the Key—Yellow light.
2. In the Attributes Manager, select the General tab.
3. Change Visible Light to Volumetric (see Figure 6.21).
4. Click on the Visibility tab in the Attributes Manager.
5. Change Sample Distance to 10, Brightness to 40%, and Dust to 50%. A lower Sample Distance number makes the rays more accurate but takes longer to render. We lower our Brightness for aesthetic reasons only. Dust is similar to an atmospheric effect of particulates in the air (see Figure 6.22).

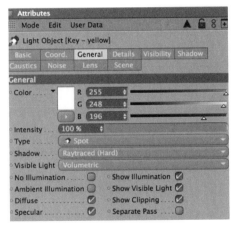

FIGURE 6.21   Key—Yellow General tab settings.

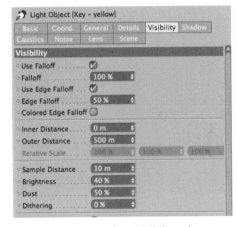

FIGURE 6.22   Key—Yellow Visibility tab settings.

Three-Point Lighting Render

It's time to render again. The quality of the renderings hasn't been very good because we have antialiasing turned off. This is good for preview renders but not so good for finals.

Use antialiasing:

1. Go to Render > Render Settings. Turn on Antialiasing (Best) in either the General or Antialiasing tab.
2. Re-render (see Figure 6.23).

FIGURE 6.23   Final three-point lighting render.

Wrap Up

Three-point lighting is very straightforward and can be applied to many situations. Remember that it is a technique and not an exact science. There are many solutions to lighting problems.

To spice up this render further, add some Ambient Occlusion in the Render Settings, turning the Accuracy way down to add some grit. With Best Antialiasing and Ambient Occlusion, the render times will increase noticeably. ✄

TUTORIAL 6.2   **AREA LIGHTING**

Later on in this chapter, we will cover GI (Global Illumination, previously referred to in earlier versions as radiosity) and HDRI, which are CPU-expensive rendering techniques that can take a significant amount of time to render. Area lighting can achieve similar results to GI without the render times.

That's not to say that area lighting won't take a long time to render. Only that it is generally faster. Render times depend heavily on how many polygons you have in your scene, light count, shadow types, materials, and texture sizes, to name just a few. It is usually true, however, that there is a direct relationship between render quality and the time it takes to render an image. That only applies if you know what you are doing. Don't expect to just crank up all your render settings and get a great image. It can take just as long to render an ugly image as a beautiful one.

Area lighting imitates the bounced and diffuse light that is achievable through GI. You place the main lights in your scene and then secondary "bounce" lights to mimic light diffusion. One of the best ways to learn how this works is with the Light Box, which is essentially a room with an object in the middle. That's our second tutorial.

In this tutorial, you will learn about the following:

- Area lights
- Shadow types
- Falloff
- Primary/secondary lighting
- Multiple selections
- Materials and lighting
- Ambient Occlusion

ON THE CD

Open the file Tutorials > Chapter06 > Chapter6-2 > area_lighting_start.c4d on the CD-ROM. You will need this file to complete the tutorial.

Scene Description

After you open the file, you'll notice a statue in the middle of a six-sided box. Looking at the Objects Manager, you'll notice each wall has been separated out and a color has been applied. The *Light object* is the light on the ceiling. It doesn't really emit light, so we'll have to add a light just below it to simulate what it would do. It has a material with the Luminance turned all the way up to help in the illusion. The Light object is the primary light prop in the scene.

The left, right, and back walls each have their own unique color applied. We will add area lights and place them over the walls. The light will be given the same color as the wall it represents. This is secondary lighting, or the bounced light we will be imitating.

The colors on the walls are intense so we can overexaggerate the effect of bounced light and make it obvious what is happening and why. If this were a real-world project, we'd tone those colors down.

As with the previous project, the camera has been disabled. Moving the camera changes how the scene would render. So, moving it is unnecessary except to edit in Side view, Top view, or Front view. Please leave the Perspective Camera as is.

Main Light

It's always important to establish the main light in a scene. Ours is obvious. It's the Light object that is above the statue and on the ceiling. But, as stated before, this isn't a real light, just a scene prop.

Our prop has area to it, so we need a light that does more than just emit from an infinitely small point, like regular Point and Spot lights. Area lights are what get this done. They mimic lights that have area or volume, which is what real lights are. So, let's add an Area light to the scene.

Add a light for the Light object:

1. Add an Area light from the nested Light icons or choose Objects > Scene > Area Light from the main menu.
2. Rename the light as *Main Light*.
3. In the Coordinates Manager, change the Y Position to 1193. In Rotation, change P to 90. Click Apply. This will place and correctly orient the Main Light just below the Light object.
4. Change Shadow to Shadow Maps (Soft) in the Attributes Manager. Later on, we will change these to a more accurate type of shadow. But Soft Shadows renders quickly, which is what we want for now.
5. In the Attributes Manager, click on the Details tab. Change Outer Radius to 300, Size X to 600, Size Y to 600 (Size X and Y changes automatically when you change Outer Radius), and Falloff Angle to 0 (see Figure 6.24).
6. Render to the Picture Viewer. The shortcut is Shift+R or Render > Render to Picture Viewer (see Figure 6.25).

FIGURE 6.24   Main Light's Details tab settings.

FIGURE 6.25   Main Light render.

Look at the render. All the major elements in the scene are visible. You can see the different colored walls. The Main Light is casting a shadow on the statue. It is also casting a shadow on the Light object. This just won't do, as that's the object that we are trying to simulate. We need to use the Scene tab to exclude the Light object from being seen by Main Light.

Exclude the Light object:

7. Select Main Light in the Objects Manager.
8. Click on the Scene tab in the Attributes Manager.
9. Click-drag and drop the Light object into the Objects list in the Scene tab (see Figure 6.26). Remember, if you just click on the Light object, you'll deselect the light, and thus lose the Scene tab. If that happens, start at step 1 and try again.
10. Re-render (see Figure 6.27).

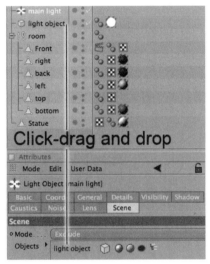

FIGURE 6.26   Click-drag and drop the Light object into Main Light's Scene tab.

FIGURE 6.27   Now Main Light doesn't see Light object, and therefore it casts no shadow.

In the previous steps, we just told Main Light to ignore the Light object. Doing so means that the Light object won't cast a shadow, which is exactly what we want. This type of light linking is extremely useful, and we'll continue to use it throughout the tutorial.

Secondary Lights

With our primary light practically finished, it's time to move on to the secondary lights. These lights mimic light coming off the walls. Even though the walls don't really emit light, in the real world, they would bounce the main light back into the scene. That is what we are going to achieve in the next steps. We need to do one for each wall. Because a wall has a fairly large surface, we will again use Area lights.

Create an Area light for the yellow wall:

1. Add another Area light to the scene (Objects > Scene > Area Light).
2. Rename it *Left—Yellow*. We use a description for location and color to better know which light represents what wall.
3. In the Attributes Manager, change the Color to 255, 201, and 0 for R, G, and B. This will give it a yellowish-orange color. More importantly, it will exactly match the color of the left, yellow wall's material. Activate Shadow Maps (Soft).
4. In the Attributes Manager, click on the Details tab. Change Outer Radius to 683, Aspect Ratio to 0.87, Falloff Angle to 0, Falloff type to Linear, and Radius/Decay to 2000 (see Figure 6.28). These settings will increase the size of the light, change it from square to rectangular, and make it so that its light falls off at a linear rate. We want this because real light behaves similarly and is especially effective for secondary lights. Falloff means that as the light gets further away, it gets weaker. At 2000m it will no longer light anything up.
5. In the Coordinates Manager, change Position to –986, 623, 0 for X, Y, and Z. In Rotation, change H to 90. Click Apply. This rotates and places the light right on top of the yellow, left wall.
6. Re-render (see Figure 6.29).

You can see from the render that it appears as if the wall is now bouncing light back into the scene. It's a little overexaggerated for clarity. There are a few strange things happening though. The Light object has a shadow being cast from the Left—Yellow light. This is not what we want because secondary light bounces would not be strong enough to cast such shadows. We'll need to tell the Left—Yellow light to ignore the Light object, just like we did with Main Light.

We are going to go one step further and add the left wall to the Exclude list for Left—Yellow because there is no reason for it to affect that

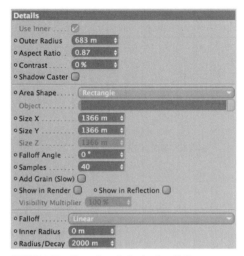

FIGURE 6.28   Details tab for Left—Yellow.

FIGURE 6.29   A render of the effects of the addition of Left—Yellow.

wall in any way. So, we want Left—Yellow to ignore both the Light object and the left wall.

Exclude the Light object:

7. Select Left—Yellow in the Objects Manager.
8. Click on the Scene tab in the Attributes Manager.
9. Click-drag and drop the Light object into the Scene tab's Objects list.
10. Click-drag and drop the left wall into the Scene tab's Objects list. The exclude list for Left—Yellow should like Figure 6.30.
11. Re-render. The shadow on the Light object is now gone.

FIGURE 6.30   The Left—Yellow light's Exclude list in the Scene tab.

Light for the Red Wall

The red wall is called *right*. For its light, we will just duplicate the Left—Yellow light, move it, change its color, and modify its Exclude list. We won't need to change its Details tab because it is just the same as Left—Yellow.

Duplicate and modify the Area light:

1. In the Objects Manager, select Left—Yellow.
2. In the Objects Manager menu, select Edit > Copy and then Edit > Paste to make a copy.
3. Rename the copy to *Right—Red*.
4. In the Coordinates Manager, change Position X to 986. Click Apply.
5. In the Attributes Manager, click on the General tab. Change Color to 168, 29, and 13 for R, G, and B.
6. Click on the Scene tab. Select Left in the list, and click Delete. Click-drag and drop the right wall down into the list. The list should now include the Light object and Right.
7. Re-render. You should now see yellow light coming off the yellow wall and red light coming off the red wall, with no shadows on the Light object (see Figure 6.31).

FIGURE 6.31   Light now bounces off the yellow and red walls.

Light for the Blue Wall

The light for the back, blue wall is very similar to the yellow and red lights. We have to edit its color, Details, and Scene tab, along with its co-ordinates.

Duplicate and modify the Area light:

1. In the Objects Manager, copy and paste Right—Red. Rename its copy to *Back—Blue*.
2. In the Attributes Manager, click on the General tab. Change RGB Color to 48, 51, and 183. This will match the back wall's blue color.
3. In the Attributes Manager, click on the Details tab. Change Outer Radius to 985 and Aspect Ratio to 0.64. This will make its area larger and more rectangular, matching the surface of the back wall.
4. In the Attributes Manager, click on the Scene tab. Delete Right from the list, and add the back wall. The list should now contain the Light object and Back.
5. In the Coordinates Manager, change Position to 0, 623m and 732 for X, Y, and Z. Zero out any Rotations. Click Apply. This places the light over the back wall.
6. Re-render. The scene now shows the influence of the yellow, red, and blue walls (see Figure 6.32). Because the blue color is rather mute, it won't influence the scene as much as the yellow and red lights, but you should see some color mixing in the corners of the ceiling and floor.

FIGURE 6.32   Light now appears to bounce off the yellow, red, and blue walls.

Light for the Front Wall

The statue is still pretty dark in the render because we are missing our last light, the Front light. Even though we can't see the front wall (it's hidden from the Editor and the camera), it would still have some influence on the scene. We will assume it has a neutral, white color, and this will help balance out the other colors in the scene, as well as light up our statue.

Duplicate and modify the Area light:

1. In the Objects Manager, select Back—Blue. Copy and paste it.
2. Rename the copy to *Front—White*.
3. In the Attributes Manager, click on the General tab, and change its Color to White. In the Details tab, change Radius/Decay to 4000. A higher radius/decay number will make the scene brighter. Click on the Scene tab, and delete the back wall. Only the Light object should remain in the list. Since we don't see the front wall, there's no reason to include it in the list.
4. In the Coordinates Manager, enter 0, 623, and –711 for Position X, Y, and Z. Click Apply.
5. Re-render. You can now see the statue better (see Figure 6.33).

FIGURE 6.33   The statue and the scene are now brighter.

Area Shadows

Our scene is mostly finished. It renders fairly quickly, with Antialiasing turned off and Soft shadows. It lacks the realism that we were seeking, though, because the types of shadows we are using aren't very accurate for this particular setup. Area shadows match our Area lighting much better. However, you should be aware that doing so adds a lot of rendering time.

We will change the shadows to Area for a greater realism. We can do this to all the lights at the same time by selecting them all in the Objects Manager.

Make multiple selections:

1. In the Objects Manager, select all of the lights (Front—White, Back—Blue, Right—Red, Left—Yellow, and Main Light).
2. In the Attributes Manager, click on the General tab. Change the Shadow type to Area. You have now done this for all of the lights.
3. Click on the Shadow tab in the Attributes Manager. Change Maximum Samples to 70 to help speed up the rendering a little.
4. Re-render. With realism comes a render penalty, so it will take significantly longer. It is just part of the game. However, our scene looks more accurate now (see Figure 6.34).

FIGURE 6.34   Area shadows are much more realistic but take much longer to render.

Area Light Wrap Up

Looking at Figure 6.34, you'll see that with Area shadows, the scene is much more diffuse and mimics real lights in a more natural way. You may notice noise on the floor, which is caused by the fact that we lowered the Maximum Samples to 70. For a final render, turn on Ambient Occlusion and Geometry Antialiasing in the Render Settings. Ambient Occlusion has already been edited for you, so all you need to do is activate it and render (see Figure 6.35).

You can also change the intensity of the floor and ceiling by editing their materials instead of adding lights. The floor already has a material named Floor. Its color has been turned down to 48% since its default was at 80%. This was too bright for the scene. It's often much more useful to edit the brightness of a material than to try and relight it. ✂

FIGURE 6.35   Final Area light render.

TUTORIAL 6.3   GLOBAL ILLUMINATION

Radiosity, now called Global Illumination (GI) in R10, calculates bounced light. Along with other techniques and a good eye, it can produce very realistic imagery. As stated before, it takes a lot of CPU horsepower to calculate. Fortunately, C4D offers a relatively good solution and ways to optimize for maximum quality and lower rendering times. Optimizing a scene is very important, and we'll talk about this as we progress.

ON THE CD

Open up the scene for this tutorial, found on the CD-ROM in Tutorials > Chapter06 > Chapter6-3 > Radiosity_start.c4d, or copy over the folder to your hard drive and open it up from there.

The scene contains a hallway, doors, sky, and a hidden light. As with the previous tutorials, there is a camera with movement and selection restrictions on it. This scene is meant to be rendered from this viewpoint. Please leave the camera in its current position.

In this tutorial you will learn about the following:

- Global Illumination (GI) settings
- Lights and GI
- Light intensity
- Sky and GI

- Ambient Occlusion and GI
- Color bleeding
- Material Illumination settings
- Auto light

Lights and Auto Light

Render the scene. Notice that you can see parts of the hallway. Now look at your Objects Manager. The only Light object in the scene is hidden, indicated by the two red dots next to it. How is it that we can see anything then, if there are no lights? C4D has what's called the Auto light, which is always on when there are no other lights present or active so you can see your objects. The Auto light is attached to the Editor Camera, so no matter where you move your view, you'll always have a light shining on the objects. This is very helpful when modeling and texturing and not so much for lighting. So, C4D automatically turns off the Auto light when you import any other light(s). However, it doesn't turn it off when you activate Global Illumination (GI). So, if you are going to render using GI, and you have no other lights in the scene, you will need to turn off the Auto light.

Turn off Auto light:

1. Open the Render Settings by choosing Render > Render Settings.
2. Click on Options.
3. Uncheck Auto Light.
4. Close the Render Settings.
5. Render the scene.

You'll now just see black with some sky poking through the openings in the ceiling and window. This is because with the Auto light turned off, there is nothing to light the scene. Sometimes you may want this, but we have another Light object ready to go.

Turn the Light object on:

6. Unhide the Light object in the Objects Manager by clicking once on both the top and bottom red dots, making the dots turn gray. These dots are found in the Objects Manager for the object and sit to the right of the object's name (see Figure 6.36).
7. Render to the Picture Viewer (see Figure 6.37).

Light Intensity

You will now see that the Light object shines through the windows and hits the floor and walls. The light has a hard shadow, which is evident on its crisp edges. Let's take a look at our Light object properties for a moment.

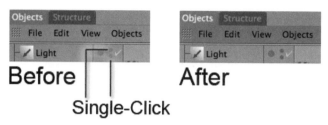

Before   After

Single-Click

FIGURE 6.36   Click on both the top and bottom red dots to make them turn gray and unhide the Light object.

FIGURE 6.37   Render of the scene with the Light object revealed.

Observe the Light object:

1. In the Objects Manager, select the Light object.
2. In the Attributes Manager, click on the General tab.
3. Notice that the Type is set to Infinite.
4. Notice that Intensity is set to 200%.

An Infinite light was chosen because it mimics sunlight fairly well. Light rays entering the hallway are mostly parallel. Omni or Spot lights would have to be moved very far away from the hallway to get similar results.

You can raise Intensity past 100%, which is useful for scenes with GI. Because the light that will bounce comes from this main Light object, we want it to be intense enough to light the hallway. There are a few other tricks we can employ along with this, which we'll talk about later.

Turn on GI:

5. Open the Render Settings by choosing Render > Render Settings.
6. Click on the words Global Illum. to activate Global Illumination (see Figure 6.38).
7. Re-render (see Figure 6.39).

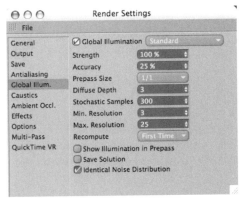

FIGURE 6.38   Render Settings for Global Illumination.

FIGURE 6.39   Rendering with GI turned on.

You will now see in the re-render that GI lets the light bounce around the room, lighting it up. To better understand the GI settings, let's go back and look at the Render Settings window and cover what some of those terms mean.

Review GI settings:

8. Open the Render Settings by choosing Render > Render Settings.
9. Click on the words Global Illum. to see its settings.
10. Observe Standard, Strength, Accuracy, Diffuse Depth, Stochastic Samples, Min, and Max Resolution (refer to Figure 6.38).

- Standard refers to the type of GI calculation C4D will use. Standard is the default setting. We will not cover every setting here, as that information is present in the Help > Help system.
- Strength refers to how strong the bounced light will appear in the scene. If you turn this down to 0, it would render as if there were no bounced light, although it's not the same as turning it off because it would still calculate GI. You can go over 100%.
- Accuracy is heavily related to how long it will take to render. A lower number will render fast, but produce lower quality. A higher number will take longer to render but will help reduce noise and artifacts associated with GI.
- Diffuse Depth is the number of bounces in the scene, so a higher number means longer render times. Each bounce has an additive effect, essentially lightening the scene as the number of bounces increases. There are other ways of increasing brightness in a scene besides Diffuse Depth, which should be considered first.
- Stochastic Samples also affects render times greatly. Think of these samples as the number of rays in the scene. The lower the number, the fewer rays there are to go around the scene to light up surfaces, so it will look grainy or have a high number of artifacts. A higher number means more rays, better quality, and longer render times.
- Min Resolution refers to the areas in a scene where the computer doesn't have to spend a lot of time calculating bounced light. For example, the middle of a wall is an area of Min Resolution. You can usually keep this number low, but there are times when it needs to be increased. Let's say you had a neon sign on a wall. The sign would light the wall up. But if your Min Resolution number was too low, it might not turn out so well.
- Max Resolution refers to the areas in a scene where the computer needs to spend more time thinking about GI. Corners and object intersections are good examples of these. The higher the number, the more time it will spend in these areas

Which Settings to Use?

So, what's the magical formula to make it all work? Well, there isn't one, except patience and trial and error. After a while, you'll pick up the instinct to make it work. One thing you should always do is try and get the best-looking image for the least amount of render time.

Ambient Occlusion

One way to do that is to use Ambient Occlusion in conjunction with GI. Ambient Occlusion darkens the areas of Max Resolution, essentially giving shadows to the places normally covered by GI. However, Ambient Occlusion doesn't bounce light, and therefore is more of a shadowing tool. In conjunction with GI, it can greatly speed rendering times while maintaining quality.

Activate Ambient Occlusion (AO):

1. Open the Render Settings by choosing Render > Render Settings.
2. Click on Ambient Occl. Click on Apply to Scene.
3. Lower Accuracy to 25% and Maximum Samples to 64. This will speed up the AO rendering (see Figure 6.40).
4. Re-render (see Figure 6.41).

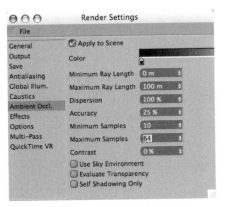

FIGURE 6.40   Ambient Occlusion settings.

FIGURE 6.41   Render with Global Illumination and Ambient Occlusion.

Looking at Figure 6.41, we see that the image is starting to come together. There is much artifacting and noise due to our relatively low GI settings. We will fix these later.

Sky as Light

Besides the Light object in the scene, the sky is also contributing to the overall lighting. To better see this, let's turn off our Light object and re-render with just the Sky.

Deactivate the Light object:

1. Locate the Light object in the Objects Manager. Click on the green check mark that sits to the right of its name. Clicking on it will turn the check mark into a red X, indicating it is deactivated.

2. Re-render (see Figure 6.42).

FIGURE 6.42 Render with just the Sky object illuminating the scene.

Now just the Sky object is lighting the hallway. Since the sky has a material with a Blue Luminance channel, the hallway takes on diffuse, blue shading. Sky objects produce such indirect lighting because they light in all directions.

Materials Illumination

Materials play a big part in GI. Each material has an Illumination channel that dictates how it will interact with GI. Let's take a look at some of our materials to understand what they are doing in the scene.

Use Hallway material:

1. Double-click on the Hallway material in the Materials Manager.
2. Click on the Illumination channel (see Figure 6.43).

Observe the Strength setting next to Generate GI. The default value is 100%. This setting of 135% means that it will produce more light than normal, essentially making the hallway brighter. Because there is no luminance to this material, the Generate GI option works similarly to the Receive GI option.

There's no real render penalty for increasing the numbers here. Remember, the Diffuse Depth setting in the GI Render Settings does something similar but at a significant render penalty, so modifying the Illumination channel for your materials is a good idea if you are just looking for ways to modify the brightness of your scene. You could also try the Strength setting in the GI Render Settings.

FIGURE 6.43   Hallway material Illumination settings.

Using Sky material:

3. Double-click on the Sky material in the Materials Manager.
4. Click on the Illumination channel (see Figure 6.44).

FIGURE 6.44   Sky material Illumination settings.

Notice how the Strength setting is set to 400% for the Generate GI. This means that the Sky object is taking a more active role in lighting the hallway than it would if it were set to its default of 100%. Materials are an important part of GI lighting.

Preparing for the Final Render

It's time to turn up some of our settings for the final render. This scene only has 257 polygons, which is an extremely low number. Regardless of this low number, a GI render might still take 10 minutes depending on settings and on the speed of your computer. However, keeping track of your polygon count is very important.

You can check scene polygon count in the Objects Manager by choosing Objects > Scene Information.

Use GI settings:

1. Turn the Light object back on by clicking on its red X, changing it to a green check mark.
2. Select the Light object in the Objects Manager. In the Attributes Manager, under the General tab, change its Shadow to Area. This will produce a more realistic shadow.
3. Open the Render Settings by choosing Render > Render Settings.
4. Click on Global Illum. to see its settings. Change Accuracy to 75%, Diffuse Depth to 4, Stochastic Samples to 600, Min Resolution to 10, and Max Resolution to 90 (see Figure 6.45).
5. Click on the General section of the Render Settings. Make sure Antialiasing is set to Best and that Reflection is set to All Objects (see Figure 6.46).
6. Render. As your image renders, see Figure 6.47 and read ahead.

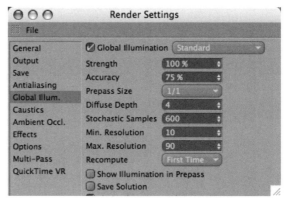

FIGURE 6.45   Render Settings and GI settings for the final render.

While your image is rendering, you will notice a few things. It first does a prepass, placing red and green dots along the areas of Min and Max Resolutions. Notice how the corners have a higher concentration of

FIGURE 6.46   Render Settings and General settings for the final render.

FIGURE 6.47   What you'll see as it renders.

dots, while the middle of the walls and floor have fewer. This again, is because of the Min/Max settings.

Global Illumination Wrap Up

GI is an incredibly powerful and amazing tool. See the images artists have contributed to this book, including the cover, to see just what beautiful renderings can be made when in the right hands. Just remember that GI is usually a beast that needs to be tamed.

ON THE CD

In the final render, Figure 6.48, notice the color bleeding (see the full-color image on the CD-ROM, or look at your own render for reference). This is most noticeable on the ceiling, which has taken on both a blue and a red hue. The blue comes from the influence of the Sky object, and the red comes from the stripes on the walls. Color bleeding is a benefit of GI. In our last exercise, we had to set all this up manually, but GI does it automatically.

FIGURE 6.48   Final render.

TUTORIAL 6.4

HDRI LIGHTING AND SHADOW CATCHING

Perhaps one of the most entertaining things to do with 3D is to take a picture of a real place, make a 3D object, and composite that object into the picture convincingly. HDRI (High Dynamic Range Image) helps achieve this by providing realistic lighting for your object. An HDRI scene with an object will most likely have four components: a background with the picture applied, a sky with the HDRI applied, a floor with the same picture as the background applied, and an object on top of the floor.

Making HDRIs

The tutorial you are about to do provides a custom-made HDRI along with the accompanying background picture. For more information on how to make your own HDRIs, visit *http://gl.ict.usc.edu/HDRShop/*. This site provides a free version 1.0 of HDR Shop, which you can use to make your own HDRIs. The site also has technical information on what HDRIs are. Essentially they are images that have a greater color and value range than can be displayed on the computer screen. They are made from many different exposures to capture as much dynamic range as possible. This tutorial uses HDRIs but does not instruct on how to make them.

This tutorial will teach you about the following:

- HDRI lighting
- Images used as background
- Frontal projection
- Compositing tag
- Material Illumination channel
- Shadow catching
- Standard vs. Stochastic GI
- Layer Browser

Getting Started

ON THE CD

From the CD-ROM, copy the folder Tutorials > Chapter06 > Chapter6-4 to your hard drive. In C4D, open the file HDRI_start.c4d that is in the folder you just copied.

Material Setup

The first thing you'll notice is there's not much in the scene: a plane, sky, background, hidden primitives, and some unfinished materials. Since this is a tutorial on lighting, we won't do any modeling, those are provided, and we won't do much in regards to materials, except to load the background and HDRI image. You don't have to make any new materials. Those have been created, but there is absolutely nothing special about them at this point.

The camera, like in previous lighting tutorials, has again been disabled. This tutorial will not work from any other angle. Please leave the camera settings as they are.

Next you need to load the images into their respective materials and link to the objects in the scene.

Load the background picture:

1. In the Materials Manager, double-click on the Background material swatch. The Material Editor opens.
2. Click on the Color channel.
3. Click on the Texture bar (or the three dots) to load an image file. Go to the Chapter6-4 folder you copied to the hard drive. Inside that folder is another folder named tex. Inside that folder is the file you

will load called BGimage.JPG. Load that file into the Texture space. This is your background material (see Figure 6.49).

FIGURE 6.49   This is the picture you have just loaded into the Background material.

Load the HDRI:

4. In the Materials Manager, double-click on the HDRI material swatch.
5. For the Color channel, load the file Atrium.hdr that is also located in the same tex directory as the Background image (see Figure 6.50a).
6. After it loads into the Texture space, click on the word Atrium.hdr to edit it.
7. Change HDR Gamma to 1 (see Figure 6.50b). This tones down the brightness of the light that the HDRI will generate.
8. Repeat steps 2 through 4, but this time, load the Atrium.hdr into the Luminance channel and adjust the Gamma setting to 1.
9. Close the Material Editor window.

The HDRI you just loaded isn't of the highest quality, but unless your scene requires a lot of reflections, it doesn't need to be. It'll do its job well enough.

Link the materials:

10. Starting at the Materials Manager, drag and drop the Background material onto the Background object in the Objects Manager.
11. Do the same with the HDRI material, dropping it onto the Sky object.
12. Do the same with the Background material, dropping it onto the Plane object. Up to this point, you should have the Background material linked to the Background and Plane objects, along with the HDRI material linked to the Sky object (see Figure 6.51).

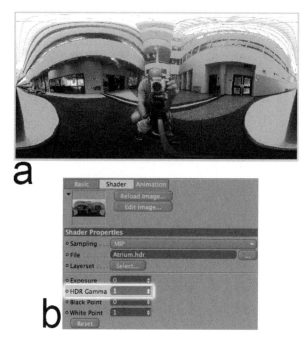

FIGURE 6.50   (a) A low-quality, homemade HDRI. (b) Set HDR Gamma to 1.

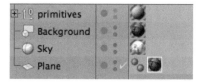

FIGURE 6.51   The Background, Sky, and Plane objects with their materials tags.

13. Select the material tag on the Background object. Notice how it's set to Frontal in the Projection. This means that the picture is simply placed on the Background and when you render, you'll just see the picture. This means that no outside compositing is necessary.

However, for the shadow catching to happen correctly, you need to change the projection type for the Plane's material tag. The Plane object shouldn't be visible, except the shadows it receives. To do this, you need to set its tag to a Frontal Projection just like the Background. That way when you render, you won't be able to distinguish Background from Plane because they'll have essentially the same material and projection. This is a good thing. Remember, we are trying to create the *illusion* that our object *belongs* in the picture.

Set Frontal Projection:

14. In the Objects Manager, select the material tag for the Plane object.
15. In the Attributes Manager, change the Projection type to Frontal (see Figure 6.52).
16. Render to the Picture Viewer by pressing Shift+R (see Figure 6.53).

FIGURE 6.52   The Plane's material tag with its Projection set to Frontal.

FIGURE 6.53   An unsuccessful and premature render.

Compositing Tag

What's happening here? The Sky object has overridden the Background object. So, instead of seeing the picture, we're seeing the HDRI, and it's not pretty. The other problem is that there is no Auto light (it has been disabled) and Global Illumination is off. That means there's nothing to light our scene. Let's fix some of these issues.

We want to hide the Sky object but still use its HDRI material to light up the scene. We accomplish this through the use of the Compositing tag. We need to add one to the Sky object and edit its settings. We will also need to turn on GI so that the HDRI can do its magic.

Add the Compositing tag:

1. In the Objects Manager, select and then right-click on the Sky object. A pop-up menu will appear (see Figure 6.54a). Choose Cinema 4D Tags > Compositing. A Compositing tag will be applied to the Sky object (see Figure 6.54b).

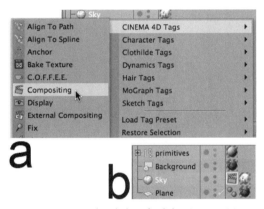

FIGURE 6.54   (a) Right-click to find the Compositing tag. (b) The tag is applied to the Sky object.

2. Make sure the newly created Compositing tag is selected. In the tag's Attributes Manager settings, uncheck Seen by Camera (see Figure 6.55). This means that when we render, the Sky object will not be visible.

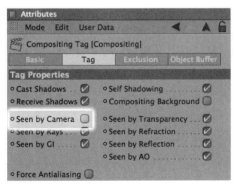

FIGURE 6.55   Turn off Seen by Camera in the Attributes Manager after selecting the tag.

3. Re-render. You'll now see the Background image, but the Plane object is still black.
4. Turn on Global Illumination in the Render Settings. You can leave the settings at the scene default. This will let the Sky object, even though it's not visible in the render, have its HDRI light the scene.
5. Re-render by pressing Shift+R (see Figure 6.56).

FIGURE 6.56   In this render, we can now see the Background and Floor object.

Illumination Channel

The render looks a lot better. We can now see our Background image, and the Floor object shows the frontal projection of the Background image too. The problem is that the floor is still visible. Remember we don't want that. We want it to be there to catch shadows, but otherwise, it should just look like the Background image.

It's brighter than the surrounding image because of the lighting, so we're going to tell it to interact differently with the HDRI lighting through its own material. More specifically, we will edit the Saturation setting in the Illumination channel.

Edit saturation:

1. Double-click on the Background material swatch in the Materials Manager.
2. Click on the Illumination channel in the Materials Editor.
3. Change Saturation to 0 (see Figure 6.57).
4. Re-render by pressing Shift-R (see Figure 6.58).

FIGURE 6.57   Saturation set to 0 in the Background material's Illumination channel.

FIGURE 6.58   Now we just see the picture, but the floor is still there, silently waiting.

Shadow Catching

Now that the Background, Sky, and Plane objects are all working, it's time to unhide our primitives and render them. The Plane object will "catch" the primitive's shadow created by the HDRI lighting. Because the HDRI was made in the same location as the primitives, the light they receive matches closely the picture.

Preparing to render:

1. Unhide the primitives' Null object by turning the red dots gray in the Objects Manager (see Figure 6.59).
2. Re-render by pressing Shift+R (see Figure 6.60).

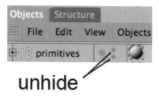

FIGURE 6.59 Unhide the primitives by clicking on the red dots to turn them gray in the Objects Manager.

FIGURE 6.60 A successful render of the primitives.

Now the primitives look like they are in the image. They cast shadows on the Plane object. That's all there is to it, really. But primitives aren't all that fun, so let's try a different object.

Layer Browser

There's a much more complicated object in the scene, hidden away in the Layer Browser. You will unhide and then render the Robotbike object next. Make sure to rehide the primitives before the final render.

Reveal the Robotbike object in the Objects Manager:

1. In the main menu, select Window > Layer Browser.
2. In the Layer Browser, click on the Show in Manager button for the blue Bike layer. That small button looks like a hierarchy representation (see Figure 6.61). This will reveal the Robotbike object in the Objects Manager.
3. In the Objects Manager, unhide the Robotbike by clicking on both red dots to turn them gray.
4. In the Objects Manager, rehide the primitives by clicking on the gray dots until they both turn red (see Figure 6.62).
5. In the Render Settings, turn Antialiasing to Geometry. Turn on Ambient Occlusion. This will let you keep the GI settings low.

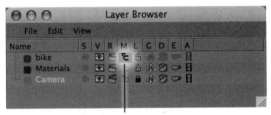

Click to reveal in Objects Manager

FIGURE 6.61 In the Layer Browser, click on the small Show in Manager button.

FIGURE 6.62 Rehide the primitives, and then unhide the Robotbike object.

HDRI Wrap Up

Another setting to consider when rendering with HDRI is changing from the Standard GI method to Stochastic (found in the Global Illum. section in the Render Settings). Stochastic renders, usually, much slower (there are exceptions). However, because it looks at each pixel, it can add grain and noise to the objects. Sometimes, this can be a good thing, especially when compositing. A little noise can go a long way. However, you should stay with the Standard method for this tutorial.

There's one more thing to do before we render the final image. We need to add a Compositing tag to the Plane object. If we render right now, the floor just won't catch a good shadow because our GI settings aren't high enough. Instead of changing the GI settings for the whole scene, we can just raise them for the Plane object.

Enable GI accuracy:

1. Right-click on the Plane object in the Objects Manager. Add a Compositing tag by choosing Cinema 4D Tags > Compositing.
2. In the tag's Attributes Manager, click on Enable to turn on GI Accuracy. Leave it at its default setting of 70% (see Figure 6.63).
3. Re-render by pressing Shift+R (see Figure 6.64).

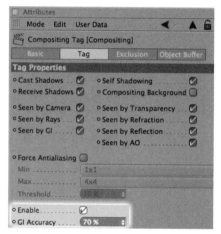

FIGURE 6.63   Enabling GI Accuracy for just the floor.

FIGURE 6.64   Final HDRI render.

The tutorial is now complete. This image (see Figure 6.64) took about 7.5 minutes to render on a dual G5 computer. Remember, HDRI uses GI for its calculations and is therefore subject to a render penalty. For an even better image (the background doesn't get antialiased with the Geometry setting), you can render with Best Antialiasing. However, it'll take around 20 minutes to render, again, using a dual G5 as the base comparison. Your mileage may vary.

CONCLUSION

3D artists often overlook lighting, but it is just as important as good modeling and texturing. This chapter has not only given you insight on how to get started using Cinema 4D's lighting system but also helped open your eyes to the world around you. Next time you look at a sunset, sunrise, bright sunny day, or even a cloudy one, look at how the objects you see are really just reflections of the moment. They are snapshots of time, exposed by the wonderful revealer that is light.

ANIMATION BASICS

In This Chapter

- Object Tool versus Model Tool
- Animation Layout
- TUTORIAL 7.1   Ball Bouncing
- TUTORIAL 7.2   Camera Animation

Animation covers a broad spectrum of meanings and contexts, from motion pictures to television, from traditional to computer generated. This chapter focuses on the very basics of animation, from both a technical and theoretical standpoint. It will teach you about C4D's style and philosophy toward animation workflow while at the same time teaching you about general physics and how objects move.

Before we dive into the tutorials, we will cover C4D's Animation layout, talk about terminology related to animation and C4D, and generally get you familiarized with the interface in preparation for the upcoming tutorials.

Next, you will learn about the basic physics of how objects move by bouncing a ball (a very common but necessary instruction). This is followed by a camera animation tutorial, which is a common request. There is a lot we could choose to include in this chapter, but space constraints limit us to the very basics.

As stated often, this chapter does not replace the manuals or Help system, and those remain a valuable source of information. During this tutorial, you are encouraged to look up more information there.

 This chapter uses the new, default R10 Icon scheme. To change to the new scheme, go to Edit > Preferences, and in the Common options, choose Light for the Scheme.

Object Tool versus Model Tool

Until now, you have mostly used the Model tool, but its time to switch over to the Object tool (see Figure 7.1). They are mostly the same, and you sometimes can get functions (namely move, scale, rotation, and so on) done without needing to worry which one you are using. However, it is best practice to model with the Model tool and animate with the Object tool. To explain why, you need to understand the difference between scale and size.

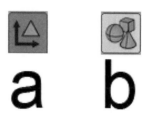

FIGURE 7.1   (a) The Model tool and (b) the Object tool.

Size versus Scale

C4D differentiates between a model's size and its scale. This can be confusing at first, as many 3D programs do not place such emphasis on this distinction. Basically, every object has both a size and a scale. Think of it this way. A house may be 40 feet long, 30 feet wide, and 20 feet tall. That is its size. However, its scale is just 1 in each direction. This is how C4D treats objects. *If you change the size of the house, you haven't changed the scale.* You could change the house to 100 feet long, 60 feet wide, and 40 feet tall, but it will still be 1 in the scale for each axis. However, if you change its scale, *you will be affecting its size too!*

Despite the last sentence's emphasis, this isn't a big deal, but it does take some getting used to. Just remember, to change *size* you use the Model tool. To change *scale*, you use the Object tool. Both scale and size are found in the Coordinates Manager for any given object (see Figure 7.2).

Size, Scale, and Rotations

It's important to understand that there are times to scale and times to resize. This becomes important when you later need to rotate an object. Let's say, for example, you have a Polygon object linked to a Null object. If you scale (using the Object and Scale tools) the Null and then later rotate your Polygon object, distortions in the object will occur (see Figure 7.3). Sometimes this can be useful, but it's usually something to avoid.

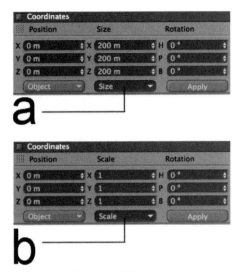

FIGURE 7.2   (a) Size and (b) Scale.

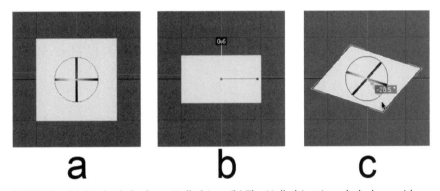

FIGURE 7.3   (a) A cube linked to a Null object. (b) The Null object is scaled, along with the child cube. (c) The cube, rotated, is now distorted.

ANIMATION LAYOUT

You'll need to be able to switch to the Animation layout for the upcoming tutorials, just like when you modeled and painted, you had to change to those layouts. To change to the Animation layout, use the main Layout button, or in the main menu, choose Window > Layout > Animation. Your layout will look something like Figure 7.4.

We can't cover every button and lever here for this layout, but you can look under Help > Help, and then Content > Manual > Reference > Animation for more in-depth coverage on the interface. We will, however, cover a few of the basics as the chapter progresses.

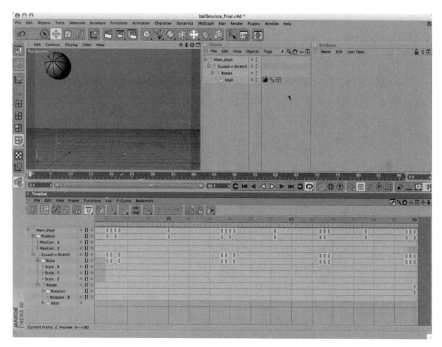

FIGURE 7.4   Animation layout.

TUTORIAL 7.1   BALL BOUNCING

This tutorial will teach you about the basic physics that we expect to see when objects are animated. That's right, what goes up, must come down. But did you know that the time an object takes to go up must equal the time it takes to get down? Did you also know that the course it takes up must be symmetrically consistent on the way down? There's more to it than just that, but you get the idea.

This tutorial will teach you about the following:

- Hierarchy
- Animation Palette
- Timeline
- Key framing
- Key management
- Key framing methods
- F-Curves
- Rendering animation

Getting Started

On the CD-ROM, go to Tutorials > Chapter07 > Chapter7-1, and open the file ballbounce_start.c4d. A prepared scene file with lighting, camera, materials, and environment already completed are ready to go but hidden so you can concentrate on animation. The camera has been locked because this project is meant to be viewed from a particular angle. In the next tutorial, you'll animate cameras.

Looking at your Objects Manager, you will notice the following hierarchy: Main_bball, Squash n Stretch, Rotate, and bball (see Figure 7.5).

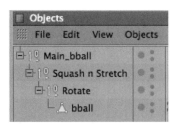

FIGURE 7.5   Hierarchy for the bball.

Hierarchy

You might think this grouping is unnecessary. But to get the ball to fall to the ground, squash/stretch, and rotate, they become very necessary. Hierarchy is critical to any successful animation. Basically, each Null object is a controller. To animate the ball's movement, you animate the Main_bball. To animate its volume changes, you use the Squash n Stretch controller, and to rotate, you use the Rotate controller. In the end, you will never animate the actual bball geometry, just its controllers.

You use so many controllers because each action the ball takes is highly dependent on center point. For example, the action of the ball squashing and stretching when it hits the ground will be successful only if the ball's center point is right at the point where the ball and ground meet, in other words, on the bottom of the ball. However, for the ball to rotate, it needs a middle axis point.

So, to give the ball two axes of rotation, you add two controllers, one with the center point in the middle of the ball and another one located at the bottom of the ball.

The third controller is for movement only. Having three controllers helps to simplify by breaking each motion down by controller. When you get to Chapter 8, "Character Setup," you'll start to understand the power of hierarchy even better, as character animation is even more dependent on these types of hierarchies.

Intro to Animation

Switch to the Animation layout by using the Layout button or by choosing Window > Layout > Animation from the main menu. The Animation layout will appear. You will notice a Perspective window, Objects Manager, Attributes Manager, Animation Palette, and Timeline (similar to Figure 7.6).

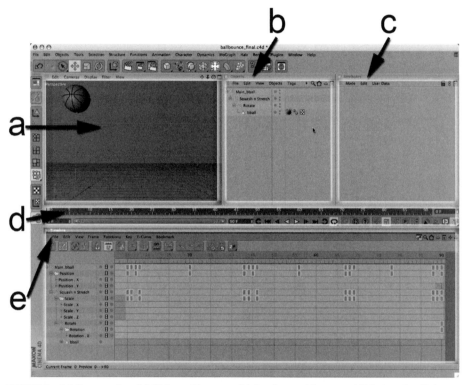

FIGURE 7.6   (a) Perspective, (b) Objects Manager, (c) Attributes Manager, (d) Animation Palette, and (e) Timeline.

We will explain the various interface elements as we proceed. So let's just dive in with the animation.

Animating the Bounce

You are going to animate, using the Main_bball controller, the up-and-down motion of the bounce. Imagine dropping the ball and what would happen to it. As it bounces, each successive bounce should become lower and lower. For now, we can just bounce the ball in place. We'll add forward motion later.

Animate the Main_bball in the *y*-axis:

1. In the Objects Manager, select the Main_bball controller.
2. In the Attributes Manager, click on the Coord button. You'll now see the controller's coordinates. Note, this is not the Coordinates Manager, but you can still edit and animate its coordinates from here.
3. Notice how P. X, P. Y, and P. Z each have an empty black circle next to them. In fact, all the coordinate elements and many other animatable items do (see Figure 7.7).
4. Put your mouse over the P. Y empty black circle and Ctrl-click. The empty black circle will become a red circle (see Figure 7.8a). You will notice that for time zero, indicated by the Animation Palette's time indicator (see Figure 7.8b), a key frame was created. This key frame is also visible in the Timeline (see Figure 7.8c).

 The "P" in the coordinates stands for Position, "S" stands for Scale, and the "R" stands for Rotation.

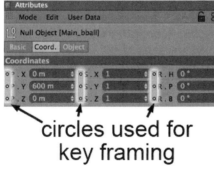

circles used for key framing

FIGURE 7.7   The empty black circles are used to create key frames.

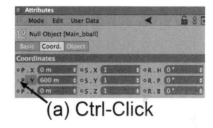

(a) Ctrl-Click

(b) Time = 0

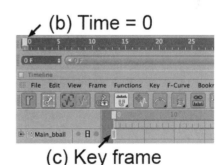

(c) Key frame

FIGURE 7.8   (a) Ctrl-click at (b) time zero to make a (c) key frame.

5. In the Animation Palette, change the frame to 15 by clicking and dragging on the Timeslider until it says 15. The Timeslider is the little green box that indicates where you are in time (see Figure 7.9).
6. In the Attributes Manager, under the Coord section, enter 0 for P. Y, and then Ctrl-click the empty red circle. After you Ctrl click, you'll

notice it change to a filled, red circle (see Figure 7.10). An empty red circle means that attribute has key frame(s) but not at the current time. A
full red circle means that there is a key frame at the given time.

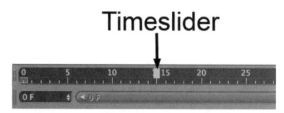

FIGURE 7.9   The Timeslider should be set to 15.

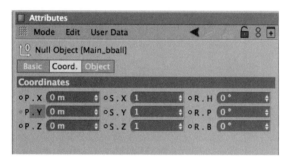

FIGURE 7.10   P. Y key framed with its value set to 0.

Animation Palette

Congratulations! You've just animated a ball in C4D (of course, there's
much more to do!). Let's review quickly. You first key framed the ball at
$y = 600$ at time 0. Then you moved the Timeslider over to 15 and key
framed it again with P. Y = 0. You did this by Ctrl-clicking on the circle
next to the P. Y in the Coord section of the attributes for the Main_bball
controller. You can tell if you've successfully animated if you see an animation path for the ball, indicated by a simple line, in the Perspective
view (see Figure 7.11).

Verify further that the ball is moving by click-dragging the Timeslider
back and forth between 0 and 15 (also called *scrubbing*). You should see
the ball moving up and down. The Timeslider is part of the larger Animation Palette. This area contains many tools for animation. Notice the playback controls. They are similar to the standard play buttons found on
most consumer devices.

FIGURE 7.11   The animation path for the ball.

Animation Tips

You will continue to animate the P. Y value for the Main_bball controller. The ball starts at 600; so the next bounce should be lower, say 500. It will progressively get lower as time moves forward.

Here's a tip for the next few steps. Instead of just moving the ball up and down, remember that the ball needs to spend a few frames on the floor. When the ball hits the ground it compresses and then uncompresses. This is its squash and stretch. If you don't keep the ball on the floor for a few frames, then you won't have time to animate that dynamic, and it will look odd.

Another thing to remember is that the time the ball takes to get up is the same amount of time it takes to get down. So, if you tell the ball to go from the floor to a height of 500 over 13 frames, then you need to key frame it on the ground again 13 frames later. This is basic physics. Time up equals time down.

Timeline

The *Timeline* is the large space underneath the Animation Palette. Refer to Figure 7.6e if necessary. In the Timeline, notice that you see the Main_bball Null object, which is displayed just as it is in the Objects Manager. Key frames that are recorded are shown here for editing. The Timeline also has its own Timeslider. It doesn't matter which Timeslider you use.

In the Timeline, open the Main_bball hierarchy until you see Position Y. You will notice that Main_bball, the Position folder, and Position. Y all have keys. For example, at time 0, all three have a key frame. Notice, however, that not all the keys are shown the same way. The Main_bball and Position folder have keys that are unfilled blue rectangles, whereas Position. Y's key is a solid blue. A solid blue key means that attribute is the one with the key frame, whereas an outlined blue key is given to the parent. They are really just the same key. You can't separate them. If you move one, you'll move the parent's as well.

Finish the P. Y animation:

1. Move the Timeslider over to frame 17.
2. Observe the Timeline. Open the Main_bball hierarchy in the Timeline until you see Position Y. You will see two key frames for Position Y.
3. Making sure that the Timeslider is still at 17, Ctrl-click-drag the key frame for time 15 over and drop it at time 17. This will create an exact copy of that key frame (see Figure 7.12).

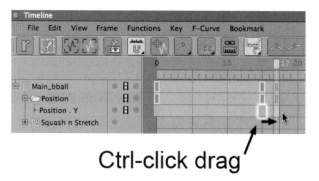

FIGURE 7.12   Ctrl-click-drag the key frame for 15 and drop it at time 17, creating a copy.

4. Move the Timeslider over to frame 30.
5. Select the Main_bball in the Objects Manager so that you can see the Coord section of the Attributes Manager. Enter 500 for P. Y, and make another key frame by Ctrl-clicking on the empty red circle. You will now see four key frames in the Timeline (see Figure 7.13).
6. Move the Timeslider over to 43. Remember, time up equals time down.
7. Enter 0 in the P. Y for Main_bball, and key frame it.
8. Move the Timeslider over to 45. Make another key frame for P. Y = 0 by either Ctrl-click-dragging and dropping the key frame at time 43 over to 45 in the Timeslider, or just Ctrl-clicking on the empty red circle next to P. Y in the Coord section.
9. Move the Timeslider to 56. Key frame 400 for P. Y.
10. Move the Timeslider to 67. Key frame 0 for P. Y.

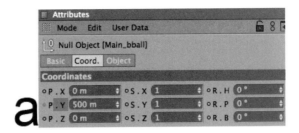

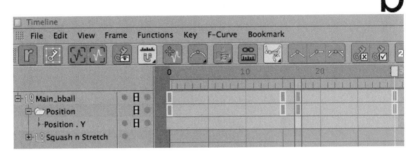

FIGURE 7.13　(a) P. Y = 500 key framed and (b) a new key frame at time 30.

11. Move the Timeslider to 68. Key frame 0 for P. Y.
12. Move the Timeslider to 78. Key frame 320 for P. Y.
13. Move the Timeslider to 88. Key frame 0 for P. Y. You should have 11 key frames at 0, 15, 17, 30, 43, 45, 56, 67, 68, 78, and 88 (see Figure 7.14).

FIGURE 7.14　Key frames in the Timeline (key frames are highlighted for clarity).

Playback

In the Animation Palette are controls for playback. Take the Timeslider back to 0, and press F8, or click the Play button in the Animation Palette to play the animation. The ball will move up and down. Press F8 again or click the Pause button to stop when you are finished viewing the animation. Return the Timeslider to 0.

F-Curves

You've probably noticed that the ball doesn't move very realistically. The biggest problem is that as it approaches the floor, it slows down. That's not how a real object falls. Gravity dictates that falling objects accelerate. So, our ball should do the same until it hits the floor. The way to change this is with F-Curves. F-Curves are found in the Timeline by clicking on the Key/F-Curve button. This button toggles from Key mode to F-Curve mode. This button resides in the Timeline on the upper-right corner of the manager. When in Key mode, it looks like an actual key. When in F-Curve mode, it looks similar to a heartbeat monitor (see Figure 7.15).

You will edit the F-Curves for Position Y so you can change how the ball moves make the ball appear to bounce.

 You can quickly toggle between the Timeline and F-Curve mode by pressing the spacebar while your mouse is over the Timeline.

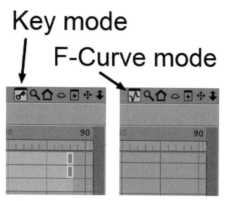

FIGURE 7.15 Key mode and F-Curve mode. This button toggles between the two.

Edit the F-Curve bottom keys:

1. Click on the Key/F-Curve toggle to change to F-Curve mode.
2. In the Timeline, select Position Y by clicking on its name. It will highlight in white.
3. In the Timeline's menu, choose Frame > Frame All. Your Timeline should now look like Figure 7.16.
4. Drag a selection box around all of the bottom keys (see Figure 7.17). These represent all of the places where the ball is on the ground. After you select the keys, you will see the Attributes Manager change to represent your selection (see Figure 7.18). You can now edit many of the attributes for these keys at the same time.
5. In the Timeline, choose Key > Zero Angle to flatten the key's handles.
6. In the Timeline, choose Key > Break Tangents. This will allow you to move the one side of the key's handle without moving the other side.

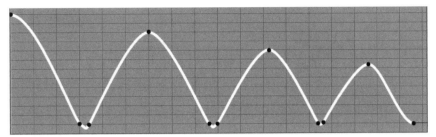

FIGURE 7.16   Framed F-Curves for Position Y. The curve and edit points have been exaggerated for clarity.

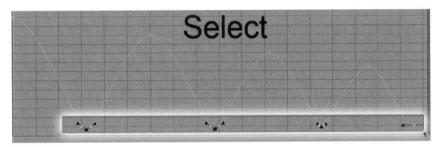

FIGURE 7.17   Select the bottom row of keys.

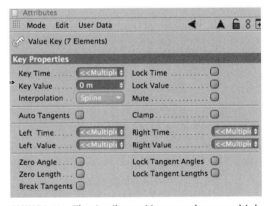

FIGURE 7.18   The Attributes Manager shows multiple selections for the selected keys.

The handles also change from having triangular to circular handles (see Figure 7.19).

7. In the Attributes Manager, uncheck Zero Angle (see Figure 7.20). This is exactly the same as going to the Timeline and choosing Key > Zero Angle. It's important you do this while all the bottom keys are still selected. Now that the handles have been set to 0, we want to be

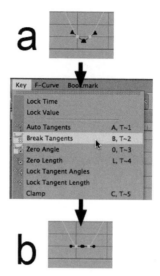

FIGURE 7.19   (a) Before Zero Angle and Break Tangents. (b) After Zero Angle and Break Tangents.

FIGURE 7.20   Uncheck Zero Angle in the Attributes Manager for the selected bottom keys.

able to give some of the handles an angle. That is why we are now turning Zero Angle off. If you try and move them while it's on, you will find that it won't move upward.

8. Select the first bottom key by dragging a selection box around it.
9. Click and drag its left handle upward until it hovers right around the 100 mark.
10. Select the second bottom key, and raise its right handle, just like the previous step. Notice how we left alone the handles in the middle. This

is because we want the curve to be flat between them. If we didn't, the ball would move up or down when we want it to be on the ground (see Figure 7.21).

11. Repeat these steps for the rest of the bottom handles (see Figure 7.22).

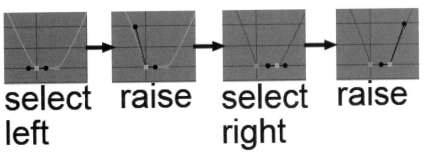

select
left

raise

select
right

raise

FIGURE 7.21   The process of selecting and raising the handles for the keys.

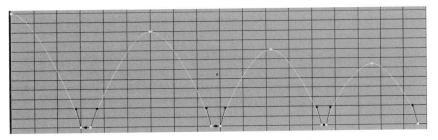

FIGURE 7.22   The bottom handles should look something like this.

You may have noticed that the F-Curve for Position Y is now looking similar to the path a ball might take on a real bounce. This is good, and illustrates a difficult concept of what the F-Curves are doing. Essentially, the more Position Y looks like a ball bouncing trajectory, the better.

Play back the animation. The ball now accelerates until it hits the ground, where it pauses, and then decelerates as it goes back up. The pause looks unnatural at this point because we haven't added squash and stretch yet. We'll do that in a bit.

You may have noticed that the ball could use a little bit more hang time when it's in the air. This is where the top keys come in because they represent the ball when it's at its apex.

Editing the F-Curve top keys:

12. Select the first top key, and move its handle to the right (see Figure 7.23).

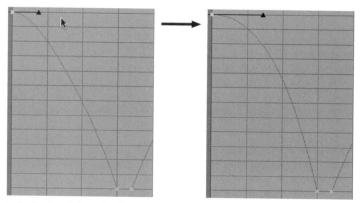

FIGURE 7.23 Select the first top key, and move its handle to the right slightly.

13. Select the next top key, and move either of its handles so that they become longer. Don't give them an angle (see Figure 7.24).
14. Repeat this process for the rest of the top handles (see Figure 7.25).
15. Play back the animation, and then adjust the top key's handles as you see fit. There is some subjectivity involved, so don't spend a lot of time here.

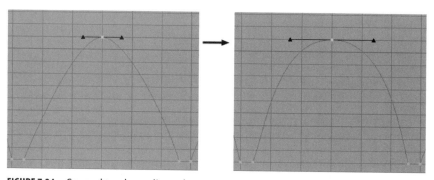

FIGURE 7.24 Second top key adjusted.

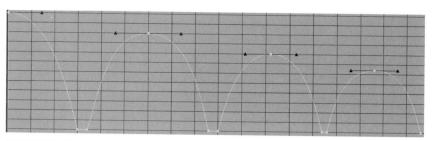

FIGURE 7.25 The rest of the top keys adjusted.

Now when you play back the animation, the ball will have more hang time. This is the power of F-Curves, and you will find yourself working with them often to do effective animation.

Forward Motion

Let's make the ball's bounce a little more apparent by moving the ball forward.

Set key frame P. X:

1. Select the Main_bball null in the Objects Manager.
2. Make sure the Timeslider is at time 0.
3. In the Attributes Manager, under the Coord section, set key frame P. X = 0 by Ctrl clicking the empty black circle.
4. Move the Timeslider to 90.
5. Enter 850 for P. X, and key frame it. See the Perspective view and Figure 7.26.

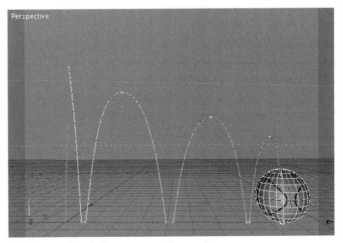

FIGURE 7.26   The ball now moves forward.

Now look at the Perspective view. Play back the animation. The ball now moves forward, and its bounce trajectory matches closely the P. Y curve. There is one slight problem. The ball's forward motion isn't linear. It speeds up and then slows down. This is how Cinema works by default. All animation is set to soft interpolation, meaning it will not move at a constant velocity.

Usually this is good but not in our case. We need to tell the ball to move forward linearly.

Use linear animation:

6. In the Timeline, select Position. X. Frame it (Frame > Frame All). You'll notice its curve is sloped, which causes it to speed up and slow down.
7. Select both the first and last key frames. You can hold down the Shift key if you need to for multiple selections.
8. In the Timeline's menu, choose Key > Linear. Now the Timeline will show you a straight line for the Position. X. Notice how the animation path for the ball in the Perspective view shows a much more realistic path (see Figure 7.27).
9. Play back the animation. Stop the play back after you review.

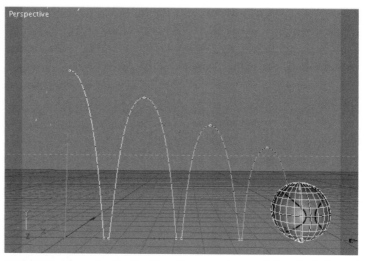

FIGURE 7.27   Changing the Position. X curve to Linear makes the ball's path more realistic.

The animation is looking better. There's nothing more to do to the ball's trajectory. There is still the matter of squash and stretch, along with rotation. We'll get to those now.

Squash and Stretch

As the ball hits the ground, it pauses. This is where we add the squash and stretch, which is the distortion that naturally happens to bouncing objects. Adding this will also make us overlook this pause; that is, it will feel more natural. The squash and stretch happens fairly quickly over just a few frames.

There is a controller null specifically for this called *Squash n Stretch*. You will animate the scale of this controller in a different way than you did the ball's movement. This is done to familiarize you with the various ways C4D handles key framing. Let's discuss the Animation Palette to understand the upcoming method a little better.

Animation Palette and Record Scale

In the Animation Palette, on the right side, are four orange buttons for Position, Scale, Rotation, and Parameter. These buttons, in conjunction with the red Record Active Object button (also found in Animation > Record Active Objects), will record those attributes for any selected object.

Rarely, however, do you ever need to record all the attributes for your objects, so you can depress those attributes you don't need to record. For example, for the upcoming operation, you only need to record the scale of the Squash n Stretch controller and nothing else. Doing so keeps the Timeline clean of unwanted and unnecessary animation and keeps the file size smaller.

Record Squash n Stretch:

1. In the Animation Palette, deactivate (by clicking) Position, Rotation, and Parameter, leaving Scale active (see Figure 7.28). This will ensure that you will only record key frames for Scale.

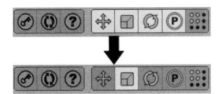

FIGURE 7.28   Deactivate Position, Rotation, and Parameter.

2. In the Objects Manager, select Squash n Stretch. Make sure the Coord section in the Attributes Manager is visible.
3. Change to Key Mode by clicking on the Key/F-Curve toggle button in the Timeline.
4. Change the Timeslider to 15. This is where the ball first meets the ground and where we want to start our scaling.
5. Click on the red Record Active Object button in the Animation Palette (see Figure 7.29). A new key is created for the Squash n Stretch controller in the Timeline (see Figure 7.30).
6. Move the Timeslider to frame 16.
7. In the Coord section in the Attributes Manager, enter 1.1, 0.9, and 1.1 for S. X, S.Y, and S. Z, respectively.

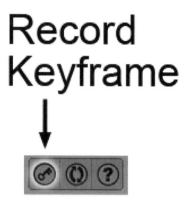

FIGURE 7.29   The Record Active Object button.

FIGURE 7.30   A scale key is created in the Timeline.

8. Click the red Record Active Object button in the Animation Palette to create another key frame at frame 16 (see Figure 7.31). You will see another key frame created at frame 16 in the Timeline.

FIGURE 7.31   Enter the values for Scale, and then click the Record Active Object button.

9. Move the Timeslider to 18.
10. Enter 1, 1, and 1 for S. X, S. Y, and S. Z. Record the key frame. You will now have 3 key frames for one squash and stretch for when the ball hits at time 15.

11. In the Timeline, select the keys at 15, 16, and 18 that you just created.
12. Move the Timeslider to 43.
13. Ctrl-click-drag copies of those key frames over to time 43 (see Figure 7.32). It's easier to just copy key frames than to key new ones.
14. Ctrl-click-drag copies of the same keys over to frame 67.
15. Ctrl-click-drag copies of the same keys over to frame 88. You've now created the Squash and Stretch keys (see Figure 7.33).

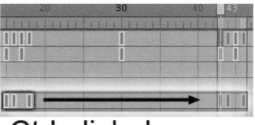

FIGURE 7.32   Ctrl-click to drag and drop copies of key frames.

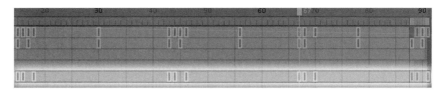

FIGURE 7.33   The key frames for the Squash n Stretch controller.

Play back the animation. The ball now has a more realistic bounce that compresses when it hits the ground, and then decompresses afterwards.

This type of key framing is different from the last type and is meant to show you the different ways of key framing. You could have just as easily done it the other way. The difference is that when you use the Record Keyframe button, even for a limited attribute like Scale, you still do so in the X, Y, and Z. However, when you selectively Ctrl-click on an attribute's empty circle, you have more control over what you animate.

Rotation

The last thing the ball needs is a bit of rotation. This is pretty easy to do, and we have a specific controller for that task. Its center point is in the middle, not like the others, which had their center points on the bottom of the ball.

You will record Rotation keys for the Rotate controller to add the last bit of animation.

Use the Rotate controller:

1. In the Objects Manager, select the Rotate controller.
2. Make sure the Timeslider is at 0.
3. In the Attributes Manager, under the Coord section, Ctrl-click the empty circle next to R. B to create a key.
4. Move the Timeslider to 90.
5. Enter 270 for R. B, and record a key.

Play back the animation. You'll notice that the rotation speeds up and slows down. We want it to have a constant rotation.

Set a linear rotate:

6. In the Timeline, change to F-Curve mode.
7. In the Timeline, open up the Squash n Stretch hierarchy. Open up the Rotate hierarchy until you see Rotation B. Select Rotation B.
8. In the Timeline's menu, choose Frame > Frame All.
9. Select all the keys for Rotation B. Choose Key > Linear.

Rendering Animation

Double-check that the animation is satisfactory, and make any changes you see fit. After you are finished, it's time to render. Rendering was covered somewhat in Chapter 6, "Lighting," but only as still frames. We now want to render to an animation format. QuickTime is the preferable format, as it provides many different compression types and is cross platform. However, AVI is also acceptable, if you are using Windows.

This scene already has lighting and texturing completed, so there is no need to add those elements. They have been hidden in the Layer Browser but will show up at render time.

Use Render Settings:

1. In the main menu, select Render > Render Settings.
2. In the Render Settings window, click on Output, and change Frame to All Frames (see Figure 7.34). If you don't change this setting, it will render to a single frame.
3. Click on the Save options. Change Format to QuickTime Movie. Click Path, and give the file a name and a place to save to your hard drive (just remember where, for later retrieval) (see Figure 7.35).

 If you are using Windows, you will need to make sure that QuickTime is installed, if you want to render to that format. You cannot save to QuickTime without giving it a path first!

It would be wise to also click on the Options setting next to QuickTime, and change the setting from Animation to Sorenson Video 3 (or another option that will lower your file size). These are the Codec settings that determine your quality and file sizes. If you have a 3-second file that is many megabytes in size, you'll know why!

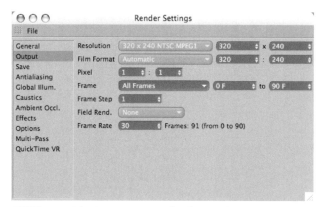

FIGURE 7.34   The Output section for the Render Settings.

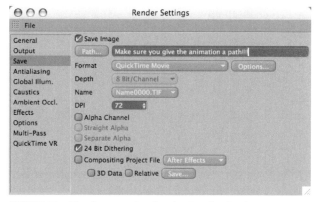

FIGURE 7.35   The Save section for the Render Settings.

4. Close the Render Settings window.
5. In the main menu, select Render > Render to Picture Viewer, or click its icon. The animation will now render (see Figure 7.36). After it's complete, review the file in the QuickTime player.

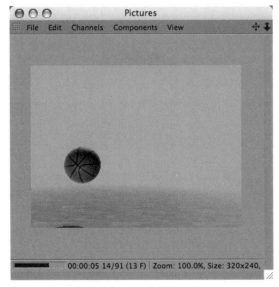

FIGURE 7.36   The rendering of the ball bounce.

Wrap Up

You learned how to key frame the different movements of the ball as it bounced. Along the way, you discovered certain physics that govern the bounce and how to achieve that through the Timeline's F-Curve editor. Even simple animation can be fun and effective.

There are many attributes you can animate. In fact, just about everything in C4D is animatable, from objects to materials, and from lighting to cameras.

You can change the length of the animation in the main menu under Edit > Project Settings. Enter the number of frames you want in the Maximum setting.

TUTORIAL 7.2   **CAMERA ANIMATION**

Animating the camera is no different from animating any other object. You first must import a camera into your scene and then switch views. C4D uses what's called the *Editor Camera* by default. This default camera is not an object you can select and then key frame, but imported cameras are.

Dos and Don'ts of Camera Animation

The simple fact of the matter is that most of the time, especially if you are relatively new to cinematography, you shouldn't animate the camera at all. Jerky movements, head-spinning twirls, and ill-timed bumps don't help your animation. Subtle camera placement and good editing will take the animation much further.

This is not a cinematography book. Nevertheless, take this warning to heart: most beginning animators move the camera when they shouldn't.

Think of a movie, any movie. Sure, the camera may move sometimes. But many scenes employ a nonmoving camera because it is often easier to see what's going on without a moving camera.

Getting Started

That being said, this tutorial will show you how to animate the camera, and even animate between cameras. C4D has a lot of tools to deal with cameras and basic editing that are fairly easy and intuitive to use. You are going to start with another prepared scene, which picks up where we left off, and animate the cameras while doing some basic editing.

ON THE CD

On the CD-ROM, open Tutorials > Chapter07 > Chapter7-2 > CA_start.c4d. A prepared scene file with the basketball animation will appear. You do not need to model, texture, or light this scene. You do not need to animate anything other than the cameras that you will import.

Looking at your Objects Manager, you will notice a camera has already been imported into the scene. You will animate this camera, and then you will import another camera and attach it to the bouncing ball. With both cameras animated, you will use the Stage object to do basic editing.

This lesson will teach you about the following:

- Auto Key
- Camera position animation
- Importing cameras
- Camera view switching
- Stage object
- Preview

Auto Key

Another way to key frame is through the use of Auto Key. Autokeying (MAXON's terminology for automatic key creation) will create key frames for any object that you edit over time. That means if you turn on Auto Key, select an object, move the Timeslider, and then move the object—keys will automatically be made for you. Autokeying usually requires fewer steps to animate objects. Autokeying is found under Animation > Autokeying.

While autokeying sounds enticing, I do not recommend it for beginners because it is too easy to do something unintentionally. Even simple scenes with seemingly simple animation can go awry because of one mistake. The reason it becomes so difficult to maintain is because you must *always* think four-dimensionally, which is a tall order for even advanced users.

Another limitation of autokeying is that it will not work with the camera pan, zoom, and dolly controls. So, if you want to animate the camera without actually selecting it with the Move tool, you'll have to use another technique.

Now that you know what Auto Key is all about, let's move on. If you want to learn more about how to use it, try opening up a blank document and animating a cube with Auto Key.

Animate the Camera

You will use the Record Active Object button instead of Auto Key to record the position of the camera. Only two keys are required for its start and end positions. You will use the Perspective view to do a simple pan that follows the ball.

Record camera position:

1. Change to the Animation layout by selecting Window > Layout > Animation in the main menu. It is important to be able to see the key frames you are about to create.
2. Select Camera Main in the Objects Manager.
3. In the Animation Palette, make sure that only Position is active (see Figure 7.37).

FIGURE 7.37   Make sure that only Position is active.

4. Make sure that the Timeslider is at time 0. Click on the red Record Active Object button (see Figure 7.38) to create a key frame in the Timeline.
5. Use the Timeslider to change the time to frame 90, the last frame.
6. In the Perspective Viewport, use the pan controls (or Alt+mmb) and pan so that the ball is roughly in the center bottom of the Viewport (see Figure 7.39).

If you make a mistake, use the Undo view command from the Viewport's Edit menu.

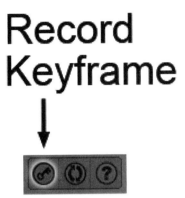

FIGURE 7.38   The Record Active Object button will record a key frame for the position of the camera.

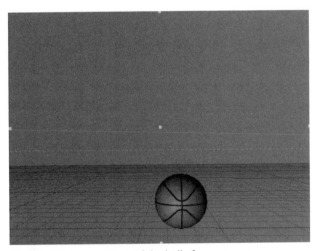

FIGURE 7.39   The position of the ball after you pan.

7. Record another key frame for time 90.
8. Play back the animation. The camera now follows, slightly, the ball bounce. After you review, stop the animation, and take the Timeslider back to 0.

Importing Cameras

You are going to import another camera, place it just over the ball, link it to the Main_bball Null object, and then switch to that view. After you do that, you'll notice that the camera will follow the bouncing of the ball.

When you import a new camera, it will be placed exactly where the current camera is. That means you'll have to adjust its position and rotation after it's imported.

Import and place a new camera:

1. Create a new camera by selecting Objects > Scene > Camera in the main menu.
2. Rename the camera to *Camera Ball* in the Objects Manager.
3. In the Perspective Viewport's menu, select Cameras > Scene Cameras > Camera Ball (see Figure 7.40). This will change the Viewport's display to the Camera Ball. Since that camera was placed on top of Camera Main, you won't notice any changes in the view.

FIGURE 7.40   Changing camera views.

4. Select Camera Ball. In the Attributes Manager, click on the Coord button.
5. Enter the following: P.X = −165, P.Y = 870, P.Z = 0, R.H = −90, R.P = −23, and R.B = 0 into the Coordinates (see Figure 7.41).

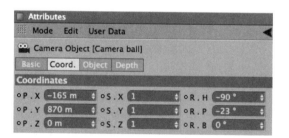

FIGURE 7.41   Coordinates for Camera Ball.

6. In the Objects Manager, drag and drop Camera Ball onto Main_bball so that it becomes a child of that hierarchy (see Figure 7.42).
7. Play back the animation. The view now follows the ball animation. Since the ball was already animated, no key framing was necessary for the camera. When you are done reviewing, stop the animation, and reset the Timeslider to time 0.

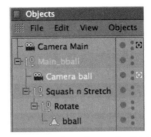

FIGURE 7.42   Camera Ball placed into the Main_bball group.

Camera Editing

You now have two animated cameras in your scene. You could render both views to an animation file and edit them in a third-party editor such as Adobe Premier or Final Cut Pro. The other option is to do basic editing in C4D with the Stage object. This allows you to switch views at the time of your choosing.

It's preferable to edit in a professional compositor such as Final Cut over doing it in C4D because Cinema can only do straight cuts between views. However, if that is all you need, then this option works quite well.

You will import a Stage object and then animate a straight cut between the cameras.

Import a Stage object:

1. In the main menu, select Objects > Scene > Stage. A Stage object will appear in the Objects Manager. Make sure it is selected.
2. In the Attributes Manager, click on the Object button to see the Stage's Object Properties. You will notice empty fields for Camera, Sky, Foreground, and so on.
3. Drag and drop Camera Main into the Stage object's Camera field. Take care not to deselect the Stage object when you do so (see Figure 7.43).

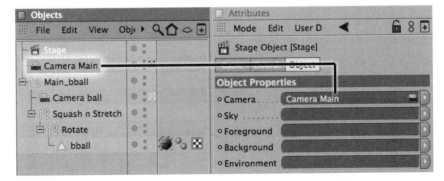

FIGURE 7.43   Drag and drop Camera Main into the Stage's Camera field.

4. Make sure the Timeslider is at time 0. Ctrl-click the empty black circle next to Camera in the Stage Objects Properties in the Attributes Manager. This creates a key frame (see Figure 7.44).

5. Change the Timeslider to frame 44. When you do so, you will notice that the Perspective has changed back to the Camera_Main view. This is because you just linked that object to the Stage's Camera setting and key framed it.

6. Drag and drop Camera Ball into the Stage's Camera field, replacing Camera Main. Ctrl-click its empty red circle to key that switch.

7. Change the Timeslider to frame 68.

8. Drag and drop Camera Main into the Stage's Camera field, replacing Camera Ball. Ctrl-click its empty red circle to key the switch.

9. Play back the animation. The view starts off with the ball bouncing. It then switches to the ball's perspective and then back again.

FIGURE 7.44 Ctrl-click the empty black circle to make a key.

Preview

This animation is ready to render. Instead of rendering using the C4D's standard rendering engine, you are going to create a *preview*. This is very useful because previews just capture the Viewport when it creates the animation. This is much quicker than rendering and is vital in checking how the animation looks without having to wait a long time.

Make a preview:

1. In the main menu, select Render > Make Preview. The Make Preview dialog box will appear (see Figure 7.45).

2. Change the Preview mode to OpenGL. Click OK. C4D will create the preview, and it will open in QuickTime Player.

3. Review the Preview, and then return to C4D.

C4D saves the preview in its own directory. If you need to find it later, use your operating system's file browser to locate the C4D application. This is usually in a folder called Maxon in the location the operating system stores applications and programs. The file it creates is called Preview.

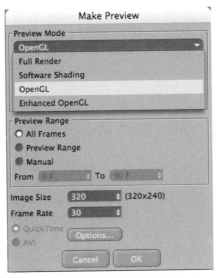

FIGURE 7.45   The Make Preview dialog box.

Wrap Up

Camera animation can be very effective but should be approached with caution. Luckily, C4D makes it a pretty straightforward process.

CONCLUSION

This chapter covered the basics of animation. It's important to understand the many methods of key framing and which one you like best. The fact that C4D has many different ways of animating is a testament to the wide variety of animators out there who have their own preference.

Remember, however, that it's good practice to keep the Timeline free from as much clutter as possible. That's why you only keyed what was needed. Keying attributes that don't get animated just slows down the application and adds to the time it will take to complete the project. Use Previews to check your animation for errors before rendering.

8

CHARACTER SETUP

In This Chapter

- TUTORIAL 8.1   Morphing
- TUTORIAL 8.2   Joints and Basic Rigging
- TUTORIAL 8.3   Controllers and Visual Selector
- TUTORIAL 8.4   Skins and Weights

Character animation is the pinnacle of the 3D artist. There is a diverse list of skills you must possess to master it. Since everyone new to character animation must start somewhere, we will cover how to build a simple rig, attach it to a premodeled and textured character, and make sure its parts will move and bend correctly. We will also cover how to do facial animation with R10's new Morph tools.

MAXON has completely redone the character tools with the introduction of R10 and MOCCA 3. Older character setup systems have to be redone to take advantage of the newer tools. However, pre-R10 scenes using bones will still work because MOCCA 3 still includes all the old tools for compatibility reasons.

This chapter will not focus on covering every new feature. With R10's new help system, there's just no need to do that. However, it covers in depth how to rig, along with tips on how to prepare your own characters for animation.

This chapter uses the new, default R10 Icon scheme. To change to the new scheme, choose Edit > Preferences, and in the Common options, choose Light for the Scheme.

| **TUTORIAL 8.1** | **MORPHING** |

PoseMixer, the previous method for doing facial animation, required you to make a copy for each of your geometry states. This made for fat scenes heavy with polygon mesh information. It could also mean an inflated Objects Manager, as you had to take care of each target mesh. PoseMixer, like many other facial morphing systems out there, also meant that further editing to the original mesh was out of the question because it requires that each mesh contain exactly the same point count.

Every single one of these problems has been bested by Morph, MOCCA 3's new morphing tool. No more worrying about 30 different mesh objects, or having to go back, fix the nose and start over. Trust me, for those of you who are just getting started with 3D, this is a wondrous windfall that will speed up your workflow dramatically. Morph is nothing short of amazing.

That being said, PoseMixer still has its place. Both systems have advantages even though superficially they appear to do the same thing. PoseMixer works well with morphing rotations on joints, like hand and finger movement.

This tutorial will teach you about the following:

- Morph tag
- Morph Targets
- Edit mode vs. Animation mode
- Rotational morphs
- Set Driver and Set Driven

ON THE CD

The file for this tutorial is located on the CD-ROM in Tutorials > Chapter08 > Chapter8-1 > Morph_start.c4d. Open this file to begin. No modeling, texturing, or lighting is required for this tutorial.

Morph Tag

Upon opening the scene, take care not to deselect or change tools, as the file is ready to go as is. You will notice a single head mesh, called Maiden, which is linked to a HyperNURBS. There are various other objects in the scene, which you need not worry about for now. You will add a Morph tag to the Maiden and then add Morph Targets to it. Think of each target as a separate action, for example, blinking an eye or raising an eyebrow.

Morphing the facial features of a full body mesh is no different from what you are about to do here to this single head. They are synonymous.

Add the Morph tag:

1. Make sure that the Maiden object in the Objects Manager is selected. Right-click on the object, and choose Character Tags > Morph from the

pop-up menu (see Figure 8.1). A Morph tag will be applied to the head. The Attributes Manager will now contain the Morph's Tag Properties (see Figure 8.2).

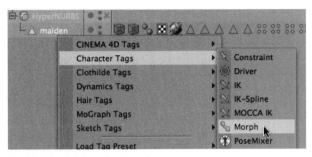

FIGURE 8.1   Adding the Morph tag.

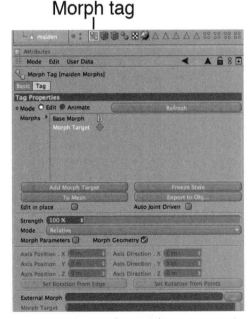

FIGURE 8.2   The Morph tag and its accompanying Tag Properties in the Attributes Manager.

2. Observe the Maiden's left eye (or right eye from your perspective) in the Viewport. Zoom in if necessary (see Figure 8.3). The points that form the bottom part of the upper eyelid should already be selected. If they are, move on to step 3. If they are not, find the Point Selection tag on the Maiden object titled left_eyelidbottom, and click Restore Selection. You can also select the points manually.

3. Using the Move and Selection tools, move the eyelid to a closed position. This will mean deselecting/selecting points and moving them. The exact position does not matter (see Figure 8.4).

 You may find that choosing Selection > Hide Unselected helps. This hides all of the unselected points and prevents accidental selection and movement. When you have finished, choose Selection > Unhide All.

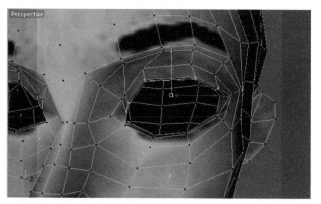

FIGURE 8.3 The upper eyelid point selection.

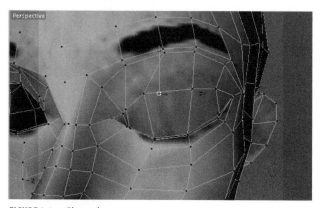

FIGURE 8.4 Close the eye.

4. In the Objects Manager, reselect the blue Morph tag on the Maiden object to see its Tag Properties (similar to Figure 8.2).
5. In the Tag Properties, locate the Strength slider (see Figure 8.5). Click and drag on the slider to see the eyelid morph back to its opened state. When you are finished, set the slider value to 0 so that the eye is open.
6. Observe the Morphs section of the Tag Properties. There you will see Base Morph with a little blue "b" next to it. Underneath that are the

words Morph Target with a target symbol next to it. Double-click on the words Morph Target, and rename it to *Left Eye Close* (see Figure 8.6).

Strength slider

FIGURE 8.5   The Strength slider dictates the morph state.

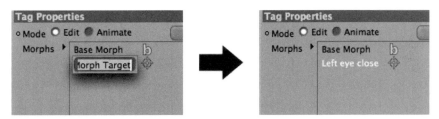

FIGURE 8.6   Rename the Morph Target to Left Eye Close.

Rotational Morphs

The first Morph Target it almost finished. This type of morph is linear in that the points from start to end move in a straight line. For many types of morphing this is just fine, but for eyelids you may want them to move rotationally, since eyelids move on the surface of the eye not linearly.

To fix this, we change the mode of the Morph Target and tell it which axis to use as it morphs.

Set rotation from points:

1. Make sure that the Morph tag is still selected and that the Tag Properties are visible in the Attributes Manager.

2. In the Mode section, change Relative to Rotational. Mode can be found right under the Strength slider (see Figure 8.7).

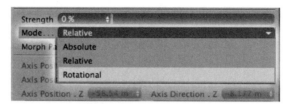

FIGURE 8.7 Change Mode to Rotational.

3. For this next operation, you must ensure that the Maiden object is selected in the Objects Manager and that you are using the Points tool and Live Selection tool. You are going to select two points. The two points will form a centerline from which the axis for the rotation can be set.

4. Zoom in on the eye area, and select a point on the inner corner of the eye. The exact point doesn't matter. Shift-select a point on the outer corner of the eye. Double-check that you have only two points selected. Again, it doesn't matter which points, just make sure that they are one from each corner.

5. After you have selected the points, return to the Morph's Tag Properties, and click on Set Rotation from Points (see Figure 8.8).

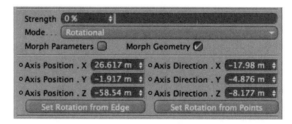

FIGURE 8.8 Click the Set Rotation from Points button.

6. A yellow line will be drawn between the points indicating the axis (see Figure 8.9).

7. Change to the Right Viewport (F3), and zoom in on the eye. Click-drag on the Strength slider to see how it now morphs rotationally (see Figure 8.10).

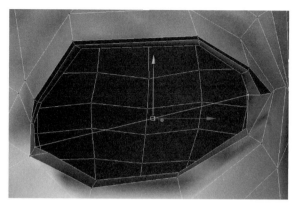

FIGURE 8.9   A rotational axis will be drawn between the points you selected.

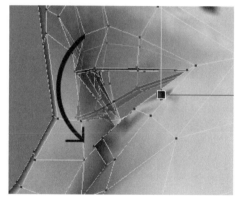

FIGURE 8.10   The eyelid can be seen to move rotationally in the Right Viewport.

Adding More Morphs

Each Morph Target can be given different parameters, independent of other Morphs. You are going to add another Morph Target for the eyebrow. That target will not be set to Rotational but will have the default mode of Relative. We want the eyebrow to rise linearly.

Add the Morph Target:

1. In the Morph Tag's Tag Properties, click on Add Morph Target. Another Morph Target will appear in the list. Rename it to *Left Eyebrow Rise* (see Figure 8.11).
2. Change to the Perspective view.
3. In the Objects Manager, locate the Maiden object. On the Maiden object are a series of selection tags (you may have to use the Manager's scroll

bar to see all the tags). Find and select the tag titled Left_eyebrow, and click Restore Selection. Make sure you are using the Points tool and Move tool; otherwise, you may not see the selection take place (see Figure 8.12). You will now see that the points that make up the eyebrow have been selected.

In R10, the Object Manager can be made to display tags vertically. Click on the View menu and enable Vertical Tags.

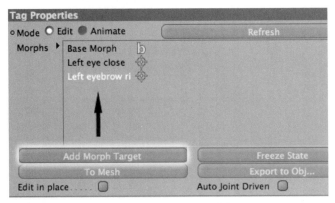

FIGURE 8.11　Add another Morph Target and then rename it as *Left_eyebrow rise.*

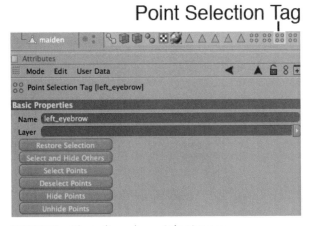

FIGURE 8.12　The Left_eyebrow Selection tag.

4. Raise the eyebrow points (see Figure 8.13).
5. Change the Strength slider to see the results.

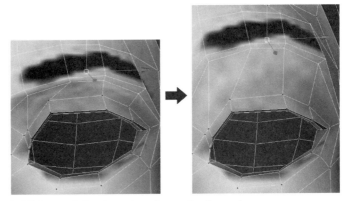

FIGURE 8.13   Raise the points that make the eyebrow.

Edit Mode versus Animate Mode

That's really all there is to it. Each time you add a Morph Target, its slider gets set to 100% and awaits your changes to the mesh. The mesh gets reset to its original state, ensuring that you don't incorporate other morphs. This is handy for editing, but at some point, you will want to mix the sliders. That is done in Animate mode.

Use Animate mode:

1. In the Tag Properties for the Morph tag, enable Animate mode by clicking its gray circle (see Figure 8.14). All of the options for the tag collapse, leaving just the sliders.
2. Test the sliders to your satisfaction. After you are finished, return each slider to 0.

FIGURE 8.14   In Animate mode, the tag collapses, showing just the sliders.

Set Driver and Set Driven

This section isn't exclusive to morphing. Rather, it applies to any animatable attribute across C4D. It is equivalent to Maya's Set Driven Key and is extremely useful in telling one attribute to animate another. In this case, you'll quickly see that the closing of an eyelid can also raise the eyebrow.

Use Set Driver and Set Driven:

1. In the Tag Properties for the Morph tag, select and then right-click on the name Left Eye Close (not its slider). From the pop-up menu, choose Animation > Set Driver (see Figure 8.15). This sets this slider as the driver. Nothing will happen yet, as C4D is awaiting you to assign a driven.
2. Right-click on Left Eyebrow Rise, and choose Animation > Set Driven (Relative) (see Figure 8.16).
3. Click-drag on the slider for Left Eye Close. You will now see that doing so raises the eyebrow automatically.

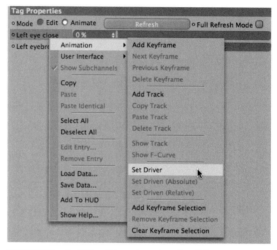

FIGURE 8.15   Left Eye Close is set as the driver.

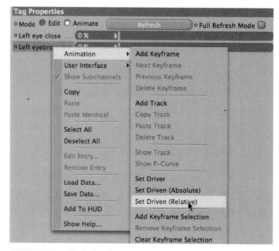

FIGURE 8.16   Left Eyebrow Rise is set as the driven.

Wrap Up

Set Driver and Set Driven can be done at any time. You will notice that a new Null object called Expression was created and placed in the Objects Manager. It has an XPresso tag that dictates the intricacies of how the driver and driven interact. If you delete the Null Expression from the Objects Manager, the link between the eyebrow and eyelid will be broken.

Morphing has taken a giant leap with R10's new tools. However, it is still good practice to do your morphs before you do any other rigging. That is why we are showing you this tutorial prior to the rigging tutorial.

If you like, use this scene to create more Morph Targets. Practice setting up mouth and facial positions. Otherwise, move on to the next section.

TUTORIAL 8.2   **JOINTS AND BASIC RIGGING**

Whenever you rig, use the Save Incremental feature in the File menu. If you come upon an unrecoverable state (and chances are, you will), you won't lose all your work. Just go back to the last save state.

Rigging and character animation is inherently complex, which means that this next section simply can't focus on any beginner issues. If you are not sure what the Objects Manager or Attributes Manager are, for example, then you need to go back to previous chapters and learn those basics first. Rigging isn't for the faint of heart, and you will need to remain patient and be willing to trek out on your own if things don't work. Don't be afraid to start over.

As always, this tutorial is step by step, so take care not to add extra steps. However, given the complex nature of rigging there might be times when you'll have to do a little bit of extra exploring to make it work. That is simply the nature of rigging.

This tutorial will teach you about the following:

- Joint tool
- Align
- Mirror tool
- IK splines
- IK chain
- Pole Vectors
- Skeleton systems

ON THE CD

From the CD-ROM, open Tutorials > Chapter08 > Chapter8-2 > Maiden_rig_Start.c4d. A file with a female character in the standard "T" pose will open.

When modeling for character animation, your character should be modeled so that the arms stick straight out, palms down. The legs should come straight down. As good practice, use a low polygon proxy that you can subdivide with a HyperNURB. This will keep things snappy. Make sure that areas that need to bend have enough loops (enough geometry); otherwise, they will collapse when bent. All of this, of course, is just a general guideline, and there are exceptions.

Joint Tool

The Joint tool replaces bones as the primary skeleton element. You place joints, starting at the base of the spine, and work your way outward (see Figure 8.17). You first do the joints for the spine, then the neck/head, and finish with the arms and legs. Joints do not have to be linked initially, and you will see there are advantages to keeping them separate. Later, you will connect them. This is as easy as parenting in the Objects Manager.

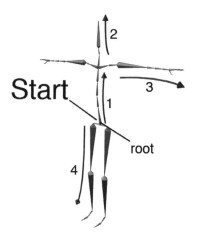

FIGURE 8.17 A diagram of how the joint system spreads outward from the root, starting with the spine.

The Joint tool has several modifier keys that you must use with it. This makes it very versatile in that you can enter joints, move them around, and split them by default. By making a series of joints, you are making the character's skeleton.

Before you make the skeleton, you need to prep the scene a little better to see what the Joint tool is doing.

Prepare the scene:

1. Maximize the Right Viewport. Make sure that the Maiden object takes up most of the Viewport.

2. On the Maiden's Null object, locate and select the Display tag. Change the Shading Mode to Lines. This will make it easier for you to see the joints as they are created (see Figure 8.18).

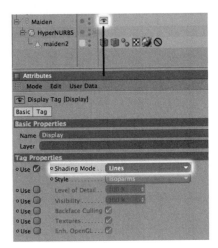

FIGURE 8.18   Use the Display tag to change the Maiden's view to Lines.

Use the floating Character palette:

3. The first thing you need to do is make a floating palette that contains the Joint tool. To do this, go to the main menu, and select the Character menu. Click on the little bar that sits just above the words *Soft IK / Bones*. This will make the Character menu float. You can place it wherever you like, but it's handy next to the Attributes Manager and Objects Managers (see Figure 8.19).

The floating palette can be docked into your layout. Once docked, clicking the middle mouse button on the line of dots will hide the menu. Left-clicking on the dots will unhide it. For more on this, see Chapter 13, "Customizing the C4D Interface."

4. In the floating Character palette, click on the Joint tool (not to be confused with another option in the palette called simply *Joint*). You will see its options appear in the Attributes Manager.

5. Set IK Chain to Spline. Uncheck Root Null. Open the Modifiers section (see Figure 8.20).

FIGURE 8.19 Make the Character menu float by clicking on the checkered bar at the top. Then drag it over so that it sits to the left of your Objects and Attributes Managers.

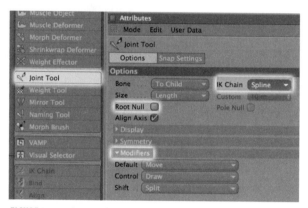

FIGURE 8.20 Set IK Chain to Spline, uncheck Root Null, and open the Modifiers section.

Joint Tool Options

Some explanation is appropriate. Root Null would mean that on creation, your joint chain would be parented to a Null object. We don't need this. You will learn later on how to organize everything.

We changed IK Chain from none to Spline because we want to set up the back spine with controllers. These controllers are based on splines and Null objects, which will control the joints that make up the back spine. It's easier to create the controllers now rather than later. There are ways of doing this manually, but it's somewhat more complicated.

Also of note is that the Align Axis option should be on by default. This will make sure that your joint's axes will all be related. This is very important for the back spine. Lots of problems may occur if the joints aren't aligned properly.

The words spine and spline are not used interchangeably here. Splines are the 2D objects that will control the spine via the IK Spline tag.

Look at the Modifiers section for clues on what is about to happen. To draw joints using the Joints tool, you must hold down the Ctrl key when you click. After that you can just click on the joints to move them around for placement. Holding down the Shift key while clicking on a joint will split it in two. There are other options here that we'll cover later.

You are going to create just the joints that make up the back spine. After you do so, you will edit the IK Spline tag that will be created. It will be created because we've set the IK Chain to Spline for the Joint tool options.

Add joints for the root spine:

1. With the Joint tool still selected, zoom in on the hip area of the character in the Right Viewport. Make sure you can still see the character's head. It's important that you create this chain in the Right Viewport because that will ensure the chain rests exactly on the *x*-axis.
2. Holding down the Ctrl key, draw five joints, starting where the bottom of the spine would go and ending at the shoulders (see Figure 8.21 for clarification). Exactness isn't too important. But try and start around the middle of the hips and end at the arms.

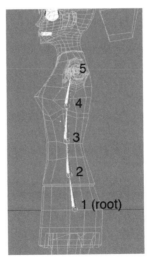

FIGURE 8.21   Draw five joints, starting around the hip area and ending around the shoulders.

3. After you've drawn in the joints, you can click and drag on the circles to move the joints around to adjust their position.
4. When finished, click on the Move tool to end your Joint tool session. This is necessary so that Joint Tool can finish creating the IK Spline tag. This tag will be on Joint in the Objects Manager. A Spline is also created.
5. Rename *Joint* to *Root*. Rename *Joint.4* to *Shoulder*. You can leave the rest at their default names.

6. Click on the IK Spline tag on Root in the Objects Manager. You will see its properties in the Attributes Manager. Make sure that the Tag and Handles buttons are active. In the Tag Properties, activate Twist (see Figure 8.22).

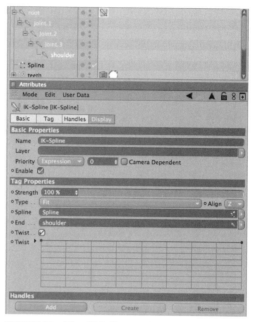

FIGURE 8.22 The IK Spline tag's properties. Make sure to activate Twist.

IK Spline Tag

Let's talk about the tag's settings. Note in the Spline field is the Spline object. This was created because we set the Joint tool to create an IK Spline. That means that the position and orientation of this joint chain is dictated by the spline. Move the spline, and you will move the chain. The chain ends at Shoulder. These fields were filled automatically for you.

We activate Twist so that later on we can rotate the shoulders and the hips. Otherwise, the spine will only be able to bend forward and sideways, without twisting.

Adding Twist later on, after all the joints have been added, often yields unpredictable results (twists in ways that make you cringe). So, it's good to work on the Spine/IK-Spline system while no arm or leg joint chains are attached. If you find that you need to create or edit significantly this IK Spline system, unparent the arms, legs, and neck from the spine, make your changes, and then reconnect.

IK Spline Handles

The points on the spline are what control the joint chain. You could click on the spline, go to points, and move them around, but this is terribly inconvenient when animating. That's where *handles* come in. Essentially, you make Null object handles for the points. The IK Spline tag will do this for you in the Handles section. It's not critical that you do this at this stage, but since we are in the tag's properties, we'll just do it now.

Create handles:

1. Click on the Handles button in the Attributes Manager for the IK Spline tag.
2. Click on the Add button to add a new section with an Index indicator. This index refers to the points on the spline. Since our spline has 5 points (index 0-4), we must choose between 0 and 4. 0 refers to the point at the root, while 4 refers to the last point at the shoulder. Leave it at its default of 0. We will create only two handles for this lesson.
3. Click on the Create button. You will see a new Null Object.0 object appear in the Objects Manager. Rename it as *Hip* (see Figure 8.23). You have now created a controller handle for the first point on the spline. It will become more obvious later what this does.

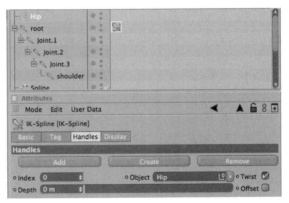

FIGURE 8.23   Clicking the Add and then Create buttons for the Handles section will make a Null object in the Objects Manager. Rename it as *Hip*.

4. Click the Add button again. A new index will appear with the value of 1. Change it to 4 to coincide with the shoulder. (You may need to select the IK Spline tag again.)
5. Click the Create button. A new Null Object.4 object will appear in the Objects Manager. Rename it as *Shoulder* (see Figure 8.24).

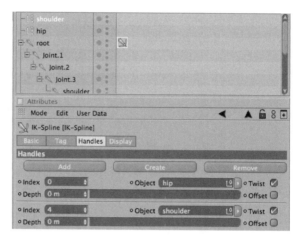

FIGURE 8.24   Do it again for the Shoulder controller.

What Type of Spline?

The default spline type for our spine is a Bezier curve. This works pretty well because you can get nice spine positions using only two handles. However, it is also inconvenient because it means you'd have to go into Point mode to edit the point's Bezier handles, which defeats the whole point of making handles in the first place. So, the next best thing is changing the spline to a B-Spline. B-Splines will make the spine bend in natural ways.

I hope you can see why we are doing all of this now. If we made a lot of changes to the spine when all of our arm and leg chains were connected, it would have a tendency to go haywire. So, do your spine chain edits first.

Change to a B-Spline:

1. Select the Spline object in the Objects Manager.
2. Change it to a B-Spline (see Figure 8.25).
3. Select the Shoulder Null object. In the Right Viewport, move it to the left. Make sure you undo this! This is just so you can see how the controller works. Again, it's important that you undo this to return the spline and controller to their original positions. The spine chain bends in a naturalistic way (see Figure 8.26).

Neck, Arm, and Leg Chains

For now, you won't see much of the effect of the spine chain because it isn't hooked to the character. That effect comes later. For now, let's move on to creating the rest of the chains.

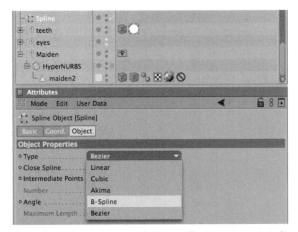

FIGURE 8.25   Change the Spline type from Bezier to B-Spline.

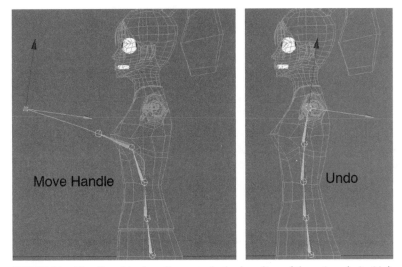

FIGURE 8.26   The Shoulder handle controls the bending of the spine chain. Make sure you undo any moving.

You will create a neck joint chain, and then one arm and leg joint chain. Later, you will mirror the arm and leg chains, which is nice because you only have to set up one set of chains.

Create the neck chain:

1. Make sure you have nothing selected. In the Objects Manager's Edit menu, choose Deselect All. If you were to have something selected, the upcoming Joint tool operation would link the joint chain to that object. We don't want that.

2. Make sure you are in the Right viewport. Select the Joint tool. Make sure that IK Chain is set to None in the Joint tool's options in the Attributes Manager. We don't want our neck chain to have an IK spline.

3. Draw a new joint chain starting at the base of the neck. You'll only need three joints. Remember that you must use the Ctrl key with the Joint tool to draw joints (see Figure 8.27).

4. Rename the new joint chain: *Joint* to *Neck*, *Joint.1* to *Head*, and *Joint.2* to *Head Top* (see Figure 8.28).

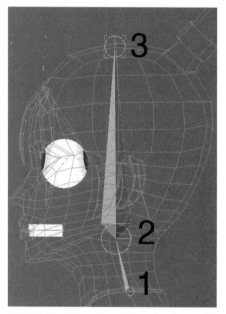

FIGURE 8.27 Draw three joints for the neck and head chain.

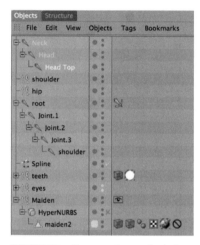

FIGURE 8.28 Rename the neck chain parts. Your Objects Manager should look similar to this.

Align

Notice the axis indicators for each of the neck joints. You may notice that they are not all pointing in the same direction (see Figure 8.29, which shows the green *y*-axis direction). The fact that they are not all pointing in the same direction is not desirable. Usually the Joint tool will automatically ensure that the axes are pointing in the same direction, but sometimes it doesn't. That's where Align comes in. Although it's important that the joints in each chain have the same axis orientation, each chain, spine, neck, arm and so on will often have different orientations when compared to each other, which is usually okay.

Align the neck:

1. Select the Neck joint.

2. Click on the Align command in the floating Character palette, or choose Character > Align from the main menu (see Figure 8.30). The command aligns the axes.

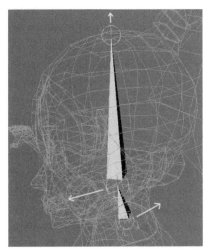

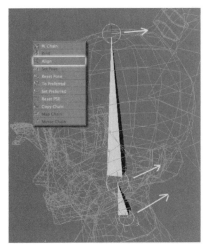

FIGURE 8.29   After you draw the joints, they may be pointing in different directions, which is indicated by the arrows.

FIGURE 8.30   The Align command fixes this.

Create the arm chain:

3. Switch to the Front Viewport, and zoom in on the character's left arm (from your viewpoint, her left arm is on the right side of the screen).
4. Make sure you have nothing selected.
5. Select the Joint tool. Make sure that IK Chain is set to None.
6. In the Front Viewport, draw four joints for the arm starting at the shoulder and ending at the fingertips. Make joints at the elbow and wrist along the way. Don't worry about making all the little finger joints. That is beyond the scope of this tutorial. You'll want to draw the joints in a fairly straight line (see Figure 8.31).
7. Switch to the Top view.
8. Make sure that you have the Joint tool selected and that you can see its Options in the Attributes Manager. Make sure that you open the Modifiers section. In that section, change Default to Move Chain. You do this so that when you click on the first part of the chain, it will move all of the child joints (see Figure 8.32).
9. Move the arm chain by clicking on the joint at the shoulder and moving it into the arm (see Figure 8.33).
10. Edit the Joint tool's Modifier again so that Default is set back to Move.
11. Move the joints so that they match the bottom part of Figure 8.33. The slight bend in the elbow is necessary for future operations.

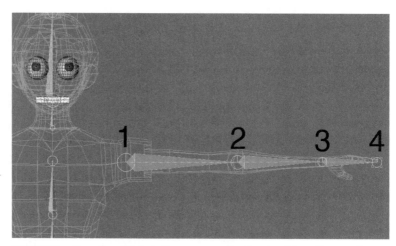

FIGURE 8.31   Draw four joints in the arm: one for the shoulder, elbow, wrist, and hand.

12. Select the first joint in the arm chain, and select the Align command.
13. Rename the arm joints to *L_shoulder*, *L_elbow*, *L_wrist*, and *L_hand*. It is very important that you include the "L_" part. When you perform the upcoming Mirror command, you can tell it to rename it to "R_" for the right arm. You'll see later.

FIGURE 8.32   Before you move the chain into position in the Top view, change the Default to Move Chain.

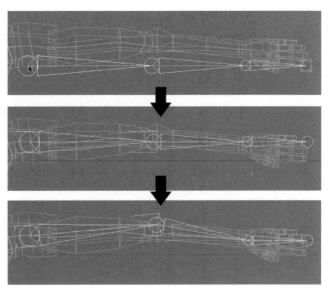

FIGURE 8.33   The sequence of events, top to bottom, from moving the arm chain into the arm to refining each joint.

Because you have positioned in at least two Viewports, the Front and the Top, you can be confident that the chain is in the arm. If you like, however, you can verify in the Perspective view. After doing so, return to the Top view.

The bend in the chain is important because later, when we add IK handles, the IK solver needs that bend; otherwise, the arm might bend the wrong way.

IK Chain

On of the most important aspects of any rig is the IK handle that you'll use to affect the arms and legs. Those handles come about through the IK Chain command. Even though we haven't finished with the skeleton, it's okay to make the IK chain for the arm. However, you could just as well wait until the leg chain was completed.

You will create an IK chain for the arm joint chain by selecting two joints and then clicking on the IK Chain command found in the Character palette.

Add the IK chain to the L_shoulder chain:

1. Select L_shoulder in the Objects Manager.
2. Holding down the Ctrl key, click on L_wrist. Now both L_shoulder and L_wrist will be selected.

3. Select IK Chain from the floating Character palette, or choose the option from the Character menu in the main menu (see Figure 8.34).

FIGURE 8.34 Selecting two joints for the IK chain.

Goals

Note that a new Null object, L_wrist.Goal, has been created. This is the IK handle that controls the arm. The controller resides outside any hierarchy, which will suffice for now.

Also note that an IK tag has been applied to L_shoulder. This is an important tag because it dictates how the IK will function.

Pole Vector

One of the problems that always arises with character rigging is how to control where the elbow and knees are pointing. This is done through poles, which are made in the IK tag. When you add a pole to the chain, you will be adding yet another Null object, to which the elbow or knee must always point.

Add a pole:

1. Select the IK tag on the L_shoulder joint. Make sure the Tag section is active in the Attributes Manager (see Figure 8.35). This is where you will add the pole.
2. Click on the Add Pole button in the Tag Properties in the Attributes Manager. The Pole field will be filled with L_shoulderPole. This new object is also listed in the Objects Manager and is linked into the L_shoulder joint chain.

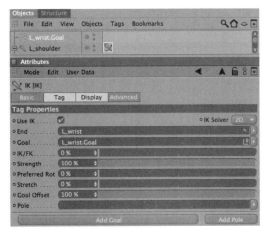

FIGURE 8.35   IK Tag Properties.

3. Drag and drop L_shoulder.Pole out of the hierarchy. It is easiest to drop it above L_wrist.Goal (see Figure 8.36).

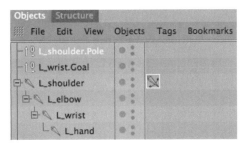

FIGURE 8.36   Drag L_shoulder.Pole out of the
L_shoulder hierarchy, and drop it above
L_wrist.Goal so that it is not linked to anything.

4. Select L_shoulder.Pole, and move it in the Top view so that it sits behind the elbow and is easier to see (see Figure 8.37).

You would not want to move the pole in other views, as you might change its Y value. Doing so would make the elbow point upward or downward. Be cautious when moving the pole. If in doubt, leave it at the elbow.

Leg Chain

It's time to do the joints and IK chain for the leg. There are a couple of hints that follow that will solve many problems down the road. Namely,

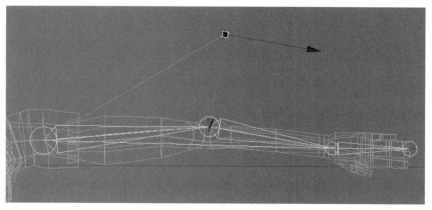

FIGURE 8.37 Moving the pole up in the Top view (or behind the elbow) makes it easier to see.

that you want the leg chain to come straight down. To do this, you will need to place the first joint in the Front view, and then finish the chain in the Right view.

Remember, our chains aren't yet linked to the back spine (root) chain. That'll happen later.

Add joints for the leg:

1. Switch to the Front view, and center the view on the root joint near the hip.
2. Deselect All.
3. Click on the Joint Tool. Make sure that IK Chain is set to None.
4. Place one joint near the root over the character's left leg (your right). This will be the left leg's hip joint (see Figure 8.38).

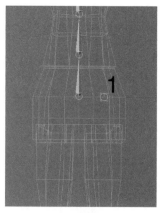

FIGURE 8.38 Make your first joint for the leg chain in the Front view, near the hip and centered over the leg.

5. Change to the Right view, and ensure that you can see the whole leg. You are still in the Joint tool and will continue to make joints in the next step.

6. Make five joints in total, one each for the knee, ankle, foot, and toe. Edit the placement of the joints so that they are similar to Figure 8.39. Remember, there needs to be a slight bend in the knee.

7. Go back to the Front view. Notice how the chain goes straight down. This will solve many problems later on (see Figure 8.40).

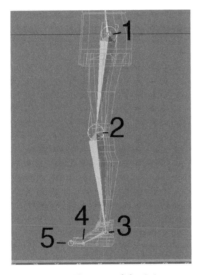

FIGURE 8.39   The rest of the joints, placed in the Right view.

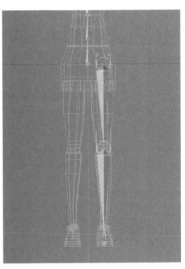

FIGURE 8.40   The leg chain is straight as is indicated in the Front view.

Leg IK

You will add three IK chains for the leg, one each for the ankle, foot, and toe. In a character rig, for arms and legs, an IK chain shouldn't span more than three joints. For example, don't create chains that might span from the hip all the way down to the toe. There are exclusions for this advice, in much more sophisticated rigs, but for more common ones, you only want to span at a maximum three.

For the arm, you linked the shoulder to the wrist, which is a three-joint span. For the leg, you will IK chain the hip to the ankle, which is also a three-joint span. You will create a link between the ankle and foot and then between the foot and toe. These are two-joint spans.

Add IK chains to the leg:

1. Rename the new leg joints to *L_leg, L_knee, L_ankle, L_foot,* and *L_toe* in the Objects Manager.

2. Select L_leg in the Objects Manager. Use Align to correct any alignment issues.
3. Select L_leg and then L_ankle (use the Ctrl key and Objects Manager).
4. Click IK Chain in the Character palette to make L_ankle.Goal.
5. Select L_ankle and L_foot.
6. Create another IK chain to make L_foot.Goal.
7. Select L_foot and L_toe.
8. Create another IK chain to make L_toe.Goal.
9. Select the IK tag on L_leg. In the Attributes Manager, in the Tag Properties, click on Add Pole. This creates L_leg.Pole, which will be linked to the L_leg hierarchy. Drag it out, and place it above the L_x.Goal objects.
10. In the Right view, select the L_leg.Pole, and move it so that it sits in front of the knee (see Figures 8.41 and 8.42 for Viewport and hierarchy details).

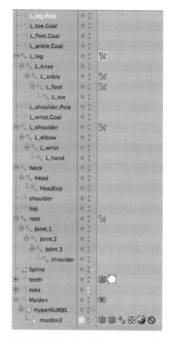

FIGURE 8.41 The hierarchy so far.

Mirror Tool

You've done most of the heavy lifting for the joints and IK chains. All that is left is to mirror the arm and leg joints. The great thing about the Mirror tool is that it will copy IK chains too. That's why we did that right after we created the joint chains.

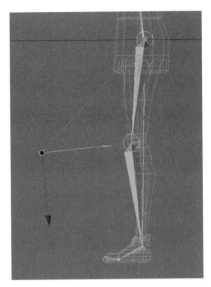

FIGURE 8.42   Moving the L_leg.Pole so that it sits in front of the knee.

After you mirror the leg and arm chains, you will link all the chains into one hierarchy.

Use the Mirror tool on L_arm:

1. Select L_shoulder.
2. In the Character palette, choose the Mirror tool. Its Options will show in the Attributes Manager.
3. In the Options, change Plane to World YZ, and change Origin to World. In the Replace field, type *L_*. In the With field, type *R_*. This makes the new copy have R_ in front of it, meaning you won't have to do any manual naming (see Figure 8.43).

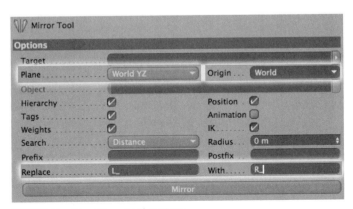

FIGURE 8.43   The Mirror tool options.

4. Click on Mirror. Check the Perspective view. You will see a new right arm joint chain in the character. In the Objects Manager, you will see the R_shoulder chain, along with R_shoulder.Pole and R_wrist.Goal (see Figure 8.44).

It's important to see that the Mirror tool copied your IK chain and also named it with the *R_* prefix.

Use the Mirror tool on L_leg:

5. Select L_leg.
6. Repeat the Mirror tool process on the leg chain. The options are the same as for the arm (see Figure 8.45).

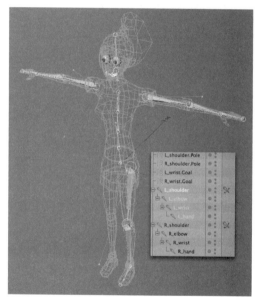

FIGURE 8.44   The Perspective view and the Objects Manager of the right arm chain.

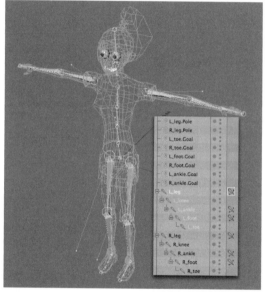

FIGURE 8.45   The Perspective view and the Objects Manager of the right leg chain.

Connecting Chains for a Complete Skeleton

Now that you have all the chains, it's time to connect them. This is all done in the Objects Manager and is just drag and drop. It's important to have the joints connected so that, for example, when you move the spine, the arms will also be affected.

Parenting joint chains:

1. Collapse the L_leg, R_leg, L_shoulder, R_shoulder, and Neck chain groups so that you don't see their children.

2. Drag and drop L_shoulder, R_shoulder, and Neck onto Shoulder. This is the last joint in the root joint chain.

3. Drag and drop L_leg and R_leg onto Root, the first joint in the root joint chain (see Figure 8.46).

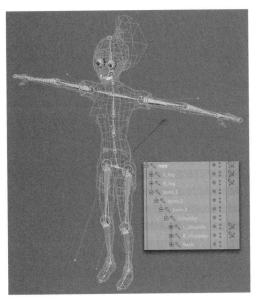

FIGURE 8.46   The Perspective view and the Objects Manager of the connected joint chains.

You will notice that after you make the links, new joints connections will be drawn between the back spine and the other joint chains.

Wrap Up

ON THE CD

The character is still not ready. Save your work and then move the wrist and ankle goals around to see how they behave. Also try the Hip and Shoulder controllers made at the beginning of this lesson. The final render of this tutorial is on the CD-ROM, and the next section picks up right where we leave off.

There's still a lot to do: set up skins, weight tags, and create and organize controllers. Move on to the next part to learn more.

The Hip and Shoulder controllers are rotatable and movable. The others are just movable.

TUTORIAL 8.3   CONTROLLERS AND VISUAL SELECTOR

Open the file Tutorials > Chapter08 > Chapter8-3 > Maiden_controller_ start.c4d from the CD-ROM.

This file leaves off almost exactly from the last tutorial, except that some linking has been done to some of the goals.

For your information, this is what has been done. You do not need to do these steps:

- An extra spine controller has been added, called *Midsection* (it controls Index 3 on the spline), and the spine Shoulder controller has been linked to it. This is so that you can either move or rotate Midsection and have Shoulder go with it. This helps with upper body bending.
- L_toe.Goal and L_foot.Goal have been linked to L_ankle.Goal.
- R_toe.Goal and R_foot.Goal have been linked to R_ankle.Goal. This will help in rotating and moving the feet.

Controllers are, for the most part, just Null objects, at least in our simple rig. There is a lot of power in how things are linked and organized in the Objects Manager, as you are about to see.

Controllers also extend into sliders and other manipulators. There are many different types and styles of character rigs, which vary greatly because every animation situation is different. Our rig is quite simple for book tutorial purposes, and therefore would not be suited for some types of animation. But after we are finished, you could get quite a decent walk cycle out of even our simple rig.

This tutorial will teach you about the following:

- Creating controllers for the arm
- Linking arm and spine
- Creating controllers for the leg
- Axis snapping
- Object Manager controller organization
- Visual Selector

Arm Control

For this lesson, you will only work on one side of the character. Everything you learn can simply be applied to the other side. We will ignore, therefore, everything that has an *R_* prefix. We will focus exclusively on the left side.

One of the problems with the current setup is getting the arm to swing. For example, during a walk, the arms would swing back and forth. They swing from the shoulder in an arc. However, right now, we only have Goal Null object controllers. Getting them to move in arcs would require a lot of work. The answer then is to create a Null object, place it over the left shoulder joint, and then link the L_wrist.Goal and L_shoulder.Pole to it.

Create a Null object for the arm:

1. Create a Null object.
2. Rename it as *L_Arm_Controller*.
3. Switch to the Move tool.
4. Press the P key to see the pop-up Snapping menu. Choose 3D Snapping. Press P again, and choose Axis Snapping (see Figure 8.47). (In R10, the P key can be held down while selecting.)

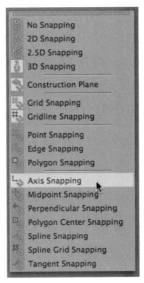

FIGURE 8.47 The "P" Snapping menu. Choose 3D and Axis Snapping.

5. In the Perspective view, move the L_Arm_Controller up to the left shoulder joint. It will "snap" in place over it. Now the controller has the exact same center as the shoulder (see Figure 8.48).
6. Link L_wrist.Goal and L_shoulder.Pole to the new L_Arm_Controller (see Figure 8.49).

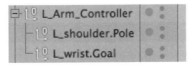

FIGURE 8.48 A Perspective view of moving the L_Arm_Controller up to the left shoulder joint.

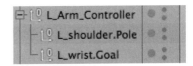

FIGURE 8.49 The new hierarchy for the Arm controller.

The left arm can now be rotated by rotating the L_Arm_Controller. It's very important to understand that this controller is for rotating and not moving. When you select it, you will notice that its X, Y, and Z values in the Coordinates Manager are not set to 0. This is a fundamental weakness that MAXON has still yet to address. It is ideal that these values be set to 0. However, notice that all the rotation values are at 0. That means all you have to do is set them to 0 for it to return to a starting position, which works for the basic needs of this tutorial.

Make sure to turn off Snapping. To bend the arm, you move the L_wrist.Goal. To rotate it, you rotate the L_Arm_Controller. Try that now, but undo every action you take (see Figure 8.50).

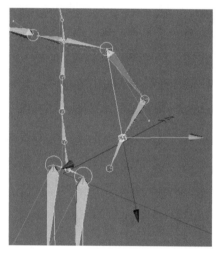

FIGURE 8.50   Moving the new controllers allows you to manipulate the arm.

Arm and Spine

If you were to move any of the Spine controllers, the arms wouldn't move with them. To rectify this, you need to link the L_Arm_Controller to Midsection. You might not be familiar with this controller, as you did not create it in the last section. Don't worry, there's nothing special about it. It was created in the exact same manner as you created the Hip and Shoulder spine controllers, except it controls the number 3 index on the spine. This was created to serve as an axis of rotation for the whole upper body.

Link arm to spine:

1. Link the L_Arm_Controller group to Midsection.
2. Rotate Midsection to see its effects. Make sure to Undo any rotations (see Figure 8.51).

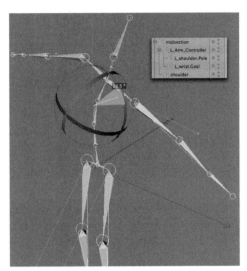

FIGURE 8.51   The Midsection spine controller will now move the left arm and the upper spine.

You may have noticed that only the left arm moves with the spine. That is because the right arm hasn't been set up and linked like the left arm.

When you rotate the Midsection spine controller you are also moving the shoulder spine along with the left arm. The result is a fairly natural bend in the upper body.

Leg Control

The leg works similarly to the arm, but it is more sophisticated because we have to account for the feet. Like before, you are simply creating Null objects, placed using Axis Snapping, over the right joints.

Create Null objects for the leg:

1. Create a Null object.
2. Rename it as *L_foot_controller*.
3. Using Axis Snapping, place it over the left ankle joint (see Figure 8.52).
4. Link the L_ankle.Goal group to L_foot_controller. This allows you to move the whole group by moving L_foot_controller (see Figure 8.53).
5. Create another Null object.
6. Rename it as L_footWpole.
7. Using Axis Snapping, snap it to the same location as before, over the left ankle joint.
8. Link L_foot_controller and L_leg.Pole to L_footWpole (see Figure 8.54).

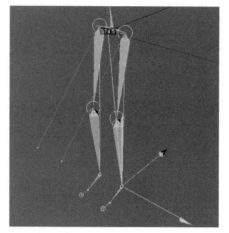

FIGURE 8.52   Moving the L_foot_controller to the ankle joint.

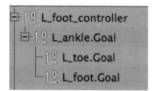

FIGURE 8.53   Linking L_ankle.
Goal to L_foot_controller in
the Objects Manager.

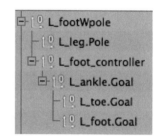

FIGURE 8.54   Hierarchy for
the L_footWpole group.

9. Create another Null object.
10. Rename it as *L_leg_controller*.
11. Snap L_leg_controller to the left hip joint (see Figure 8.55).
12. Link L_footWpole group to L_leg_controller (see Figure 8.56).

Now that you have the controllers, it's time to see what they do. Select L_foot_controller and using the Move tool, move it upward using the green *y*-axis handle (disable Snapping, if needed). You can see that it moves the left foot upward while the left knee bends (see Figure 8.57). Undo this after you have seen what it does.

L_footWpole does something very similar except that it would move the pole vector along with it. This hierarchy simply gives you the option to move it with or without the pole.

You might be asking when you would need to move the foot and the pole. Well, imagine rotating the foot outward. If you want the knee to rotate with it (and you would), you would use this controller and the Rotate tool. Try this, undoing any operations when you're finished.

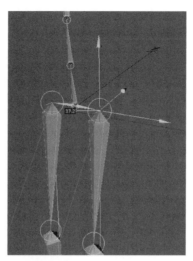

FIGURE 8.55   Snapping the L_leg_controller to the left hip joint.

FIGURE 8.56   The L_footWpole is linked to the L_leg_controller.

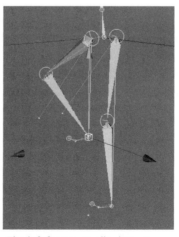

FIGURE 8.57   The left foot controller lets you move the foot.

Select the L_leg_controller. Using the Rotate tool, rotate the leg using the red axis handle. You can see that it rotates the whole leg forward and backward (see Figure 8.58). This is useful for things like kicks. Undo the operation after you've reviewed the controller.

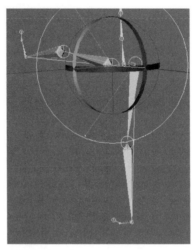

FIGURE 8.58 The leg controller rotates the whole leg using the left hip as its center of rotation.

Visual Selector

Many rigging solutions involve lots of controllers and sliders that are placed in the Viewports. This makes it convenient when animating, in that you don't have to go to the Objects Manager. However, it also can make for some serious clutter in the Viewport.

Visual Selector allows you to create links to your controllers in a separate window. These links can be modified and placed anywhere in the window. When you click on them you are actually clicking on the controllers.

Let's explore this fun and exiting new tool.

Use the Visual Selector tag:

1. Create a Null object, and rename it to *Visual Selector*.
2. Right-click on the newly created Visual Selector, and choose Character Tags > Visual Selector from the menu (see Figure 8.59). A new Visual Selector window will also appear (see Figure 8.60).

Create visual links:

3. From the Objects Manager, drag and drop L_Arm_Controller onto the Visual Selector window. You will notice a Null objects icon appear.

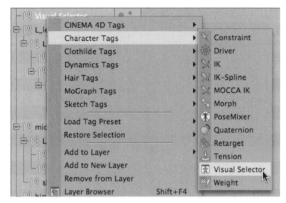

FIGURE 8.59   Applying the Visual Selector tag.

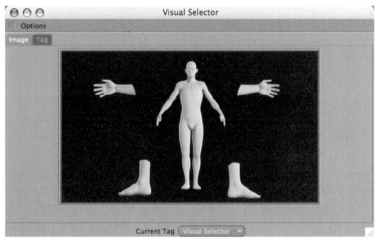

FIGURE 8.60   Visual Selector window.

4. Place the icon over the character's left shoulder (your right) (see Figure 8.61).

Edit visual links:

5. Click on the Tag tab.
6. Click on the HotSpots button. HotSpots is the name given to the visual links.
7. Click on the Null Object icon next to L_Arm_Controller. A new Visual Icon Selector window will appear. You can choose any icon from this menu. Since this controller should only be rotated, choose the white circle and click OK (see Figure 8.62).

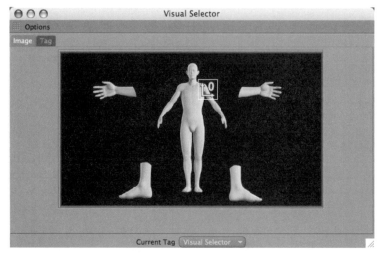

FIGURE 8.61   You create visual links by dragging and dropping from the Objects Manager.

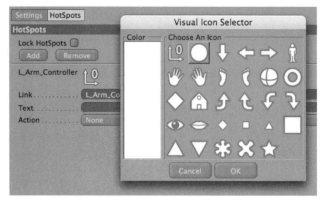

FIGURE 8.62   You can choose from a variety of icons for your selectors.

8. In the Actions section, choose Rotate. This means that every time you click on this icon, it will not only select the controller, but it will also change to the Rotate tool. Very handy!

9. Click on the Image tab to see that the Visual Selector has now changed the icon for the Left Arm controller to a circle (see Figure 8.63).

10. Drag other controllers to the Visual Selector (see Figure 8.64) and edit them.

 Use icons that will indicate the action you want the controller to take. For example, use circles for rotation, nulls for movement and points for the Spine controllers. What you use is up to you, of course.

For some controllers, you may not want to add rotate or move to the action because some controllers can do both, for example, L_footWpole. Controllers for the hips and shoulder should normally just rotate and not be moved, IK handles should be moved but not rotated, and so on.

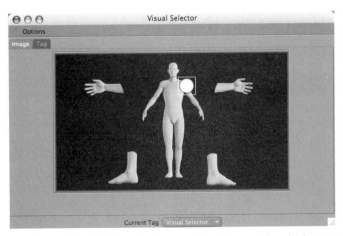

FIGURE 8.63   The Null icon has been replaced by a circle, which is more indicative of what the selector does.

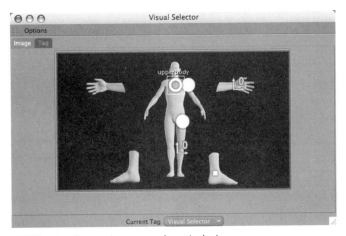

FIGURE 8.64   Customize to your heart's desire.

Wrap Up

Controllers are extremely important in any character's rig. We've only scratched the surface of the power that C4D gives you. We could have set up many more controllers, but space limits us to just the basics.

As you can see, Visual Selector is a welcome addition to the animator. No more clutter in the Viewports!

Now that you've completed a basic rig, it's time to learn about the importance of weighting.

TUTORIAL 8.4   **SKINS AND WEIGHTS**

For you to get the skeleton and controllers to move the character, you must link a Skin object from the Character menu to the Maiden geometry. Also, you must apply a Weight tag to the same, and then link all the joints to the tag. Only then will you be able to use the controllers and have the Maiden move with it. This tutorial will teach you how to do this.

Getting the character to move is one thing; getting it to move correctly (or to your satisfaction) is quite another. That's where weighting comes in. *Weighting*, sometimes called *Paint Weighting*, is where you tell the joints how much influence they should have over certain vertices. C4D does a pretty good job of getting close to where you need things to be. However, some weighting will usually be necessary, and this tutorial will teach you how to change those weights.

ON THE CD

Open the file Tutorials > Chapter08 > Chapter8-4 > Maiden_Skin_Start.c4d from the CD-ROM.

This tutorial will teach you about the following:

- Bind
- Skins
- Weight tag
- Auto Weights
- Reset Pose
- Weight tool

Skins

When the file opens, take a look at the Objects Manager. Even though there is much more in the scene, only the objects you will need are visible.

A Skin object will be applied to the Maiden geometry. Skins are what tell the geometry to be subject to joints and controllers. It is not always necessary to have the skin be a child of the geometry to be deformed. The skin has an Include list, where objects can be placed. This is extremely useful because it means that you can deform many different objects with the same skeletal system. You should not use the Force option in the Include list when using skins and regular geometry. That option is for deforming nongeometry objects that have points, such as other deformers.

For convenience, our skin will simply be linked to the Maiden geometry. Further, you will learn how to apply a Skin and Weight tag at the same time.

Use binding:

1. Open the Character menu in the main menu, and make it a floating palette (see Figure 8.65).

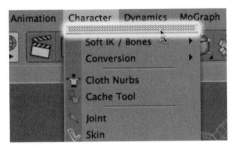

FIGURE 8.65   Make the Character menu a floating palette.

2. In the Objects Manager, select Main_Joint. This is the first joint in the joint group.
3. In the Objects Manager's menu, choose Edit > Select Children (see Figure 8.66).

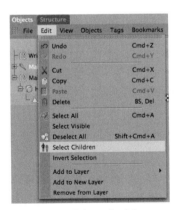

FIGURE 8.66   Select all of the Main_Joint's children.

4. Hold down the Ctrl key, and select Maiden. You should now have all the joints and the geometry selected.
5. From the floating Character palette, select Bind. A Skin object will be linked to the Maiden geometry. A Weight tag has also been applied (see Figure 8.67).

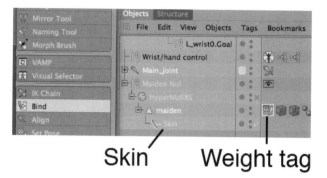

Skin   Weight tag

FIGURE 8.67   Choosing Bind from the Character palette will apply the skin and weights.

Weight Tags

The Weight tag is the link between the joints and the geometry. Select the tag (see Figure 8.67). Look at the Attributes Manager. Make sure that Tag and the Joints buttons are active. In the Tag Properties, you will see four buttons: Auto Weights, Clear Weights, Reset Pose, and Set Pose. In the Joints, you will see an Objects list that contains all the joints of the skeletal system (see Figure 8.68).

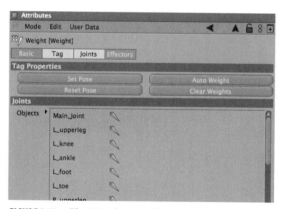

FIGURE 8.68   The Weight tag's Tag and Joint properties.

When you used the Bind command, the C4D used the Auto Weights to link the joints to the vertices of the geometry. Clear Weights will make it so that the joints have no influence over geometry. It will also undo any weight changes you might make later, so use with caution.

Set Pose was also applied to the position of the joints when you bound the skin. This is important because as you use the controllers, you may want to return it to the bind pose. Use Reset Pose for this. Note, there are limits to this: Null object and Goal controller, if moved, will override the Reset Pose. You must turn off Expressions to return the joint to its pose after you've linked and moved goals and controllers. If you don't return the goals and controllers to their original positions, the skeleton will simply return to the position it had before you applied the Reset Pose. Returning all the controllers is not very fun or useful. A workaround for this is to give each controller and goal a key frame at time 0. You should also keep a copy of your characters in the default pose with their controller systems in a separate file, so that you can always return to it if you run into problems later when animating.

Weight Tool

You will need to know how to change the Auto Weights. In this file's rig, we only have two joint chains that control four fingers. That means that it's sure not going to work with just Auto Weights. You will use the Weight tool to change how the finger joints control the finger geometry.

PoseMixer was used to create the joint movement for the fingers. The Help system has details on how to use this if you are looking to set up hand and finger movements. In the Help system, look under Reference > Modules > MOCCA > MOCCA Tags > PoseMixer for more information.

Checking finger geometry:

1. In the Objects Manager, locate and select Wrist/hand control.
2. In the Attributes Manager, click on the PoseMixer button. The PoseMixer options will appear (see Figure 8.69).

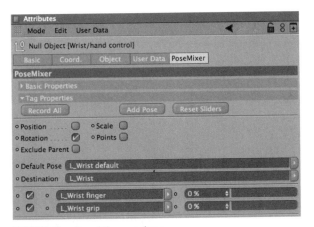

FIGURE 8.69   PoseMixer options.

3. Locate the L_Wrist finger slider. Click on the slider, or enter a value in the slider field. Note that the left hand fingers bend, minus thumb and index. Also note that only part of the three fingers bends. Part of the middle finger stays next to the index finger. This is because the joints in the index finger are also controlling part of the middle finger (see Figure 8.70).
4. Return the slider for L_Wrist finger to 0.

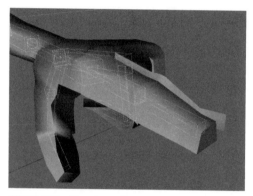

FIGURE 8.70 The three fingers don't bend correctly.

Use the Weight tool with finger joints:

5. Change to and then maximize the Top view. Make sure that the left hand is roughly centered.
6. In the Objects Manager, open the Main_Joint hierarchy. Locate and select L_hand. This is one of the joints in the hand, so it is pretty far down the hierarchy list.
7. In the floating Character palette, choose the Weight tool (see Figure 8.71).

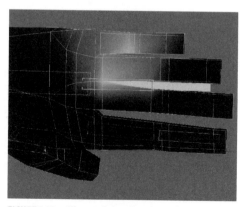

FIGURE 8.71 The weights for the L_hand on the fingers.

8. Observe the Viewport. The hand has turned to a grayscale interpretation, which shows how the joints are influencing the geometry. You have L_hand selected. That means you are seeing where this joint influences, indicated in white and shades of white. Black is where it has no influence.

9. In the Weight tool's options in the Attributes Manager, change the Strength to 100%. Make sure that Visible Only, in the Painting section, is unchecked (see Figure 8.72).

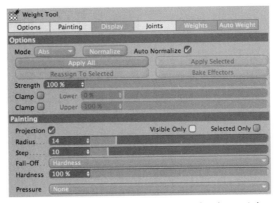

FIGURE 8.72   Change Strength to 100% for the Weight tool.

10. Paint over the vertices, as shown in Figure 8.73. Since you have Visible Only turned off, it will paint over unseen vertices on the bottom of the hand.

11. Change the Strength to 50% in the options for the Weight tool.

12. Paint over the vertices, as shown in Figure 8.74.

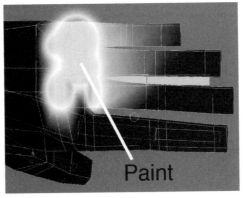

FIGURE 8.73   Paint over the indicated vertices. They turn white as you paint since the paint is set to 100%.

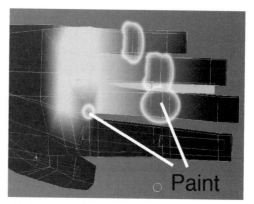

FIGURE 8.74   Paint over the indicated vertices. They turn gray as you paint since the paint is set to 50%.

13. In the Objects Manager, click on L_fingers_up. This is the next finger joint.
14. Click on the Weight Tool.
15. Change the Strength to 100%. Paint over the tips of the three fingers. Do not paint over the index finger.
16. Change the Strength to 50%. Paint over the middle knuckles, as shown in Figure 8.75.

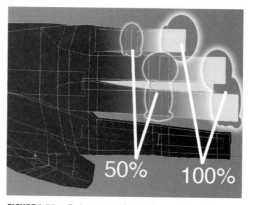

FIGURE 8.75   Paint over the indicated vertices, 50% for the knuckles and 100% for the tips.

Wrap Up

Go back to the Wrist/hand control, and move the L_Wrist finger slider again. The three fingers now bend better. Since we are controlling three fingers with only two joints, the bend is still a little rough, but the joints are now controlling the appropriate geometry. Try enabling the parent HyperNURBs object and moving the sliders as well.

CONCLUSION

There is a more finalized version of the Maiden rig on the CD-ROM in Tutorials > Chapter08 > Chapter8-4 > Maiden_final.c4d. It contains a more detailed Visual Selector, and you can use it to animate.

Cinema's older MOCCA systems were much more difficult to work with. MOCCA 3 represents a giant leap forward in both usability and ease of use. Ease of use is, of course, a matter of experience. Character rigging and animation is still hard, but, with time, patience, and study, you can master its intricacies. Good luck!

DYNAMICS

In This Chapter

- TUTORIAL 9.1   Rigid Body Dynamics
- TUTORIAL 9.2   Soft Body Dynamics

One of the most difficult things to do as an animator is to mimic real physics. For example, animating a bowling ball that hits the pins, making them bounce around, might sound easy enough. But to animate the ball, plus 12 pins, and do so convincingly, would be exceedingly difficult and time consuming. That answer to this dilemma is Dynamics, a module developed for the purpose of simulating real-world physics.

Dynamics has been designed to simulate two types of interaction: hard bodies, referred to as Rigid Bodies, which are surfaces like billiards, bowling pins, and so on; and soft bodies, which are objects whose surfaces are flexible, such as flesh, flags, sails, and Jell-o.

You need to understand that, as with every simulation, Dynamics is an approximation, meaning that it will take quite a bit of tweaking to get things to work. Look and feel is more important than worrying about setting numbers.

This chapter will teach you about both types of dynamic simulations. We start off with Rigid Bodies (see Figure 9.1).

 This chapter uses the new, default R10 Icon scheme. To change to the new scheme, choose Edit > Preferences, and in the Common options, choose Light for the Scheme.

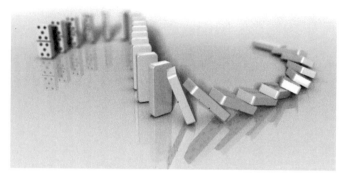

FIGURE 9.1 The upcoming Rigid Body tutorial.

| TUTORIAL 9.1 | **RIGID BODY DYNAMICS** |

Rigid bodies are surfaces that don't bend. Dynamics, in these kinds of simulation, only needs to worry about mass, velocity, and collision detection for the objects involved. However, there are quite a few subsets of these topics, and Dynamics can be very finicky. One small change can make the whole thing work or ruin a working simulation.

C4D has a *Save Incremental* feature in the File menu that will save the project file without overriding the previous file, meaning you'll get a series of project files. This is very useful for any project, but even more so for Dynamics, where one small change can mean success or failure. It's recommended that you practice using this feature as you do the Dynamics tutorials.

This tutorial will teach you about the following:

- Rigid Bodies
- Solver object
- Forces
- Rigid Body Dynamic tag
- Collision detection
- Low polygon proxy
- Bake Solver
- Layer Browser

ON THE CD

Open the project file Tutorials > Chapter09 > Chapter9-1 > domino_start.c4d. A prepared scene, complete with light, floor, background, and the objects you'll need to animate is now ready. This scene is a domino simulation. Dominos are good to start with because they are roughly rectangular. The dominos are hidden. In their place are low polygon proxy objects. You will not animate the dominos because their polygon counts are too high. Dynamics performs slowly with high poly counts where collision detection is a necessity. So, you will animate the cubes instead. The dominos, even though you can't see them, are linked to each cube. Later, after you've set up the simulation, you will simply reveal them.

Dynamics objects are located in the Dynamics menu in the main menu. Dynamics tags are located in the Objects Manager by choosing Tags > Dynamics. You will need a combination of Dynamics objects and tags to get the simulation working.

Solver Object

Dynamics requires a Solver object. The Solver will eventually be the parent of everything you want to be a part of the simulation. All geometry in the Solver must have a Dynamics tag. Dynamics only works on polygons and splines. It doesn't work on NURBS or Parametric (Primitives) objects!

You will add a Solver object to the scene. Though the simulation requires that you link the objects to the Solver, you will wait until later to do this. A brief explanation of its important settings will be given.

Add a Solver object:

1. In the main menu, select Dynamics > Solver Object (see Figure 9.2).
2. Click on the Solver object, and observe its attributes. Make sure that the Main and Details buttons are active (see Figure 9.3).

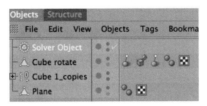

FIGURE 9.2   The Solver object.

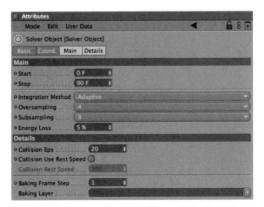

FIGURE 9.3   Solver object attribute default settings.

Solver Settings

In the main section of the Attributes Manager, you'll see Start and Stop. This is where you tell Dynamics how long the simulation should be. Next you'll see Integration Method, Oversampling, Subsampling, and Energy Loss.

Integration Method has five options. These are covered in the manuals and Help system, but all you need to know is that these are different methods Dynamics uses to calculate. The methods are progressive in speed and accuracy starting with Euler, which is the quickest and least accurate, whereas Adaptive is the slowest but most accurate. The sampling settings dictate how much time the computer should take, with any given Integration Method, to calculate the simulation.

Energy Loss is an important setting because it simulates entropy (in a loose sense) in the system. If there were no energy loss, then objects would not behave like normal objects. Also, Dynamics can sometimes add energy into the system. Energy Loss compensates for this. In real-world terms, this value can help increase or decrease the energy in the simulation.

In the Details section, the only part we will discuss here is Collision Eps. This is the distance buffer Dynamics uses to separate colliding objects. For example, when the dominos fall to the floor, they won't actually hit it because of this buffer. A value of 20 means that 20 meters (or whatever unit of measure you are using) will separate the colliding objects. Collision Eps is useful in helping objects to not pass through each other, which can happen even with collision detection.

Edit the Solver settings:

1. In the Objects Manager, select the Solver object. Make sure that Main and Details are visible in the Attributes Manager.
2. Change Stop to 120. This will lengthen the time of the simulation.
3. Change Integration Method to Midpoint. This will speed up the calculation.
4. Change Oversampling to 16.
5. Change Energy Loss to 6%. Increasing the energy loss will help the dominos to not move around too much, which they tend to do.
6. Change Collision Eps to 4. This will decrease the distance of the buffer between the dominos and the floor.
7. Activate Collision Use Rest Speed. Change Collision Rest Speed to 5. This also helps the dominos to come to rest (see Figure 9.4).

Forces

Forces are objects that exert some kind of influence on Dynamic geometries. The three options are Gravity, Drag, and Wind. As you can imagine, gravity is going to be necessary in our domino setup. Drag will also be important. When the dominos fall, drag will keep the dominos stable. You

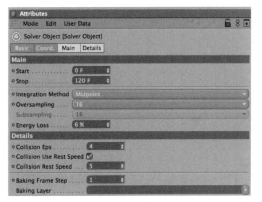

FIGURE 9.4   Solver object attribute settings, modified.

will find that Dynamics is much like a wild horse, with a mind of its own and difficult to tame. Forces are key to reining it in.

You will add gravity and drag to the scene. Do not yet link them to the Solver.

Add forces:

1. In the main menu, select Dynamics > Gravity.
2. In the main menu, select Dynamics > Drag.
3. Select the Gravity object. In the Attributes Manager, make sure that the Field option is active. Change Strength to 10.
4. Select the Drag object. In the Attributes Manager, make sure that the Field option is active. Change Strength to 50. Change Mode to Axial.
5. In the Attributes Manager for Drag, click on the Shape button to see its properties. Change Shape to Cube. Edit the Dimensions to X = 3000, Y = 100, and Z = 3000 (see Figure 9.5).
6. Change the Drag object's Position coordinates in the Coordinates Manager to X = -570, Y = 0, and Z = 700. This will center the Drag object on the dominos.

Force Settings and the 200-Meter Tall Domino

One question you may have is why set Gravity's strength to 10. You might think that its default setting of 1 should be the most accurate in any simulation. The problem is one of size. Our dominos aren't modeled to scale. They are 200 meters tall! Ask yourself, "How long would it take a 200 meter tall domino to fall?" The answer is that it would take a lot longer than a normal, tiny domino. To compensate for our lack of accurate scale, we increase the Gravity strength.

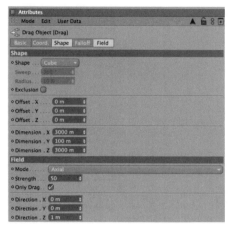

FIGURE 9.5 Drag settings.

The other setting of note is the Strength for the Drag. We set it very high so that the dominos will stop after they fall. Drag, because we changed its shape, will only affect the cube's center of mass when it crosses into its area of influence (indicated by its green box). Because the edge of the Drag is near the ground, it will only affect the cubes after they fall to the ground.

Rigid Body Dynamic Tag

As it stands, our simulation isn't ready. The proxy cubes don't have the necessary Rigid Body Dynamic tag. Without this tag, there is nothing to tell them how to interact with the Solver and Force objects. You will add this important tag to the first cube. After you've edited its settings, you will copy it to the rest of the cubes.

Add and edit the Rigid Body Dynamic tag:

1. In the Objects Manager, open the group Cube 1_copies to see its hierarchy.
2. Select and right-click on the first Cube 1 in the hierarchy. In the pop-up menu, select Dynamics > Rigid Body Dynamic (see Figure 9.6). The tag will be applied. Select the new tag, and make sure that Mass and Collision settings are active in the Attributes Manager.
3. In the Mass section, change Rotational Mass to 4%. This is, possibly, one of the most important changes. If you were to leave this setting at 100, it would make it very hard for the dominos to fall down because it would take a lot of force to rotate them. Lowering this makes it easier.
4. In Collision, change Collision Detection to Box. Change Elasticity to 10%, Static to 50%, and Dynamic to 40% (see Figure 9.7).

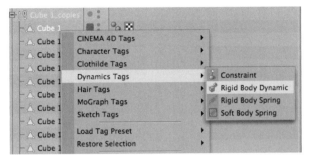

FIGURE 9.6   Adding the Rigid Body Dynamic tag.

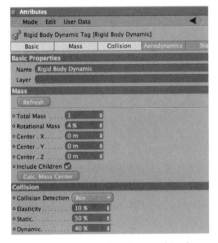

FIGURE 9.7   Settings for the Rigid Body
Dynamic tag.

5. Copy the Rigid Body Dynamics tag that is on Cube 1 to the rest of the cubes. The easiest way to do this is to select the tag in the Objects Manager. Then, while holding down the Ctrl key, drag and drop the tag onto the cube below. When you do this, a copy of the tag will be made. Repeat this process until all the cubes, from Cube 1 to Cube 1.24, have this tag (see Figure 9.8 and Figure 9.9). Do not use the Copy Tag to Children command because it will not work.

6. In the Objects Manager, select Plane. Right-click, and apply a Rigid Body Dynamic tag to the Plane object. Select the tag.

7. In the Attributes Manager, ensure that the Mass and Collision settings are active. Change Total Mass to 0. Change Collision Detection to Box, Elasticity to 0, Static to 50%, and Dynamic to 40% (see Figure 9.10).

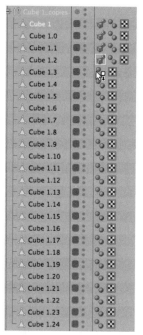

FIGURE 9.8   Copy tag to all of the cubes through Ctrl-drag and drop.

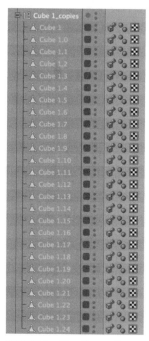

FIGURE 9.9   The Dynamic tag, applied to the cubes.

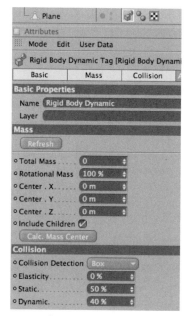

FIGURE 9.10   Dynamic settings for the tag, which was applied to the Plane object.

Rigid Body Settings

Some explanation of the settings for this tag is important:

- Total Mass dictates how much the object will react to the Gravity and Drag forces. The proxy dominos were given a mass of 1. The Plane was given a mass of 0 so that it wouldn't fall due to gravity.
- Rotational Mass determines how much force must be applied to rotate the object. This number was important to lower on the domino proxy cubes; otherwise, they would have too much rotational mass to tip over.
- Collision Detection was set to Box, and this is a fairly fast way to calculate it. For more accurate setting, you would choose Full. Because our cubes are just boxes, we didn't need that setting.
- Elasticity is how much bounce or spring an object has. High elasticity would make the dominos bounce when they hit. The floor was given a 0 value. This was to tame the dominos and keep them from going wild.
- Static is a simulator of friction, the force that tries to keep objects stationary. Without it, our dominos would glide like skaters on ice. Static refers to the force a stationary object must overcome to begin moving.
- Dynamic is also a simulator of friction but for moving objects. Because it's easier to move moving objects than stationary ones, the Dynamic number should be lower than Static. That's why we gave Static 50% and Dynamic 40%.

Hierarchy

The simulation will not work until the forces and objects are linked to the Solver object. Once linked, the Solver will control the objects, which means they can't be moved. If you want to move them, you must turn the Solver off, move them, and then choose Dynamics > Initialize All Objects before turning the Solver back on.

Select all the objects and forces, and link them to the Solver object (see Figure 9.11).

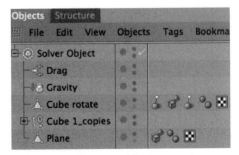

FIGURE 9.11   Objects and forces must be linked to the Solver object.

Bake Solver

Play back the animation, starting at time 0 (the animation may play slowly as your computer makes the necessary calculations). The cubes should fall like dominos, one on top of the other. You will see that a floating cube (called *Cube Rotate* in the Objects Manager) gets them going by striking the first one. It will be hidden when you render it. If the simulation is not as desired, go back and review the steps.

When the simulation is acceptable, it is time to bake it. Once baked, the animation will play back without the Dynamics calculations.

Bake the Solver object:

1. Select the Solver object.
2. In the main menu, select Dynamics > Bake Solver to start the animation. Let it finish. Once completed, you will note that the Solver object will be off. The baking is now complete.
3. Play back the animation. It should play much faster (see Figure 9.12).

To undo the baking, select the Solver object and choose Dynamics > Clear Solver. Turn the Solver back on. This will return it to its prebaked status.

It's important that you set the time to 0 before you clear the Solver. Otherwise, the cubes will remain in their position.

If the simulation is working, you do not need to clear it. This is for your information only.

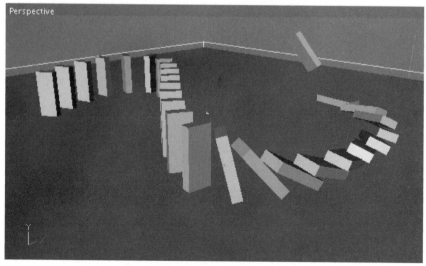

FIGURE 9.12 Baking turns the simulation into a regular key frame-based animation.

Layer Browser

There is a lot more to the scene than meets the eye. We don't want to render Cube Rotate or the Plane because there are other objects in the scene that will add to the quality of the render. Leave those objects hidden to the renderer (or as is).

The Layer Browser is where you can unhide the scene objects and dominos.

Use the Layer Browser:

1. In the main menu, select Window > Layer Browser (see Figure 9.13).
2. The Layer Browser window appears. You will notice three "layers": Blocks, Dominos, and Scene. Each will have a color by it, along with many icons (see Figure 9.14).
3. Each icon has a letter above it. These letters are S, V, R, M, L, G, D, E, and A. A detailed explanation of these is available in the Help section. For now, we will worry about three sections: V, R, and M. V stands for visible in the Editor, R stands for visible in the renderer, and M stands for visible in the Objects Manager.

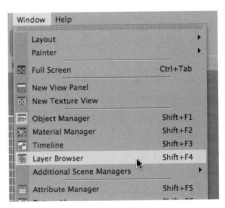

FIGURE 9.13   Selecting the Layer Browser.

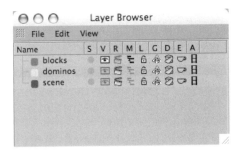

FIGURE 9.14   Layer Browser and its layers.

4. Activate the V and M icons for the Dominos layer.
5. Activate the V and M icons for the Scene layer.
6. Deactivate the V icon for the Blocks layer (see Figure 9.15).
7. Deselect all objects in your scene. The dominos will now be visible in the Perspective view (see Figure 9.16).

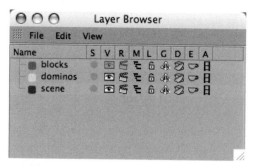

FIGURE 9.15   Editing the Layer Browser layers.

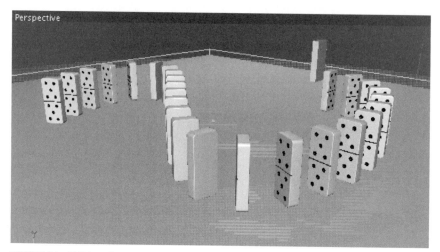

FIGURE 9.16   Editing the Layer Browser layers reveals the Scene objects in the Perspective view.

Wrap Up

ON THE CD

The scene is now ready to render to an animation file. All you need to do is enter a path in the Render Setting's Save section, and then Render to Picture Viewer. The animation can also be found on the CD-ROM and is called domino.mov.

Rigid Body simulations apply to all sorts of situations and can really add depth to your animations. Like everything 3D, practice and experimentation are critical aspects of the learning process.

TUTORIAL 9.2   SOFT BODY DYNAMICS

Soft Bodies are objects whose vertices are controlled by springs. Imagine placing an actual spring between points on a cube. These springs want to retain their shape, so when the cube is dropped and collides with an object, these springs will squash and stretch. That is the basic idea behind Soft Body Dynamics.

From the CD-ROM, open the file Tutorials > Chapter09 > Chapter9-2 > jello_start.c4d.

It's easiest to start with cubes when experimenting with Soft Bodies. Our experiment involves dropping cubes of Jell-o onto planes. The planes already have Rigid Body Dynamic tags that control their surface friction. So you don't have to add those tags. If you have questions on Rigid Bodies, refer to the previous tutorial. Remember that friction is determined by the Static and Dynamic numbers in the Collision setting for the tag. The *Platform Smooth* objects have no friction, whereas the *Platform Rough* has a very high friction. This will ensure that when the Jell-o cubes fall, they will slide on the sloped planes but come to a quick stop on the horizontal plane.

This tutorial will teach you about the following:

- Soft Bodies
- Soft Body Spring tag
- Springs
- Initialize objects
- Solver object
- Gravity

Soft Body Springs

As mentioned before, Soft Bodies are based on the concept of springs. These are added and edited through the Soft Body Spring tag. This is added in the same way as you add the Rigid Body Dynamic tag. The difference is that the Soft Body Spring tag has its own window and is not edited in the Attributes Manager.

You will add a Soft Body Spring tag to *Jello1*. You will then copy the tag to the rest of the *Jello* objects.

Add a Soft Body Spring tag:

1. Select Jello1.
2. Add a Soft Body tag to the Jello1 object by right-clicking on it. In the pop-up menu choose Dynamics Tags > Soft Body Spring (see Figure 9.17).

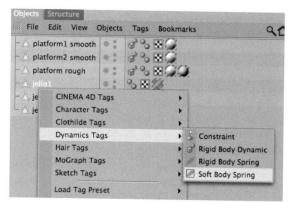

FIGURE 9.17   Adding the Soft Body Spring tag.

3. The Soft Body window appears with its own menu. Select Springs > Add Soft Springs from the Soft Body window. Remember, Soft Bodies won't work without springs (see Figure 9.18).

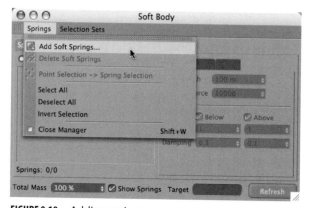

FIGURE 9.18   Adding springs.

4. The Add Soft Springs window appears. In the Method section, choose All. There are many types of springs, and each behaves differently. For our Jell-o, we want to add all the types of springs. This will give the Jell-o the resilience it needs while still being flexible (see Figure 9.19).
5. Click OK to close the Add Soft Springs window.
6. In the Soft Body window, make sure the Springs tab is active (it is by default). For Stiffness, under the Above section, enter 20. For Damping, enter 0.8 (see Figure 9.20). These settings make it so that the spring will want to retain its shape much more so than the default setting.

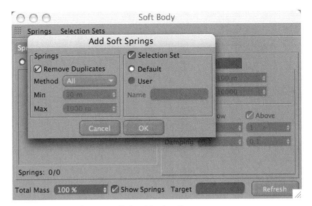

FIGURE 9.19   Choose All for Method.

FIGURE 9.20   Enter 20 and 0.8 for Stiffness and Damping, respectively.

7. Click on the Collision tab. Change Collision Detection to Full, Elasticity to 200%, Static Coeff to 60%, and Dynamic Coeff to 50% (see Figure 9.21).
8. Close the Soft Body window.

The Collision settings are very similar to the Rigid Body tag settings. Elasticity is how bouncy the object is when it meets other surfaces. Static and Dynamic Coeff determine its friction.

Initialize Objects

You will copy the Soft Body tag to the rest of the Jell-o objects. If you were to then link the objects to a Solver object, it would make Jello2 and Jello3 overlap Jello1. We want them to have their own starting positions. The Initialize Objects in the Dynamics menu will make it so that each

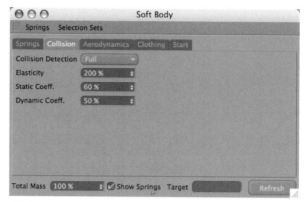

FIGURE 9.21 Collision and friction settings.

Jell-o object can have its own starting position. Initialize is also necessary every time you want to change an object's position. Remember, you must turn off the Solver object to move objects. Since our scene doesn't have one, we don't have to turn it off.

Initialize the Jell-o:

1. Copy the Soft Body Spring tag from Jello1 to Jello2 and Jello3 (see Figure 9.22).
2. In the main menu, choose Dynamics > Initialize All Objects (see Figure 9.23).

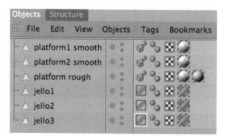

FIGURE 9.22 Copy the Soft Body tag to the rest of the Jell-o objects.

FIGURE 9.23 The Initialize All Objects command resets objects' positions.

Solver Object

The Solver object is necessary in any Dynamics simulation. You will add the Solver object and Gravity. You will then link everything to the Solver object.

Add hierarchy and the Solver object:

1. Add Gravity by choosing Dynamics > Gravity.
2. Add the Solver by choosing Dynamics > Solver Object.
3. Select Gravity.
4. Change its Strength to 3 in the Field section of the Attributes Manager.
5. Select Solver Object.
6. Make sure that Main and Details sections are active in the Attributes Manager.
7. Change Stop to 180 to lengthen the animation time.
8. Leave Integration Method set to Adaptive. Change Oversampling to 8 and Subsampling to 8. Change Energy Loss to 1%.
9. Change Collision Eps to 5 (see Figure 9.24). A brief explanation of Integration and Soft Bodies follows.
10. Link up the 3 Jell-o objects, the 3 Planes, and the Gravity object by making them child objects of the Solver object in the Objects Manager (see Figure 9.25).

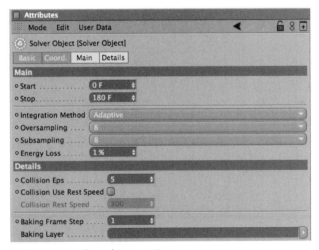

FIGURE 9.24   Solver object settings.

Wrap Up

Play back the animation. The Jell-o cubes bounce onto the diagonal platforms until coming to a rest on the horizontal platform. The horizontal platform has a lot of friction, so you will see a difference in how the Jell-o interacts with it.

Adaptive was used on the Integration Method. There is a Soft Body option there that is much faster than Adaptive. However, not every Soft Body solution will work with that setting. You can use it, and since our

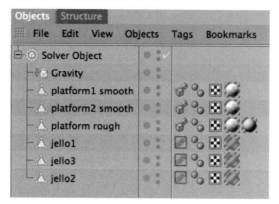

FIGURE 9.25   Solver object hierarchy.

scene has few polygons, it has a negligible impact on speed. Soft Bodies are particularly sensitive to the Integration Method. Changing it will give you drastically different results. Soft Bodies tend to explode or fly off, so once you find an Integration that is working for you, do a Save Incremental before further experimenting.

CONCLUSION

ON THE CD

The final animation is included on the CD-ROM, or you can render it out on your own.

Jell-o is a common theme in teaching Soft Bodies because it is the substance that most easily resembles how Soft Bodies naturally work. Round objects have a much more difficult time and will require much more tweaking than square or rectangular ones.

As you have seen, Dynamics is extremely powerful in aiding your animations with life-like physical interactions. You can mimic many real-life objects such as clocks, gears, and driving cars. Whatever you choose, Dynamics will prove to be an invaluable tool.

10

CLOTH

In This Chapter

- TUTORIAL 10.1   Cloth

O nly several years ago, cloth was very difficult to do in most 3D applications. MAXON has really outdone itself with this fantastic
implementation. Now animators (and modelers too!) have a
powerful new tool to work with.

No cloth simulation, at this point, is perfect, and C4D's cloth is no exception. But this tool has a lot to offer, and getting good results is readily
achievable. This tutorial will cover the basics of getting cloth to work,
along with a few tips on tweaking.

The objectives of this tutorial are to teach you about:

- The Cloth tag
- The Collider tag
- Modeling tips for cloth
- Forces
- Dressing cloth onto characters
- The Belt tag
- Tweaking for animation

*This chapter uses the Classic interface for the figures. For this tutorial, it is recom-
mended that you switch to the Classic scheme, which you can do by choosing Edit >
Preferences. In the Common section, change the Scheme to Classic.*

TUTORIAL 10.1 CLOTH

ON THE CD

The idea is to take a very basic model and let the Cloth simulator do most of the work. Remember that cloth will only work on polygon objects. It is wise to have the model devoid of N-Gons, but this is not required. Quadrangles will work best for you.

So, let's take a look at a model you are going to use for this tutorial. On the CD-ROM, open the file Tutorials > Chapter10 > clothmodel.c4d.

After you open the file, you'll notice a basic character along with a rudimentary cape that was modeled around the character's neck. Observe that, for the moment, the cape doesn't look like much, and the area around the neck is far too big (see Figure 10.1). Also notice that there is plenty of space between the neck and cape. Cloth will fix that for us later.

FIGURE 10.1 The cape model.

But as far as modeling the cape, the number of polygons is only 65. You don't need a high polygon count, and in fact, is not advisable. That's what the Cloth NURBS (found under Character > Cloth NURBS) is for. It is similar to the HyperNURB but works slightly differently and was designed specifically for cloth. It will raise your poly count and round out the cloth model. Leave it turned off until you are ready to render.

Cloth Tag

Cloth works by using at least two tags. The first can be found by right-clicking on the model you want to make into cloth and choosing Clothilde Tags > Cloth. Note that this tag is already applied to the cape model in the scene you just opened (see Figure 10.2), so you don't have to apply it.

FIGURE 10.2   The blue Cloth tag is highlighted in red.

The second tag, Collider (right-click and choose Clothilde > Collider), is applied to the objects you want the cloth to interact with. In this case, it's our hero. The Collider tags have already been applied to the subparts of the character model.

Let's get the cape ready to be placed onto the character. You will copy and paste the cloth model into a scene that already has an animated character.

Copy and paste the cloth:

1. In the Objects Manager, select the Cloth NURBS object, and select File > Copy (from the Objects Manager's menu), or use your operating system's shortcut for copying (see Figure 10.3).

FIGURE 10.3   Copying the object.

ON THE CD

2. Open the file Tutorials > Chapter10 > clothstart.c4d from the CD-ROM.
3. Paste (Edit > Paste) the object into the newly opened scene. The cape model will surround the character's neck, just like before (see Figure 10.4). The character already has Collider tags applied to the surfaces that will be interacting with the cloth (see Figure 10.5).

Collider Tags

Adding Collider tags isn't difficult and was done as a matter of convenience. To add a Collider tag to any object, right-click and then choose Clothilde Tags > Collider. These tags tell the cloth where not to penetrate. You do not have to do this step, as the tags are already applied to the character.

Dressing for Success

The cape is ready to be placed on the character. This is where the magic of cloth comes into play. It does a lot of the work for you.

FIGURE 10.4 The cape, pasted into the new scene. (Screwball model and animation by Naam.)

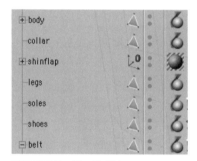

FIGURE 10.5 The Collider tags.

Use the Dresser button:

1. In the Objects Manager, open the Cloth NURBS hierarchy, select the Cape object and then select the Blue Cloth tag to see its Properties in the Attributes Manager.
2. Click on the Dresser button (see Figure 10.6).
3. Click on the Polygon tool, or press V and then choose > Tools > Polygons. You will notice that the cape has polygons around the neck area already selected. If they are not, reselect them manually or use the selection tag already on the model (see Figure 10.7). Otherwise, leave them selected.

Setting Dress State and Seam Polys:

4. In the Dresser options, click Set next to Dress State. (If you had to reselect the polygons manually, you will need to reselect the Cloth tag to see the options for Dresser.) This will ensure that you can return the model to the form it is in now. (Do not click on it now, but that is what the Show button is for.) You will also notice X's drawn on the

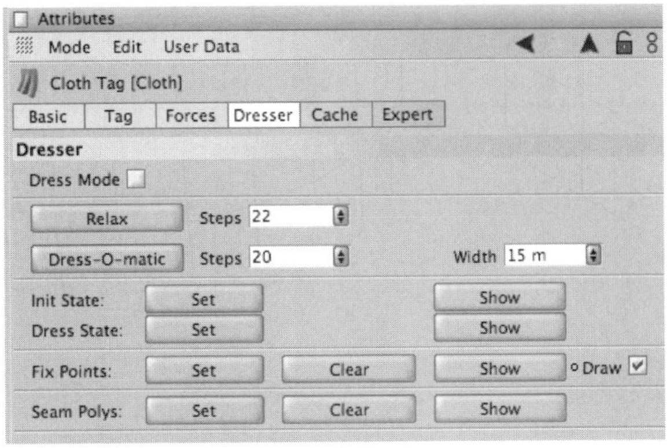

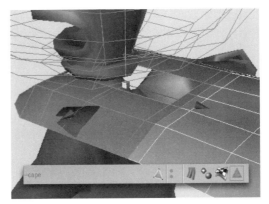

FIGURE 10.6   The Dresser button options.

FIGURE 10.7   Make sure that the polygons that surround the neck are selected.

polygons in the Editor window, and Dress Mode has been check marked in the Dresser options. The Cloth tag will turn yellow, also indicating it is in Dress mode.

5. Next to Seam Polys, click Set. This makes the selected polygons the seams for the cape. Yellow X's will fill the selected polygons, indicating that those are the Seam Polys (see Figure 10.8). Seams will shrink around the objects they interact with. For example, if you were to model a shirt, you would want the neck and arm areas to be seams.

Use Dress-O-matic:

6. Next to Dress-O-matic, make sure Steps is set to 20, and Width to 15. Click on Dress-O-matic. The Seam Polys will now collapse around the neck of the character. It will go through 20 frames before stopping. Width determines how big the Seam Polys will be, in this case, 15.

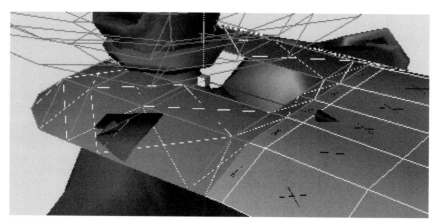

FIGURE 10.8 The Seam polygons.

7. Next to Relax, make sure Steps is set to 22. This tells the simulation how many times to calculate the position of the cape. Click on Relax. The cape will now hang around the character's neck and body (see Figure 10.9).

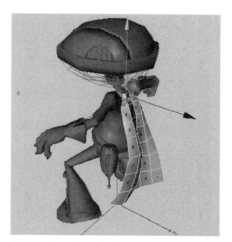

FIGURE 10.9 Screwball is now officially a caped hero.

8. Click Set next to Init State. The position the cape has formed is now its "start" position. The X's will disappear, indicating that you are no longer in Dress mode. You need to be out of Dress mode before animating.

Belt Tag

If you went ahead and did the simulation now, you would get some strange results. The area around the neck would bounce and stretch. You might also have wondered how you might model pants and other garments that on first glance don't hang on anything. That's where the Belt tag comes in handy. Belt tags were introduced in R9.5.

But you don't want the cape to be connected to his belt; you want it connected to his collar, which functions very similarly to a belt. You will add a Belt tag to the cape and then tell the cape to stick to the collar.

Fix points to the collar:

1. Select the cape. Right-click and choose Clothilde Tags > Belt. A Belt tag will be added. Make sure the tag is selected. You will see its Tag Properties in the Attributes Manager.
2. Locate the Collar object in the SCREWBALL hierarchy (SCREWBALL > Base > Deform > Welded Symmetry > Group > Collar). Do not deselect the Cape or the Belt tag. If you do, reselect them before moving on.
3. Drag the Collar object into the Belt On field (see Figure 10.10).

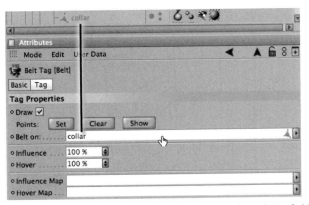

FIGURE 10.10   Drag the Collar object down into the Belt On field.

4. Now it's time to tell it which points of the cape will be tied to the collar. This works with points, so you have to convert the polygons you have selected to points. From the main menu, select Selection > Convert Selection. You want to go from Polygons to Points. Click Convert (see Figure 10.11).

A quick method is to Ctrl-click on the Points Tool icon.

5. In the Belt tag, click on Set above Belt Points. Those points will now turn yellow, indicating they are belt points (see Figure 10.12).

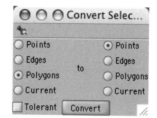

FIGURE 10.11   Convert the Cape's polygon selection to points.

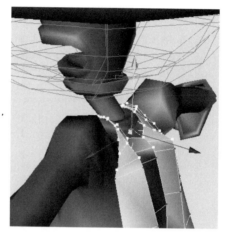

FIGURE 10.12   Clicking on Set next to Belt Points "attaches" those points to the collar.

Letting It Fly

It's time to let Cloth do its thing. A few things to note, you probably won't be satisfied with the first few simulations. There are lots of things to tweak, so don't be disappointed if it doesn't come out just the way you want it the first time. Fortunately, tweaking is pretty straightforward. But first, let's see what the cape animation looks like.

Calculate Cache:

1. Switch to the Cache button for the Cloth tag.
2. Click on Empty Cache. This will ensure any simulations are not in memory. You may want to run the simulation, then empty the cache, and rerun it to make sure.
3. Click on Calculate Cache (see Figure 10.13). The simulation will run, and the cape will interact with the character and predefined animation. When experimenting, empty the cache before each simulation. When you like the result, leave the cache full. This lets you scrub through the

animation with the cloth simulation. You can stop the calculation at any time by clicking the Stop Caching button that appears.

4. Use the Render > Make Preview feature to render out quick animation of the cloth. It's important to be able to see the animation played back in real time. Cloth is a CPU-intensive task and effects playback speed negatively.

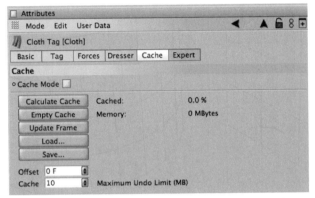

FIGURE 10.13   The Calculate Cache button starts the simulation.

Tweaking

For any given problem, there are many solutions. This is definitely a good example of that. The results for cloth can vary drastically depending on the settings you provide. Don't be afraid to redress the cloth too. Sometimes a slightly different Init State can give you the results you want.

Use forces:

1. Click on the Forces button for the Cloth tag. Notice that Gravity has been set to −30 (see Figure 10.14). Of course, this is much higher than the default −9.81 because lower values tend to make the cape flop too much. This is a good place to start when trying to get the weight of the material down. Don't worry that it's not −9.81. This is just a simulation. Use whatever gives you the best results.

2. Notice Wind and Air resistance numbers. These values can be handy when trying to change how the cape reacts to the air around it.

3. Click on the Tag button for the Cloth tag.

4. Notice Stiffness, Flexion, Rubber, Bounce, and Friction. You can control how the cloth will simulate materials with these values.

5. Try changing the Cloth tag values, and experiment with different simulations.

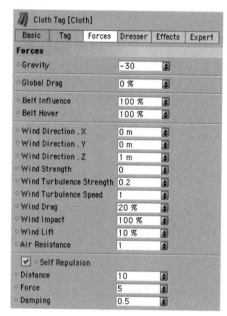

FIGURE 10.14 Forces settings.

CONCLUSION

In the same directory on the CD-ROM for the project files, you'll find a cloth movie made with the character and cape. That was achieved without too much tweaking. Remember that cloth is also good for modeling. But, no doubt it will be used for a variety of purposes. Either way, it is a powerful and fun tool that can make your animations or images shine.

HAIR

In This Chapter

- Render Settings
- TUTORIAL 11.1   Hair

Historically speaking, computer generated fur and hair has been difficult to do convincingly. Hair in most 3D applications can still be a tedious process, with users tied down in memory hog and CPU-intensive plug-ins or programs. Computations and renderings can take hours for single frames, and making changes is often like chewing on glass. So, when I tell you that MAXON's implementation is intuitive to use, renders quickly (relatively), and doesn't take up anywhere near the memory of other systems, you should be skeptical. But it's the truth!

Don't misunderstand; hair still requires some skill, and renders will be noticeably longer when using it. Chances are, if you've never used hair before, you'll never know what a fabulous job MAXON has done. Regardless, hair can be a lot of fun, and this tutorial will introduce you to some basic techniques for its use.

Hair can be used for a variety of things besides hair. Grass, shaggy rugs, or grains of wheat are all things hair could be used for (see Figure 11.1).

The objectives of this tutorial are to teach you about the following:

- Render Settings for quick renders
- Interactive Render Region
- Hair object
- Hair materials
- Selecting hair
- Editing hair
- Hair Render Settings
- Lighting hair

343

FIGURE 11.1   A futuristic combine plows through a field of grain, which was created using hair. (Image by Anson Call.)

ON THE CD

To get started, open the file Tutorials > Chapter11 > Hair_start.c4d from the CD-ROM. You will see a prepared file, complete with model, textures, and lighting. The scene has one additional camera, which is the default view. Since the scene is meant to be rendered from this perspective, you cannot move the view. Later on, while editing hair, you will switch to the Editor Camera.

Our character, an old, raggedy and unhappy man with a hat, is in desperate need of some facial hair to match his mood and style, of course.

This chapter uses the Light interface for the figures (except where indicated). For this tutorial, it is recommended that you switch to the Light scheme by choosing Edit > Preferences. In the Common section, change the Scheme to Light.

RENDER SETTINGS

Render the scene (see Figure 11.2), and then open the Render Settings (Render > Render Settings). Make sure you are in the General settings, and let's take a look at what these options will do for you as far as speeding things up.

It's important, when doing things like hair, to have the renderer going as fast as possible because you will need to make changes often. Having feedback quicker means less time waiting in-between changing hair settings.

FIGURE 11.2   In this first render, a lot of detail is missing.

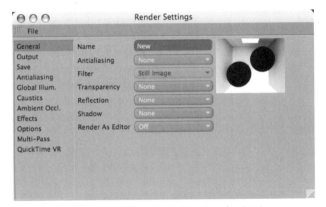

FIGURE 11.3   The General section of the Render Settings.

Looking at either Figure 11.3 or the Render Settings window, notice that Antialiasing, Transparency, Reflection, and Shadow are all set to None. This is important, as it means the renderer doesn't have to worry about doing those CPU-intensive calculations. It also means that our image will lack any depth or finishing touch, which is apparent in the render you just made or Figure 11.2.

Click on the Options section. Notice that Sub-Polygon Displacement is off. This scene uses this feature extensively, which subdivides the face, shirt, and hat so that fine details can be added. This takes a very long time to calculate, so for quick rendering, it has been disabled. Other options, such as Ambient Occlusion (also found in materials), Global Illumination, and Caustics should be turned off when you don't need them.

TUTORIAL 11.1   HAIR

Hair can be applied to nonpolygonal objects, such as NURBS and Primitives, but you will get the most flexibility with polygons. Hair functions are controlled through the Hair menu in the main menu, Hair materials, Hair tags, and Hair Render Settings. Adding hair is as easy as selecting the object and choosing Hair > Add Hair.

That command would apply hair to every part of the object. Since we only want the man to have some facial hair, we can select those polygons beforehand.

Add hair:

1. Select the Head object in the Objects Manager. It is linked to Hyper-NURBS.
2. Select the Polygon tool.
3. On the Head object are several polygon selection tags. Find the one that says Side_Head, and then choose Restore Selection in the Attributes Manager. This will select the sideburn polygons (see Figure 11.4).
4. In the main menu, choose Hair > Add Hair. In the Viewport, you will see some lines with end points coming off the area you had just selected. The length of the lines indicates the length of the hair (see Figure 11.5). These lines are called *Guides*.

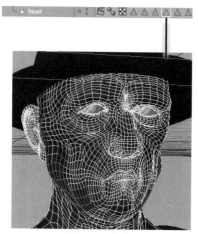

FIGURE 11.4   The Polygon Selection tag and its corresponding selection on the face.

FIGURE 11.5   Hair Guides are now visible on the face.

Notice that you did not have to do anything special to get the hair to be linked to the selection tag, other than choose your selection first. C4D will take whatever you have selected and apply hair to it.

For now, the hair is way too long. If you were to render now (go ahead!), you'd see what looked like a man who ate a gigantic bowtie made out of white bristles. Not good. But don't expect hair to look exactly the way you want it at such an early stage.

A Hair object, along with a Hair Mat, has been added to the scene. These both will be edited, along with the Guides to get the hair looking more respectable.

Hair object settings:

1. In the Objects Manager, select the Hair object. Rename it to *Hair side-burns*. Then observe the Attributes Manager.
2. Make sure the Guides button is active. Look at the Link field. Side_head is there. This is the Polygon Selection tag that was on the head. You could drag any object or tag into this field if you wanted the hair to affect it (but do not do so at this time).
3. Look at Count. This is how many Guides have been made. You do not have to change this.
4. Enter 37 for the Length. This will shorten dramatically the length of the Guides (see Figure 11.6).
5. Click on the Hairs button. Note the count is 5000. This is the actual number of hairs that will be rendered. If you find that hair looks too thin, you can increase the number here. Doing so will increase your render times, so for previews, its wise to keep this low. For now, we will leave it.

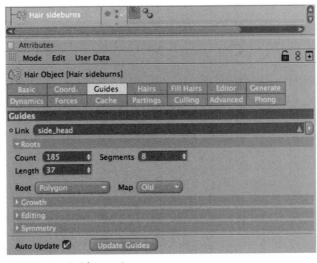

FIGURE 11.6   Guides settings.

Selecting Hair

Hair can be moved, brushed, cut, and more. You can edit the Guides directly through the Hair menu. You will need to move the Hair Guides downward. But before you do this, you need to select them. Guides are not selected using the normal selection tools but use equivalents from the Hair menu. This means you are going to be using this menu a lot.

To facilitate the process, you will create a floating Hair palette. From the palette, you will select and move the Guides.

Select and move:

1. Create a floating Hair menu. You do this by opening the menu and then clicking on the checkered line that sits above the first option (see Figure 11.7).
2. From the palette, click and hold on Live Selection to see its nested options. Choose Rectangle Selection (see Figure 11.8).

FIGURE 11.7 Create a floating Hair palette.

FIGURE 11.8 Rectangle Selection.

3. After choosing Rectangle Selection, you will see its options appear in the Attributes Manager. Make sure Visible Only is unchecked. You will need to be able to select all of the Guide points.
4. Draw a rectangle selection around all of the Guide points (see Figure 11.9). After doing so, the ends will turn orange, indicating they are Draw a rectangle selection around all of the Guide points (see Figure 11.9). After doing so, the ends will turn orange, indicating they are selected.
5. From the floating Hair palette (or the Hair menu), choose Move.
6. In the Viewport, click-drag downwards to move the hairs. You will notice the guides bend instead of staying straight. This is what we want (see Figure 11.10).

FIGURE 11.9 Selecting all of the Guides.

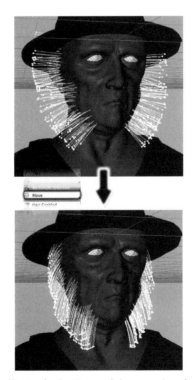

FIGURE 11.10 The effects of selecting and then moving the Guides downward.

Interactive Render Region

The Interactive Render Region (IRR) is very similar to Render Region, except that the region stays and updates as you make changes. This allows you to see rendered results of the changes you make to part of your scene, without having to do a full render and without having to use Render Region over and over. Since you are going to be making lots of changes to the Hair material settings, now would be a good time to use this tool. However, if your computer is not fast enough, or you find the process cumbersome, you can skip to the next section that details the Hair material settings and just use Render Region.

Add IRR:

1. Locate the three Render icons in the top icon palette. Click and hold on the middle Render Icon, and choose Interactive Render Region (see Figure 11.11). This can also be done through Render > Interactive Render Region.
2. Click-drag a Render Region box around one side of the man's face so that you can see part of the beard. The box will stay and render that part of the image. You can change the size of the box at any time. A quality triangle sits in the middle right of the box. Click-dragging this slider up and down will increase and decrease the quality of the render, respectively (and also the time it takes to render; you should choose a relatively snappy setting) (see Figure 11.12). You can also right-click on the triangle to see a variety of options. For more information on these options, including saving the IRR image, go to Help > Help Manual > Reference > Rendering Menu > IRRegion.

FIGURE 11.11   Adding Interactive Render Region.

Hair Material

Hair's look is largely determined through its material. You can do so many things here. As you can see in the IRR render, the hair is overexposed because we have a lot of lights in the scene. You will open and edit the Hair Mat's Color, Specular, Transparency, Thickness, Length, and Kink settings. For a complete list of Hair material settings, look to the Help system.

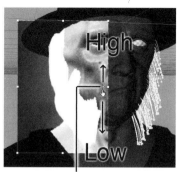

FIGURE 11.12   IRR box with quality triangle. Moving the triangle up increases render quality. Lowering it decreases render quality. Right-click on the triangle to see IRR options.

Edit Hair Mat:

1. Open (double-click) the Hair Mat in the Materials Manager. Its Material Editor window will appear. Change its name to *Hair sideburn* (see Figure 11.13).

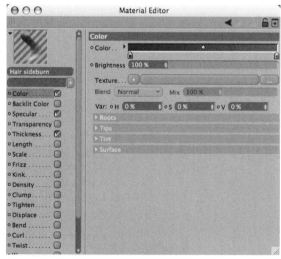

FIGURE 11.13   The Hair material and the Material Editor.

2. In the Color Channel, change Brightness to 15%. Leave the colors as they are. Notice how the IRR render has changed slightly. It's still too overexposed because the Specular settings are too high.

3. In the Specular channel, change Strength to 6%, and Sharpness to 16. In the Secondary settings, change Strength to 30% and Sharpness to 30 (see Figure 11.14).

4. Activate Transparency. In the Transparency Gradient section, slide the Black marker over slightly and then make a new marker in its place. You make new markers simply by clicking right underneath the gradient where you want them to be. Change the marker color (by double-clicking on it) to about 75% white (see Figure 11.15). The gradient will now tell the hair to be somewhat transparent at both the root and the tip.

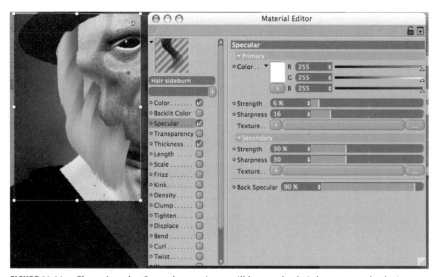

FIGURE 11.14 Changing the Specular settings will lower the brightness on the hair.

5. Make sure Thickness is active. Change Root to 0.1 and Variation to 0.05. This will make the hairs thinner. The Variation number will ensure not all hairs have exactly the same thickness (see Figure 11.16).

6. Activate Length. In the Texture space, add a Noise shader via the Texture Triangle. Click on the word *Noise* to see its settings. Change the Noise type to Dents and Brightness to 50% (see Figure 11.17). Noise on the length will ensure that not all the hairs have the same length. In fact, using Dents will make sure that they are very uneven. Raising the Brightness setting makes it slightly less uneven though. All this makes the hair more scraggly.

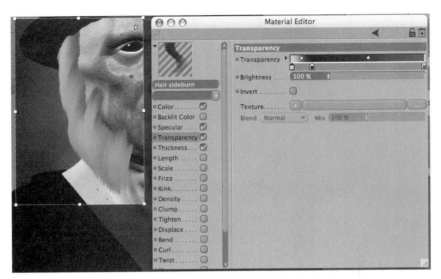

FIGURE 11.15   Transparency settings.

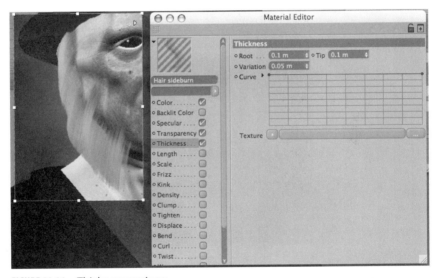

FIGURE 11.16   Thickness settings.

7. Activate Kink. You can leave the settings at their default. Kink un-
straightens the hair and makes for a more uncombed appearance (see
Figure 11.18).

As you can see, the material settings are very important. Without too
much tweaking, we were able to do quite a bit. The IRR feedback makes
for a quicker understanding of what each setting does.

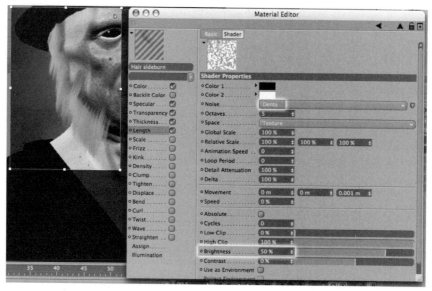

FIGURE 11.17 Length settings.

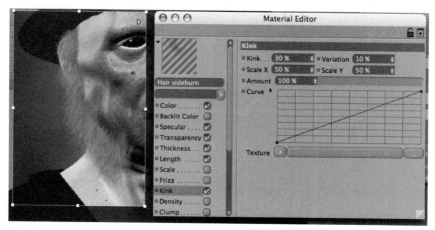

FIGURE 11.18 Kink settings.

Use IRR, Render Settings, and shadows:

8. Revisit the Render Settings. Open the Render Settings (Render > Render Settings), and look at the General section.

9. In the Shadow, change it to All Types. Now the IRR will update to show the hair with shadows. It looks much more realistic and takes significantly longer to render, but this is more telling of what the final render will look like (see Figure 11.19).

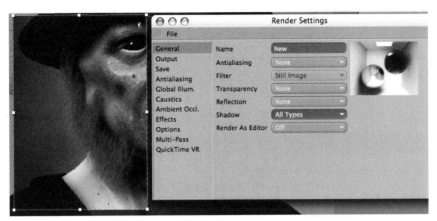

FIGURE 11.19   Shadows turned on and the IRR result.

10. Close the Render Settings.
11. Close the IRR by choosing Render > Interactive Render Region from the main menu. You are going to edit the hair, so you don't want it in the way now.

Cutting Hair

Even 3D characters need a haircut. Remember that the more you cut off, the less scraggly he'll look, so how much you take off is up to you. This is where you might want to change to the Editor Camera so that you can see it from all angles. Just remember to change back to the Camera Main when you are finished.

Use the Cut tool:

1. Change to the Editor Camera. In the Perspective Viewport, choose Cameras > Editor Camera.
2. From the floating Hair palette, choose Move > Cut to get to the Cut tool, or from the main menu, choose Hair > Tools > Cut. The Cut tool's options will appear in the Attributes Manager. Make sure that Radius is not too small or too large. A value of 10 to 20 works well.
3. In the Viewport, put your mouse over the points of the hair you want to shorten. You can click or click-drag for a painting motion. You can undo any action (see Figure 11.20).
4. After you are finished, go back to the Camera Main, and do a Render Region render on the hair to see if it is satisfactory. Make cutting adjustments as needed (see Figure 11.21).

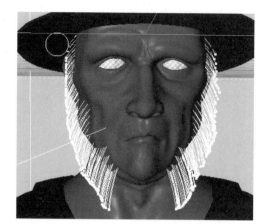

FIGURE 11.20   Cutting the hair Guides.

FIGURE 11.21   A Render Region of the cut hair.

Eyebrows

The hair for the beard is mostly finished. You will add hair for the eyebrows, and along the way, you will learn how to brush the hair so it will flow in the direction you want. You'll add hair to the brows with the same process as before. First, you will choose a selection set from the head and then add the hair.

Add hair for the brows:

1. Select the Head object in the Objects Manager. Make sure you are in Polygon mode. Select the Eyebrow Polygon Selection and choose Restore Selection in the Attributes Manager. You will see the Polygon Selection for the eyebrows on the man.

2. Choose Hair > Add Hair.
3. Rename the new Hair object to *Hair eyebrows*.
4. In the Attributes Manager, in the Guides section, change Length to 8 (see Figure 11.22). In the Hairs button, change the Count to 1000.

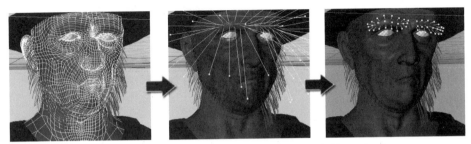

FIGURE 11.22   The process of selecting polygons, adding hair, and shortening it.

Editing hair for the brows:

5. Change to the Editor Camera, and zoom in on the brow hairs.
6. Choose Hair > Tools > Brush (see the Brush Options in the Attributes Manager). Activate Collision. Change Radius to around 20 to 30. Collision will ensure that the Guide points don't break through the surface.
7. Click and drag in the Viewport in the direction you want the eyebrows to go. Start inward and paint outward on the Guide points (see Figure 11.23 and 11.24). This brushing action will move the points and give the eyebrow hair a more realistic direction.

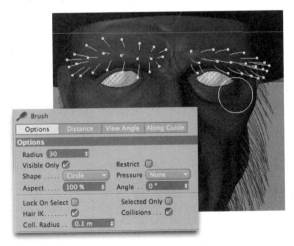

FIGURE 11.23   Brush Option settings and brushing the eyebrows.

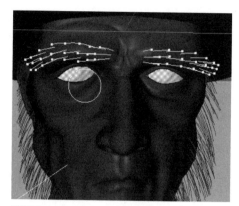

FIGURE 11.24 Brushing finished.

8. Using the Hair Selection tools, select the end group of points on one side of an eyebrow. It doesn't matter which side.
9. Choose Hair > Tools > Clump.
10. Click and drag in the Viewport to make the selected Guide Points come together. Repeat this selection and clumping on the other eyebrow (see Figure 11.25).
11. Choose Hair > Tools > Cut. Cut the inner parts of the eyebrow (see Figure 11.26).

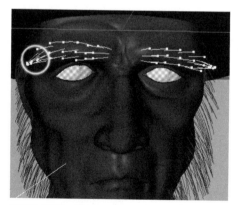

FIGURE 11.25 Clump the ends of the eyebrows so that they come to more of a point.

Eyebrow Hair Material

When you created the Hair for the brows, you created a new Hair Mat to go with it. But because you want the brow hair to have some similarity with the beard, it is easier to duplicate the *Hair sideburn* material and use that for the brows. You can edit the duplicate so that it better fits the brows.

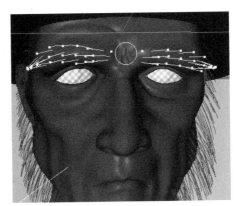

FIGURE 11.26   Trimming the inner parts of the eyebrows.

Edit eyebrow hair material:

1. Select the *Hair sideburn* material in the Materials Manager. In the Materials Manager's Edit menu, choose Copy and then Paste to make a duplicate.
2. Double-click on the duplicate (far left in the manager), and rename it to *Hair eyebrows.*
3. In the Material Editor, uncheck Kink. Check Frizz and Bend. These will help distinguish the brow hair from the sideburn hair (see Figure 11.27).

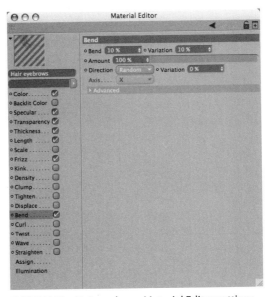

FIGURE 11.27   Hair eyebrow Material Editor settings.

4. Drag and drop the Hair eyebrow material onto the Hair eyebrows material tag in the Objects Manager. This will replace the tag with the newly edited material (see Figure 11.28).

5. Perform a Render Region to see the Hair object for the eyebrows (see Figure 11.29).

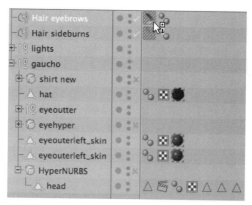

FIGURE 11.28 Replacing the old tag with the new Hair eyebrow tag.

FIGURE 11.29 The render results for the eyebrow hair.

Lighting Hair

Render a larger Render Region for the head. Notice how you can still see part of the sideburn hair, even though it should be in shadow (see Figure 11.30). This is because there are lots of lights in our scene. Some of these lights light up the man, and others light up just the background. This sort of light linking happens in the Scene tab for the lights. This is where you dictate what objects will be affected by that light.

Incorrect Shadows

FIGURE 11.30   A part of the sideburns is in shadow but is still being lit. This is not accurate.

The problem with Hair is that it ignores the Scene tab for the lights. So, if you try and use light linking in that way, it won't work. To fix this, you'll need to go into the Hair Render Settings and tell it which lights the Hair renderer should consider or ignore.

Hair Render Settings:

1. Open the Render Settings (Render > Render Settings). Click on the Effects button on the left-hand column.
2. Click on Hair Render in the Effects list.
3. Click on the Lights button. You will see an empty light list.
4. In the Objects Manager, open the lights hierarchy to see the child lights.
5. Drag and drop Light Eye Reflection, Background Light Low, and Background Light into the Light list (see Figure 11.31). Now those lights will be ignored (Excluded) from the Hair Render.

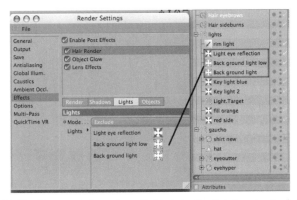

FIGURE 11.31   Drag and drop these lights into the Hair Render Exclude list.

6. Click on the General section in the Render Settings. Turn on Transparency, Reflection, and Shadows. Leave Antialiasing off for now (see Figure 11.32).

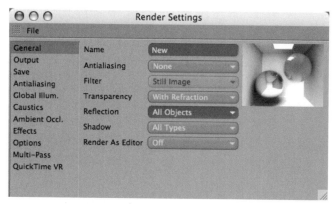

FIGURE 11.32 Turn on Transparency, Reflection, and Shadow in the General section of the Render Settings.

7. Render to the Picture Viewer. On a MacBook Pro, this takes about 38 seconds (see Figure 11.33). This render time is simply amazing. It means that Hair isn't really adding much render time to the scene.

FIGURE 11.33 A more complete render.

CONCLUSION AND FINAL RENDER

ON THE CD

The final scene (located on the CD-ROM) goes a little further and adds hair to the chest and eyelashes. For the final render, all the HyperNURBS are turned on. Displacement is turned back on in the Render Settings. The

Diffusion channel is activated for the Goucho material, which has some Ambient Occlusion. Antialiasing is set to Best. The scene takes about 14 minutes to render (see Figure 11.34). Now you know why it's so important to turn all that stuff off for previews.

Hair can really be fun and can add depth and realism to your scenes. You should know that this tutorial doesn't get into any of the animation features of Hair, which are quite extensive. Hair sports its own Dynamics engine, so hair can sway in the wind or flow over surfaces. Its powerful features are at your fingertips. Good luck!

FIGURE 11.34   This final render took around 14 minutes. Most of the render penalty is non–hair-related.

SKETCH AND TOON

In This Chapter

- TUTORIAL 12.1   Ray Gun with Style

Through the past decades of CGI renderings, there has been a quest for realism. Each year brought new techniques, software, and faster computers to help achieve that goal. Think back to some of the early CGI works, like the motion picture *Tron*, and then think of just about any movie released in today's age, and you'll realize that realism has made leaps and bounds.

Underneath all of that progress toward more realistic renderings a counter movement has been brewing. Many people simply don't want that result. But the fact of the matter is that today's rendering software is built on the premise of realism. Enter Sketch and Toon. This module was designed specifically for the artist, those looking for a unique, uncanned look that previously was difficult to achieve.

Sketch and Toon is a powerful tool that has many different rendering options available (see Figure 12.1 and Figure 12.2). There are so many, in fact, that there could be a whole book on it. Obviously, then, this chapter won't cover every feature, but it will show you the basics, along with a few tips and techniques on using some of the shaders and what to look out for.

FIGURE 12.1 An object example of a Sketch and Toon rendering. (Image by Anson Call.)

FIGURE 12.2 A scene example of a Sketch and Toon rendering. (Image by Anson Call.)

TUTORIAL 12.1 **RAY GUN WITH STYLE**

The following tutorial will walk you through a scene and show you how to apply Sketch materials. It will also show you how to use the Spots shader that is a part of the Sketch and Toon module. This tutorial assumes you have at least some basic knowledge of materials and lighting. If not, give Chapter 5, "Materials and Textures," and Chapter 6, "Lighting," a try first.

We'll also talk about the importance of material and lighting, which go hand in hand with sketching. You'll get a sense of the importance of exploration as well. Sketch and Toon, although not difficult to use, can easily give canned results. It can also just as easily give unique results, with a little bit of discovery and practice.

ON THE CD

To begin, load the file Sketch_start.c4d in Tutorials > Chapter12 from the CD-ROM.

You will learn about the following:

- The Spots shader
- Layering Spots shaders
- Using standard lights and GI with Sketch and Toon
- Sketching the background
- Adding a Sketch material to a scene
- Applying Sketch materials to individual objects
- Important Sketch material settings

This chapter uses the Classic interface for the figures. For this tutorial, it is recommended that you switch to the Classic scheme by choosing Edit > Preferences. In the Common section, change the Scheme to Classic.

The Spots Shader

You will start off by making a new material and applying a Spots shader to the Color channel. This will be applied to the floor for the background. The scene already has an object, in this case the Ray Gun, a Sky, and Floor. There is also a camera, which has a Protection tag applied to it. This scene is meant to be rendered from a particular angle, so leave the Camera view as it is. There is also preset lighting, which we'll talk more about later.

Create the Spots shader and Floor material:

1. From the Materials Manager's File menu, select File > New Material.
2. Double-click it to see the Material Editor window. Rename the material as *Floor*.
3. In the Color channel, load the Spots shader by selecting the Texture Triangle > Sketch > Spots (see Figure 12.3). After you select it, the word *Spots* will appear in the Texture bar.
4. Click on the word *Spots* in the Texture bar to see its properties.
5. Change the Spot properties so that they match Figure 12.4. Shape = Grid; Spot Color = 14, 38, 33; and Scale = 20%, 20%, 20%. Activate Camera and Shadows.
6. Close the Material Editor window.

FIGURE 12.3 Loading the Spots shader into the Color channel.

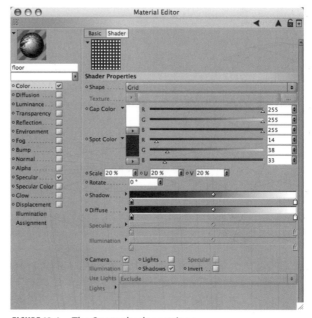

FIGURE 12.4 The Spots shader settings.

Apply the material to the floor:

7. Drag and drop the Floor material onto the Floor object in the Objects Manager.
8. Select the newly created material tag, and change the projection to Frontal. This type of projection is ideal when using static cameras. You will see a checkered background appear if you have Gouraud Shading enabled (it is not necessary that you do, as you will eventually see it in the renderer).
9. Render to the Picture Viewer (Shift+R) to see the results. Your render should look similar to Figure 12.5. Notice how the shader reacts to the shadows.

FIGURE 12.5   Render of the Spots shader for the Floor object. Notice how the shader reacts to the light and shadows.

Use the Spot Shader for the Ray Gun:

10. Make a new material, and call it *Spots*.
11. Load a Spots shader into the Color channel, just like before.
12. Change the setting to match Figure 12.6. Spot Color = 178, 98, 0 and Scale = 40%, 40%, 40%. Move the black diffuse marker over until it is almost in the middle. Make sure Camera and Lights are active.
13. Add a Spots shader to the Alpha channel. The only thing you need to change for these Spots settings is Scale = 40%, 40%, 40%. Make sure that Camera and Lights are active. Leave everything else at its default.
14. Close the Material Editor window.

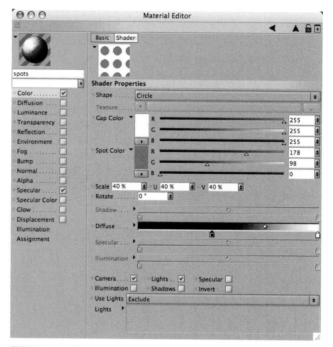

FIGURE 12.6   The Spots shader settings.

Apply the material to the Ray Gun:

15. Drag and drop the Spots material over to the Ray Gun object in the Objects Manager (see Figure 12.7). Make sure you drop the material onto the name of the object and not the tags.

FIGURE 12.7   The Spots tag. Make sure you change its projection to Frontal.

16. Change the Projection for that tag to Frontal in the Tag Properties in the Attributes Manager.
17. Render (Shift+R) to the Picture Viewer. You'll now see spots on the Ray Gun, and it already feels like the image is coming together (see Figure 12.8). Because you selected Lights for the shader, it is reacting to the light in the scene.

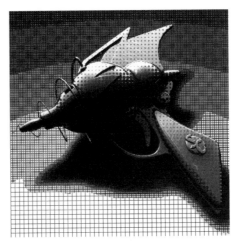

FIGURE 12.8   The rendered Spots material on
the Ray Gun.

You now have layered shaders on the Ray Gun. Because the Spots
material has an Alpha channel on it, you can see the Metal material underneath. We are going to add one more new material to the group that
will highlight the Ray Gun's contours. This will provide some nice contrast in the image.

Add Contours for the Ray Gun:

18. Create a new material, and name it *Contours*.
19. In the Color channel, change the RGB values to 14, 38, and 33.
20. Deactivate Specular.
21. Activate the Alpha channel, and load a Spots shader into the Texture
    space, similar to before.
22. Change the Spots shader settings. Shape = Grid and Scale = 40%,
    40%, 40%. Make sure that Camera is active.
23. Close the Material Editor window.

Apply the material to the Ray Gun:

24. Apply the material Contours to the Ray Gun.
25. Change its projection to Cubic.
26. With the tag still selected, select Tags > Fit to Object in the Objects
    Manager's menu set (see Figure 12.9). Click Yes to "Do you want
    sub-objects to be included?" This will make the contours have better
    spacing on the Ray Gun.
27. Re-render. Now the contours will show up on top of the Spots mate-
    rial. That is because the contours tag is "on top" (or in this case, to the
    right of) the Spots tag.

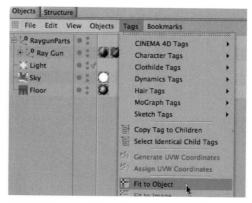

FIGURE 12.9 The Fit to Object command found in the Objects Manager. You must have the Contours material tag selected for it to work.

Shaders and Lighting

The Spots and Hatch shaders both have settings that allow them to react to both standard lights and Global Illumination (GI). The scene you are working with already had a standard light in it. It has a soft shadow that is evident when you render. The scene is a little dark but that's because it's waiting for you to activate GI.

Activate GI:

1. Activate Global Illumination in the Render Settings (Render > Render Settings). Leave the settings the way they are. The nice thing about using GI with Sketch and Toon is that it often doesn't need high settings (see Figure 12.10).

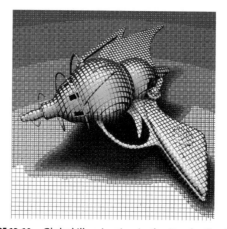

FIGURE 12.10 Global Illumination in the Render Settings.

2. Re-render the scene. Now the brightness is better, and GI has added some subtle shading. It should render relatively quickly because of the low GI numbers (see Figure 12.11).

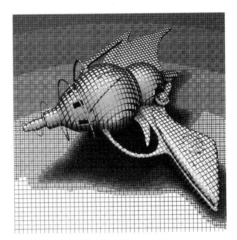

FIGURE 12.11   The Ray Gun now has contours and lighting.

Sketch Materials

Sketch and Toon has two parts to it. First are the shaders that we've been working with, like the Spots shader. Second, it also has the capability to draw many kinds of lines on objects. These lines can be turned on in the Materials Manager by adding a Sketch material. When you do this, you automatically turn on Sketch and Toon in the Effects section of the Render Settings.

Turn on Sketch materials:

1. In the Materials Manager, select File > Sketch Material. This will import a Sketch material swatch into the Materials Manager (see Figure 12.12). Sketch and Toon is now active.

FIGURE 12.12   The Sketch material swatch in the Materials Manager.

2. Re-render. You will now see the default Sketch lines around the Ray Gun. This Sketch material is automatically applied to all renderable (but not Floor or Sky objects) objects in the scene.

3. To add Sketch materials to individual objects, simply drag them to the objects in the Objects Manager. They work similarly to materials, except they have their own tags and properties. You do not have to do this step for this tutorial.

Sketch Material Presets

Normally presets aren't desirable, but there are so many that it is easy to diverge and make something uniquely your own. You will open the default Sketch material and change the settings to get a better idea of the enormous potential that lies at your fingertips.

Change the Sketch material settings:

1. Double-click on the default Sketch material swatch to open the Material Editor.

2. In the Main section, make sure that Control Level is set to Advanced. This will reveal more channels on the left.

3. Change the Presets to Marker (Edge). You will see the preview reflect this change (see Figure 12.13).

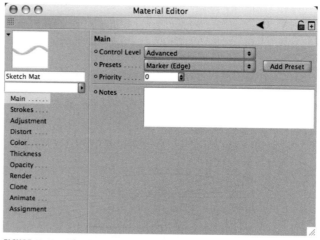

FIGURE 12.13   The Material Editor for the Sketch material. Change the Presets to Marker (Edge).

4. Click on the Color channel. Change the main color to RGB = 50, 159, 11 and Brightness to 47%. In the Modifiers section, activate Along Stroke. You will see a new section called Along Stroke appear below, along with a Gradient section.

5. Open the Gradient by single-clicking on the little black triangle next to the word *Gradient*.
6. The Gradient has two markers. Single-click on the first one (left one), and change its RGB values to 103, 151, and 121. Click on the second marker (right one), and change its RGB values to 27, 51, and 0 (see Figure 12.14). The color will now change over the length of the Stroke. That is what the Along Stroke modifier does.
7. Close the Material Editor window.

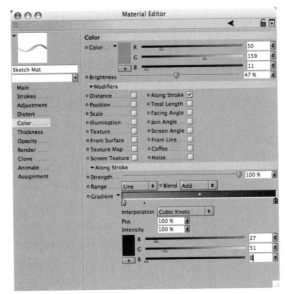

FIGURE 12.14   The Color settings for the Sketch material.

Render Settings

Before you render, let's take a look at the Sketch and Toon settings. Note that you can change how the lines behave, along with Line quality. There are too many settings to cover here, so for a more detailed understanding, please refer to the Sketch and Toon Manual in the Help system.

Open the Sketch and Toon Settings:

1. Open the Render Settings.
2. Change to Effects.
3. Select Sketch and Toon in the Effects list.
4. Observe, but don't change the settings. After the tutorial, you are encouraged to explore these settings (see Figure 12.15). More information is available in the Help system.

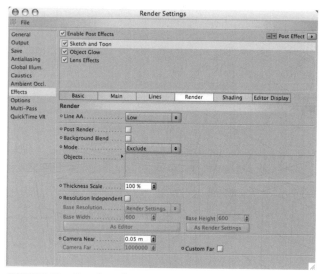

FIGURE 12.15   Sketch and Toon render settings.

CONCLUSION

ON THE CD

Go ahead and render the scene. On the CD-ROM, you'll find the finished version of this file, along with another project example of other explorations with Sketch and Toon (see Figure 12.16 and Figure 12.17). You are encouraged to check these out and play with them.

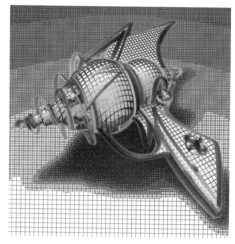

FIGURE 12.16   The finished render.

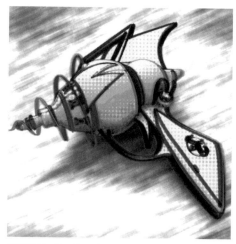

FIGURE 12.17   Another variation.

13

CUSTOMIZING THE C4D INTERFACE

In This Chapter

- Customizing Manager Size and Location
- Individualized Workflow
- Command Palettes
- Menu Manager
- Saving a Custom Layout
- Preferences
- Heads Up Display (HUD)
- Collapse/Unfold Managers

Now that you've been exposed to the various tasks and capabilities C4D has to offer, it's time to learn how to make it work *for you*. The interface you see in C4D is not set in stone. Completely customizable, the interface can be modified and optimized to fit you and your style of working.

CUSTOMIZING MANAGER SIZE AND LOCATION

The managers share screen space with the Viewport and the command palettes. The location and size of the managers is customizable. By moving your mouse to the edge of a manager (see Figure 13.1), you can resize the manager to fit your needs. In some cases, you may want to make it smaller (for example, if you need more space for the Viewport), and at other times, you'll need more space for the manager (for example, if many tags are attached to objects within the Objects Manager). When the mouse pointer is over the edge of a manager, the pointer changes to a double arrow, indicating that C4D is ready to resize a window. Click-drag the double arrow, and you can resize the window within certain parameters.

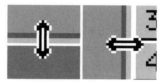

FIGURE 13.1   Resize window arrows allow you to give more screen space to a given manager or window.

The Grasp Icon

The windows and managers within the interface are *docked*. Notice that in the corner of the Viewport and the various managers is a small, checkered icon. This represents that this window (or manager) is temporarily docked at this location in the interface. If you don't like having it there, simply click on the Grasp icon, and drag the window to a more appropriate location. As you drag, you'll notice that a dark line appears near to your mouse pointer, indicating possible new locations to dock the window you are moving. Remember that by moving windows around in this way, you still maintain one monolithic overall windowed interface where you don't have any floating windows or palettes, and everything is nested into its own spot.

Undocking Windows

If you prefer to work with multiple floating windows (similar to those found in previous versions of C4D), you can *undock* windows or managers so that they float along the top of your interface. To do this, right-click on the Grasp icon, and select Undock from the resultant pop-up menu (see Figure 13.2). The result will be a new window that appears separate from the main interface.

Docking Windows

There are several important things to remember about undocking. First, after a window is undocked, it can always be "docked" again. To do this, simply click-drag the Grasp icon on the now undocked window to the new location where you want to dock it. (A dark line will appear indicating the locations at which it can be docked.) When the window is re-docked, the windows around it will resize to fit. Note that you can also dock directly to a group of managers represented by tabs. When you are click-dragging the Grasp icon, simply move your mouse pointer over the

Grasp Icon

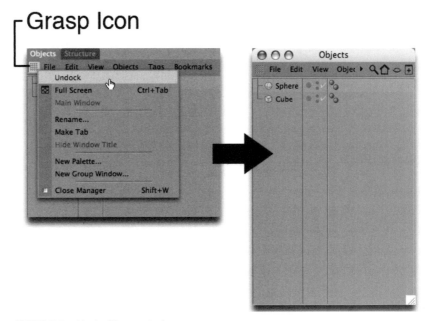

FIGURE 13.2   Undocking a window or manager.

Grasp icon of a manager grouped with others in tabs. Your mouse pointer will change to a pointing hand. Upon mouse release, the window will be docked and tabbed in the group you have selected.

While we're at it, let's look at the other options that are part of the Grasp pop-up menu:

Rename: Self-explanatory method of renaming a manager if you so desire.

Make Tab: When a manager is undocked, you can add other windows to the floating window. You can choose to tab this manager from the beginning.

New Icon Palette: Using this tool, you can create a new floating window (which can be docked later) that contains a custom set of tools. To actually place tools in this new palette, you must use the Command Manager, which we'll look at later in this chapter.

New Group Window: The term "group" as used here refers to more than one manager that shares a window. As we discussed earlier, you can swap between managers through tabs at the top of the Group Window. Creating a new Group Window allows you a new space to place multiple managers.

Close: Closes the window or manager.

INDIVIDUALIZED WORKFLOW

Depending on your working style, the managers you want to be available will differ greatly. Some artists work with two monitors and have managers open everywhere because they have enough room. Other artists working with more restricted space may choose to group into tabs a large group of their managers, or even to hide some completely.

COMMAND PALETTES

In C4D, the pop-up menus are said to contain *commands*. Each of these commands performs different functions that allow you to work in and manipulate the digital 3D space. Along the top and left side of the default C4D interface are *command palettes* (see Figure 13.3). These palettes are set up to allow you to reach often-used commands quickly.

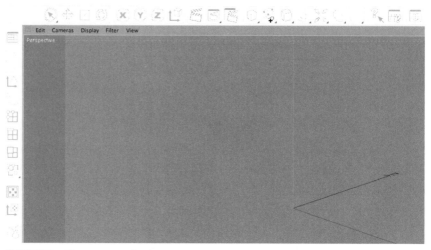

FIGURE 13.3   The command palettes.

Docking and Undocking Command Palettes

The command palettes that C4D has set up by default are docked within the interface. Like windows and managers, command palettes can be either docked or undocked. To undock a palette, simply right-click and select Undock.

Once these command palettes are undocked, you may dock them again. To do this, grab the command palette by clicking on the double, dotted line at the top of a vertical palette or the left end of a horizontal palette (see Figure 13.4a), and drag it to where you want it docked. Similar to docking managers, a heavy black line will appear, indicating the possible docking positions as you near one (see Figure 13.4b). The docked palette will now take the space you've chosen (see Figure 13.4c).

FIGURE 13.4   (a) "Docking handle" for palettes.
(b) Dark lines indicate potential docking locations.
(c) The result of the redocked Command palette.

Creating Command Palettes from Scratch

There is only so much room available for the default command palettes. C4D seems to assume that you have a monitor that displays at least 1024 × 768. At that resolution, all the default command palettes are visible. However, you may have a bigger monitor or two monitors and would like to create additional palettes that contain your most-used commands or commands that aren't available by default. Here are some ways to create a new command palette:

- Select Window > Layout > New Palette.
- For managers, right-click on the Grasp icon, and select New Palette from the pop-up menu, or right-click anywhere in the Manager's space, and choose New Palette from the pop-up menu.
- For palettes, right-click, and select New Palette from the pop-up menu.

Command Manager

New command palettes are undocked and empty. To add commands to palettes, you must first activate the *Command Manager.* In empty palettes, right-click on the words *Empty Palette,* and choose Edit Palette from the pop-up menu. Right-click again on Empty Palette, and choose Command Manager. The Command Manager window will appear with the Edit Palettes option turned on. When this is selected, a big change comes over your interface. The Command Manager appears in the foreground, and all the existing commands in existing command palettes are surrounded with blue boxes (see Figure 13.5). C4D is letting you know it's ready to move tools.

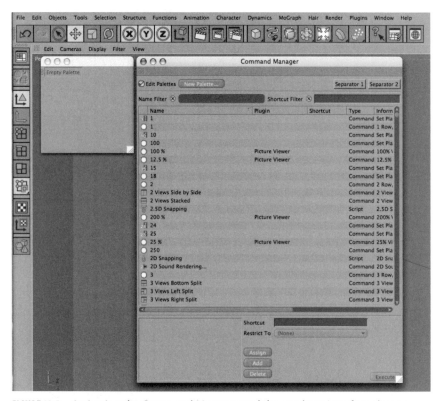

FIGURE 13.5 Activating the Command Manager and the resultant interface change.

Now you can grab command icons from existing command palettes and place them into the new palette. When you attempt to place commands in a new command palette, note that the location to which you click-drag the command palette is very important. In the empty palette, the words *Empty Palette* appear within a sunken region (see Figure 13.6).

When you move new commands into this palette, the commands must be dropped within this sunken region. Trying to place them anywhere else will result in your mouse pointer being substituted by the forbidden symbol. After the first command is placed within a new palette, subsequent commands can just be dropped next to existing commands.

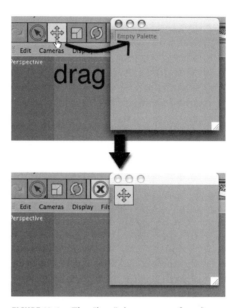

FIGURE 13.6   The "hot" drop zone of new command palettes.

There is another way to invoke the Command Manager: Window > Layout > Command Manager. When the Command Manager emerges this way, note that the command palettes aren't automatically ready to be altered. If you use this method, you must click the Edit Palettes button at the top-left corner of the Command Manager.

Power at Your Command

The Command Manager is an incredibly versatile and powerful tool. You've already seen how, by activating it, you can shift commands. However, it is also important to note that Command Manager contains a large list of commands that may not even be listed in existing command palettes. The Command Manager actually contains all the commands available in C4D. To help you find commands, R10 now has a filtering option. Say you want to find the command for Save. All you need to do is type the word *Save* into the filter. All commands that contain this word or part of this word will be displayed.

To use the commands from the Command Manager in your custom palettes, make sure that Edit Palettes is activated, and then simply click-drag the command from the Command Manager to the command palette of choice. A yellow line will indicate where C4D is planning to place the new command.

Command Manager: Editing Keyboard Shortcuts

The Command Manager also provides the capability to alter keyboard shortcuts for any given command. When a command is clicked within the Command Manager, it will appear in the bottom section of the Command Manager. If the command has a keyboard shortcut assigned to it, the shortcut will appear here under the Current input field (see Figure 13.7a). If you want to change the keyboard shortcut for the command, click the Delete button next to the shortcut to erase it (see Figure 13.7b).

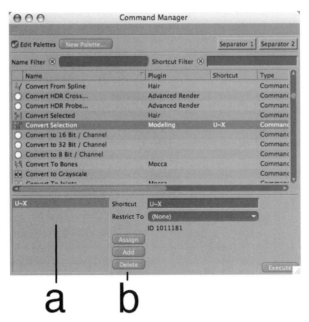

FIGURE 13.7   (a) If a command already has a keyboard shortcut, the Command Manager will display it. (b) Erasing assigned keyboard shortcuts.

To assign a keyboard shortcut, click in the Shortcut input field. You can now enter any keystroke or combination of keystrokes. If this keystroke already is assigned to another command, you will be alerted immediately with an error message that tells you what the conflicting command is and ask if you want to reassign it (see Figure 13.8). You can add multiple keystrokes to the same command by clicking on the Add button after entering a new keystroke.

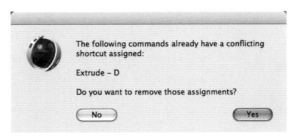

FIGURE 13.8   Click Yes if you want to remove the assigned shortcut and apply it to your own.

Note that when a new keyboard shortcut has been assigned, it not only shows up in the Current input field, it also shows up within the Command Manager above and in the pop-up menus of the general C4D interface (see Figure 13.9) as long as the Show Shortcuts option is enabled in the Preferences on the Interface page. This is a perfect example of how C4D's managers are intertwined.

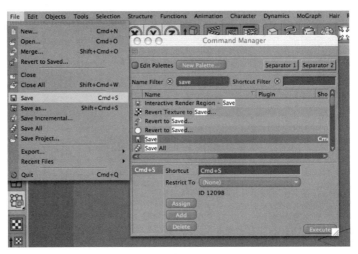

FIGURE 13.9   The places where C4D incorporates changes made within the Command Manager.

Back to the Command Palettes

Within a newly created palette, there is a slew of further customization that can be done. Right-click within any of the commands in the command palette, and you'll be given a new pop-up collection of functions to optimize the look and function of the palette. These options include ways to fold or unfold commands (make nested groups of commands), make your commands appear as simple text, make your commands appear as text and icons, make your commands appear in rows or columns, change the number of rows or columns, delete commands, and change the size of the icons within the palette. Because these are effectively described in the manual, we won't repeat how to do them here.

MENU MANAGER

Besides being able to alter the command palettes, C4D allows you to even alter the pop-up menus organization of commands. This allows you to create new menus and submenus. The *Menu Manager* works in much the same way as the Command Manager. With simple drag-and-drop methods, you can move commands from one manager to another. Pop-up menus are the least efficient way of accessing commands, so we won't spend much time here discussing how to alter the extant menus. It is strongly suggested that you organize your most-used tools into appropriate command palettes and assign good, easy-to-remember keystrokes.

SAVING A CUSTOM LAYOUT

So what happens when you have adjusted your layout just the way you want it? You want to be sure that you can access this same layout the next time you open C4D. You might also want to create a variety of layouts for different parts of your work process—one for modeling, one for animation, and so on. To save a custom layout that you have created, go to Window > Layout > Save Layout As. This will allow you to save a layout file that you can call up at will. Similarly, you can use Window > Layout > Save as Startup Layout to make your custom layout the one that always is called up when you launch C4D.

PREFERENCES

The Preferences dialog box is another location within C4D that allows for further customization of the interface's look and feel. To access the Preferences dialog box, select Edit > Preferences from the main menu, or use the keyboard shortcut of Ctrl+E (Command+E for Mac). Most of the available settings within this dialog box are beyond what we need to alter, and this area is covered extensively in the manual. However, there are a few areas of importance that we should look at.

When Preferences is first selected, you are given a dialog box with several areas listed to the left. The number of editable areas will vary depending on which modules you have (see Figure 13.10). In the Common section, you can change the Scheme to Light, Dark, or Classic, which will implement systemwide changes to your interface. Of particular note are the Interface and Viewport sections.

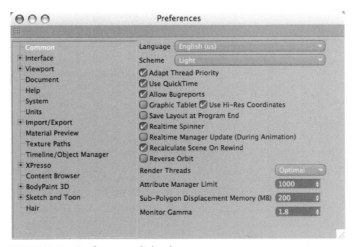

FIGURE 13.10   Preferences dialog box.

Interface

The Interface section and the Colors subsection allow you to make some changes to how the interface acts and looks. This is mostly a subjective matter, so we won't talk too much about it here; but if you don't like gray, for example, or you are working on a Mac when you are used to using a PC (or vice versa), you can come here and make it all change.

Viewport

Expanding the Viewport section provides some very useful tools. Just clicking the word *Viewport* will bring up a collection of options. Clicking the little cross next to Viewport will expand it to show other subsections that allow you to further work with your Viewports. Within the Viewport section, you will find a collection of options that allow you to customize what sorts of visual interactivity and guides are included in your interface (see Figure 13.11).

R9 has moved Render Safe, Action Safe, Title Safe, Semi-transparent Axes, and Scale Axes to the Configure settings found in the Viewport Editor window File menu. R10 adds a System setting.

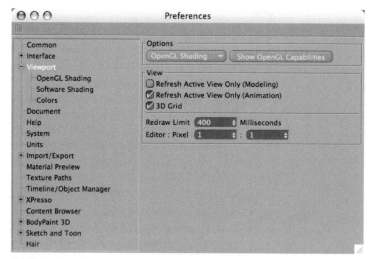

FIGURE 13.11 Viewport options within the Preferences dialog box.

Viewport Options

By default, C4D tries to use your video card through OpenGL. This is a hardware-accelerated method of drawing 3D in your Viewports. It's faster than the other option, Software Shading. The other option is Show OpenGL Capabilities. This is important for users to check and see if your video card is compatible with Enhanced OpenGL.

OpenGL

After you have selected OpenGL shading in the Options drop-down menu of the Viewport section, you can alter the OpenGL settings. OpenGL is a technology that has been developed specifically to assist in quick rendering of 3D worlds. It is used heavily in games and can be of great benefit in 3D animation. OpenGL is hardware driven (driven by the video card), and is much faster than the software-driven alternative. Most upper-end computers have video cards that utilize hardware-driven OpenGL acceleration. If you are lucky enough to have significant hardware acceleration, the rest of the settings can assist in defining how you want to use the extra horsepower. You'll need to read carefully the information included with your hardware to see if it actually supports the options listed in the OpenGL section.

Enhanced OpenGL

Cinema's Enhanced OpenGL takes the standard OpenGL a few steps forward. You can check to see if your video card supports this feature by clicking on Show OpenGL Capabilities in the Viewport options in the Preferences. Enhanced OpenGL can be turned on in the Display menu for each Viewport. You can then turn on Transparency, Shadows and Post effects. If your video card supports these, they will be displayed in the Editor window, without having to render.

Refresh Active View Only

When you have toggled views to more than one view panel, you can move an object in one view panel and instantly see it moved in the other view panels. This is because the Refresh Active View Only option is turned off by default. In most cases, it's important to be able to see how things are being positioned, rotated, and scaled within other views. However, when your projects get very large, this extra effort of drawing the changes immediately in four windows instead of one can contribute to a significant slowdown in your interface speed. If Refresh Active View Only is selected (as you may need to do with big scenes), C4D will wait to redraw the other view panels until after you have finished whatever function you are performing in the active window.

HEADS UP DISPLAY (HUD)

The Heads Up Display (HUD) places useful information into the Viewports. For that reason, its controls are found in each of the Viewport's Configure settings. You can access the Viewport Configure settings through the Viewport menu by choosing Edit > Configure or pressing Shift + V (see Figure 13.12). After which, you will see the settings in the Attributes Manager (see Figure 13.13).

The Help system covers very well what each of these settings do, but it is recommended turning on at least Projection, which puts the title of the view on the Viewport Editor window. If you work with polygons, turn on the polygon options as well. You can move the information boxes around in the Editor window by Ctrl-dragging them. Not all the settings provide immediate feedback. You have to be doing certain things to see the information displayed (see Figure 13.14). Regardless, it can be a wonderful time saver. Remember that you can configure the HUD for all Viewport windows (Configure All) or just specific ones.

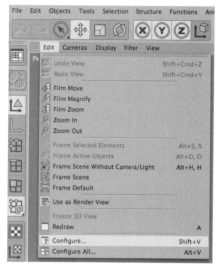

FIGURE 13.12 Choose Edit > Configure, or use the shortcut, Shift + V.

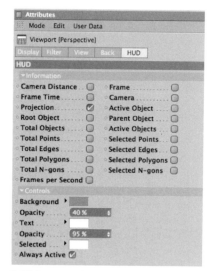

FIGURE 13.13 The HUD settings.

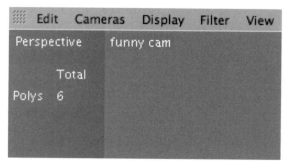

FIGURE 13.14 HUD information boxes. You can move them around by Ctrl-dragging.

COLLAPSE/UNFOLD MANAGERS

You can middle-click on any of the Grasp icons, and collapse the palette or manager (see Figure 13.15a). After it is collapsed, you can middle-click its grasp icon again to unfold, or restore it. A text box will appear indicating what is there before you unfold it (see Figure 13.15b). This is a great way to get things out of the way quickly.

Tear Off Menus

You can tear off any menu in C4D by clicking on its checkered bar at the top of the drop-down menu. For example, let's say you wanted to create

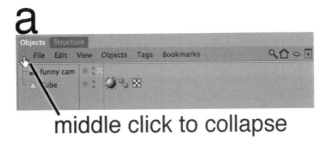

middle click to collapse

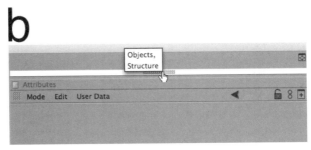

FIGURE 13.15   (a) Middle-clicking on the Grasp icon will collapse the manager(s). (b) Putting your mouse over the Grasp icon will display the hidden contents. Middle click to unfold.

a floating palette for the Character menu. You would choose the Character menu, and click its checkered bar (see Figure 13.16). This would create a floating palette for that menu (see Figure 13.17). The floating palette can then be reinserted anywhere in the interface you choose.

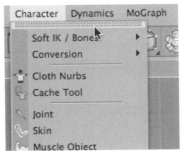

FIGURE 13.16   The checkered bar at the top of each menu can be clicked to create a floating palette.

FIGURE 13.17 A floating palette.

Conclusion

Customizing the interface can help tremendously with your workflow. You can save any interface changes by choosing Window > Layout > Save Layout As. Later, you can load it by choosing Window > Layout > Load Layout. This allows some portability because you can save your layouts next to your project files and take them to other computers.

If you are new to C4D, it is recommended that you use the default interfaces provided by MAXON. After you have learned the basics of modeling, texturing, animating, lighting, and rendering, you will have a much better understanding of not only how Cinema 4D works, but how *you* work. You'll find that customizing can greatly reduce the time it takes to complete projects. Ultimately, this will make you a more efficient and competent 3D artist. Whether your endeavors are professional or just for entertainment, good luck and have fun!

A

ABOUT THE CD-ROM

The CD-ROM included with *The Cinema 4D R10 Handbook* includes all of the files necessary to complete the tutorials in the book. It also includes the images from the book in full color, and demos for you to use while working through the tutorials and exercises. Please download the Help system files from Maxon's website: *www.maxon.net*.

CD FOLDERS

Images: All of the images from within the book in full color.

Tutorials: All of the files necessary to complete the tutorials in the book including backgrounds, textures, and images.

Bonus Tutorials: A few extra tutorials from previous *C4D Handbooks*. They should still work, with minimal fuss.

Print Me: contains printable files that can be used as references, such as keyboard shortcuts.

C4D Demo: Includes Mac and PC installation files for the C4D demo. These do not include the Help files.

SYSTEM SUGGESTIONS

Mac

- Mac OS 10.3.9
- G3 Processor or higher
- 512 MB Ram (1 GB Recommended)
- 1 GB Hard Drive Space
- 32 MB Video Card
- DVD-ROM Drive
- QuickTime 6.1 or higher
- Cinema 4D R10 or later

PC

- Windows XP
- PIII Processor or higher
- 512 MB RAM (1 GB Recommended)
- 1 GB Hard Drive Space
- 32 MB Video Card
- DVD-ROM Drive
- QuickTime 6.1 or higher
- Cinema 4D R10 or later

CINEMA 4D 10

Maxon, Inc., *www.maxon.net*

Cinema 4D is a leading 3D software program used for print, film, video production, web, game development, and illustration and is world renowned for its ease of use yet powerful toolset.

Extra Applications You Might Need

- Macromedia® Flash™
- Adobe® Photoshop®
- Adobe Acrobat®

Demo Installation

To install C4D, double click on "cinema_4d_r100_macdemo.zip" on a Mac or "cinema_4d_r100_windemo.zip" on a PC. Then just follow the prompts on your screen. You may need a .zip extractor.

INDEX